Thinking in
the Past Tense

Thinking in the Past Tense

Eight Conversations

ALEXANDER BEVILACQUA & FREDERIC CLARK

The University of Chicago Press   Chicago and London

The University of Chicago Press, Chicago 60637
The University of Chicago Press, Ltd., London
© 2019 by Alexander Bevilacqua and Frederic Clark
Published 2019
Printed in the United States of America

28 27 26 25 24 23 22 21 20 19   1 2 3 4 5

ISBN-13: 978-0-226-60117-5 (cloth)
ISBN-13: 978-0-226-60120-5 (paper)
ISBN-13: 978-0-226-60134-2 (e-book)
DOI: https://doi.org/10.7208/chicago/9780226601342.001.0001

Library of Congress Cataloging-in-Publication Data
Names: Bevilacqua, Alexander, 1984– author. |
    Clark, Frederic, 1985– author.
Title: Thinking in the past tense : eight conversations /
    Alexander Bevilacqua and Frederic Clark.
Description: Chicago ; London : The University of Chicago Press, 2019. |
    Includes bibliographical references and index.
Identifiers: LCCN 2018037451 | ISBN 9780226601175 (cloth : alk. paper) |
    ISBN 9780226601205 (pbk. : alk. paper) | ISBN 9780226601342 (e-book)
Subjects: LCSH: History—Philosophy. | Historians—Interviews. |
    Historiography.
Classification: LCC D16.8 .T4476 2019 | DDC 901—dc23
LC record available at https://lccn.loc.gov/2018037451

♾ This paper meets the requirements of ANSI/NISO Z39.48-1992
(Permanence of Paper).

Contents

Introduction

In 1980, intellectual history was left for dead. In a survey of intellectual and cultural history, the historian of France Robert Darnton registered that the field had lost the spark that had once animated it.[1] In the preceding two decades, the French Annales school of social history had won followers on both sides of the Atlantic, and quantitative methods were the ne plus ultra of historical inquiry. Meanwhile, a new strain of research, influenced by anthropology, had turned to the study of popular culture.[2] The history of ideas—the field that Arthur O. Lovejoy had named in the 1930s—came to seem to many a relic of the past.[3] Who at that time could have predicted that in just a matter of decades intellectual history—the study of past human efforts to think and to know—would become one of the most vibrant areas of historical research?

In fact, in countercultural fashion, even at the zenith of social history, individual scholars continued to investigate

---

1. Robert Darnton, "Intellectual and Cultural History," in *The Past before Us: Contemporary Historical Writing in the United States*, ed. Michael Kammen (Ithaca, 1980), 327–28; see also Dominick LaCapra and Steven L. Kaplan, eds., *Modern European Intellectual History: Reappraisals and New Perspectives* (Ithaca, 1982). And see the discussion in Anthony Grafton, "The History of Ideas: Precept and Practice, 1950–2000 and Beyond," *Journal of the History of Ideas* 67, no. 1 (2006): 1–32.

2. Clifford Geertz, *The Interpretation of Cultures: Selected Essays* (New York, 1973); Natalie Z. Davis, *Society and Culture in Early Modern France* (Stanford, 1975).

3. Arthur O. Lovejoy, *The Great Chain of Being: A Study of the History of an Idea* (Cambridge, MA, 1936). Also important in this respect is R. G. Collingwood, *The Idea of History* (Oxford, 1946).

the history of intellectual activity. And they sought new ways of pursuing it, whether through the history of science, of humanistic scholarship, or of political thought. Since then, the renewal of intellectual history has taken place against the backdrop of a boom in the writing of cultural history, a shift that has been both studied and celebrated at some length.[4] Historians have often conceptualized this change, which began in the 1980s, as a "turn."[5] Yet the notion of a unified cultural turn does not adequately explain the revival of intellectual history, whose genealogy is both more diverse and of longer standing. It reaches back to rich strains of mid-twentieth-century scholarship, which were likewise in dialogue with much earlier antecedents.[6] Intellectual history did not return ex nihilo; rather, its resurgence in the last few decades has depended in great measure upon a recuperation of older traditions that was under way even during social history's ascendancy.

From being considered old-fashioned, perhaps even stuffy, intellectual history has attracted a growing number of ambitious early- and midcareer scholars who have produced a body of innovative work. The field boasts an increasing number of journals and scholarly associations, and its present state and prospects have lately occasioned several reflections.[7] Insights from such diverse areas as the history of science, the history of the book, reception studies, and the study of material culture have all enriched the field. In the process, the *history of ideas* has become *intellectual history*. Intellectual history no longer embraces abstractions as readily as it once did, and it treats the work of the mind as a form of human activity with costs and rewards not solely intellectual but also personal, political, and social. It no longer ascribes ideas merely to the solitary philosopher or scholar, the "genius." Nor does it restrict them to the preserve of elite culture. Monolithic categories like the West, and simplistic notions of tradition, the canon, and the classics, have grown more complex, nuanced, and heterogeneous. But if the study of intellectual life no longer embraces these old verities, of

---

4. E.g., Lynn Hunt, ed., *The New Cultural History* (Berkeley, 1999). See also the essays collected in Victoria E. Bonnell and Lynn Hunt, ed., *Beyond the Cultural Turn: New Directions in the Study of Society and Culture* (Berkeley, 1999).

5. "Historiographic 'Turns' in Critical Perspective," forum, *American Historical Review* 117, no. 3 (2012): 698–813.

6. See, for instance, Marc Bloch, *The Historian's Craft*, trans. Peter Putnam (Manchester, 2004), published originally in Paris in 1949 as *Apologie pour l'histoire ou métier d'historien*.

7. Darrin M. McMahon and Samuel Moyn, eds., *Rethinking Modern Intellectual History* (Oxford, 2014); Samuel Moyn and Andrew Sartori, eds., *Global Intellectual History* (New York, 2013). See also Peter E. Gordon, "What Is Intellectual History? A Frankly Partisan Introduction to a Frequently Misunderstood Field" (Projects at Harvard, Harvard University, Cambridge, MA, March 2012), http://projects.iq.harvard.edu/files/history/files/what_is_intell_history_pgordon_mar2012.pdf.

what does it now consist, and how do its practitioners define their enterprise? Is it enough merely to complicate older simplistic narratives? With what—if anything—are they being replaced?

Thinking in the Past Tense offers a collection of reflections on these questions. It presents interviews with eight historians, some of whom have been active since the 1960s or '70s, and others who have made their mark more recently. In informal conversations, conducted between 2014 and 2017 in Berlin; Cambridge, Massachusetts; London; New York; Paris; and Princeton, New Jersey, these scholars reveal how they came to define their intellectual agendas, how they work, and what they hope for the future of their field. In contemporary academia, both disciplinary genealogy and secrets of the craft are largely transmitted person-to-person; they are topics on which historians do not normally touch except in private conversation. By publishing these interviews, we hope to make public the "private science" of historical scholarship.[8] To put it another way, this book is the one that we wish we had been given as first-year graduate students in intellectual history. It did not exist, so we had to create it ourselves.

The interview format is ideal both for demystifying the craft of the historian and for sketching out a rough draft of the history of recent historical work. This is a book about practice in two senses: it not only lifts the veil on the practice of researching and writing intellectual history, but also examines how many intellectual historians have come to understand their undertaking as a history of practice. Our interviewees labor to reconstruct the *work* of other, earlier minds. To be clear, this emphasis on practice does not imply that, in the parlance of another time, externalists have triumphed over internalists; on the contrary, the consensus of the historians whom we have interviewed is that that once-famous opposition is obsolete.[9] Content and context are no longer mutually exclusive. Intellectual historians these days have to do it all: they must be mindful of the political and social dimensions of their subject without losing sight of its intellectual content, however technical or arcane it might be.

Our selection of interviewees is by no means arbitrary, but it is constrained by the requirements of producing a readable and concise book. We would have liked to conduct many more conversations than could

8. The notion of "private science" comes from Gerald L. Geison, *The Private Science of Louis Pasteur* (Princeton, 1995).

9. For background on debates between internalists and externalists in the history and sociology of science, see the introduction to *The Cambridge History of Science*, vol. 7, *The Modern Social Sciences*, ed. Theodore M. Porter and Dorothy Ross (Cambridge, 2003), 1–10.

fit between these covers. As it is, our historians have been chosen to represent different branches of intellectual history: the history of the book (Blair); the history of science (Daston); the history of non-Western intellectual traditions (Elman); the history of scholarship (Grafton); the history of philosophy (Kraye); the history of antiquarianism and material culture (Miller); the history of religion (Quantin); and the history of political thought (Skinner). (The interviews are organized alphabetically by last name.)

It is difficult to draw generalizations about eight distinct individuals looking back upon their lives and careers. Yet the conversations do reveal some common modes or dispositions of inquiry. More often than not, our interviewees recount gradual processes of reconfiguration rather than dramatic reversals of perspective. And, more than once in what follows, they warn us to take their retrospective reconstructions with a grain of salt. Historical memory, in all its forms, can be fragile. Nevertheless, our scholars relate how they reached back to a surprisingly deep and diverse range of intellectual inheritances to help them solve the problems that interested them. And many of them recount how chance encounters—with teachers, colleagues, and books—unexpectedly shaped their intellectual development. These recollections, moreover, accord with how many of them write intellectual history: as a complex process of negotiation with available intellectual resources, rather than as a sequence of lightbulb moments and field-changing manifestos.

Our approach treats intellectual history as its own specialty, rather than merely as a form of cultural history. This former is not merely a subfield or subcategory of the latter. As our interviewees emphasize, intellectual history now embraces not only written documents but also architecture, art, knowledge of nature, literature, music, religion, and ritual—in sum, all the products of human culture. Yet the distinction between intellectual and cultural history is more than a semantic one. Intellectual history identifies a set of approaches and techniques rather than of sources. In its emphasis on thought, knowledge, and information, and on the interpretation of the world, intellectual history is a distinct mode of investigating such products of culture, whether they be texts or rituals or material objects.

A focus on intellectual history brings the contours of some important yet neglected changes in historical thinking and practice into sharper definition. Intellectual history over the past few decades has been especially methodologically inventive. In part, scholars have expanded the primary source base of intellectual history. Quentin Skinner's studies of Ambrogio Lorenzetti's frescoes and Shakespeare's plays have shown that the history of political thought should range well beyond the prescriptive tract or treatise. This expansion of remit has also involved looking in more offbeat places, especially for periods in which treatises were not the main genre of intellectual production. As Jill Kraye says, "the history of philosophy never had any gaps." She and other scholars have delved into forgotten genres, such as the critical edition and the commentary. Among early modern European humanists—the scholars who revived classical learning in the Renaissance and after—it was rather unusual to write a stand-alone treatise or narrative history. Instead, many humanists produced commentaries upon, as well as editions and translations of, preexisting texts, especially ancient ones. These works, often dismissed as secondary or derivative, were formerly neglected by intellectual historians, who thereby ignored the vast majority of the Renaissance humanist word count. Commentaries and editions—as responses to, and reconstructions of, preexisting texts—may not seem like revolutionary documents. Yet they afforded their authors great freedom to discuss thorny issues including textual authority, historical criticism, and religious revelation. Erasmus of Rotterdam produced a great stir not by writing an iconoclastic treatise on the New Testament but simply by producing a new edition of the text, in which he silently removed—and hence treated as spurious—a verse from the Gospel of John that served as a key biblical support for the doctrine of the Trinity.[10] Excavating traditions of editing, exegesis, criticism, and commentary has not only proven useful in itself but also provided a fruitful context for understanding stand-alone works that are iconic to modern readers, from Lorenzo Valla's attack on the Donation of Constantine to Thomas Hobbes's *Leviathan*.[11]

In the Chinese tradition, the civil service examination essay, an available but long neglected source, proved in Benjamin Elman's hands to be a powerful barometer of the geopolitical concerns of the Chinese elite. For Anthony Grafton, a now defunct discipline whose fruits appeared mainly in commentary form—historical chronology—provided a window into how early modern scholars weighed evidence, compared traditions, and sought to reconcile historical data with religious belief. Lorraine Daston has explored the history of abstract ideas such as

---

10. See, e.g., Joseph Levine, "Erasmus and the Problem of the Johannine Comma," *Journal of the History of Ideas* 58, no. 4 (1997): 573–96; Grantley McDonald, *Biblical Criticism in Early Modern Europe: Erasmus, the Johannine Comma, and Trinitarian Debate* (Cambridge, 2016).

11. Both Valla and Hobbes were also translators and commentators: Valla translated Homer and produced notes on the New Testament that proved crucial to Erasmus; Hobbes translated Thucydides. See Homer, *Ilias*, trans. Lorenzo Valla (Brescia, 1474); and Thucydides, *Eight Bookes of the Peloponnesian Warre*, trans. Thomas Hobbes (London, 1629).

rationality and objectivity through concrete and unexpected objects and genres, whether collections of curious objects, botanical illustrations or, most recently, medieval cookbooks and sumptuary laws.

In addition, current practitioners of intellectual history have sought to reconstruct the material, institutional, and cultural contexts of scientific and humanistic knowledge at given moments in time. Ann Blair has traced how the proliferation of encyclopedias and reference works in early modernity constituted a response to the sense of "information overload" that the rise of print technology occasioned. And Jill Kraye has shown how the history of Renaissance philosophy cannot be grasped without appreciating the Aristotelian basis of university curricula; to understand a figure like René Descartes, we must recover in detail what he learned as a student, even if he made a show of rejecting such training. Historians have also paid increasing attention to genre, register, rhetoric, and intellectual self-fashioning. Quentin Skinner has reconstructed the long afterlife of the Roman rhetorical tradition—the *ars rhetorica*—demonstrating that it remained a robust discourse well into early modernity, utilized in everything from politics to plays. Jean-Louis Quantin has explored how the genre of ecclesiastical history differed from its civil or secular counterpart not only in its subject matter but also in its methods, geared as it often was toward adjudicating theological controversy among dueling divines.

Analogously, intellectual historians have increasingly trained their attention on scholarly working methods and the effects of intellectual communities and networks. Ann Blair's current research on amanuenses and "hidden helpers" reveals a collaborative dimension of intellectual production that was largely (and deliberately) obscured by authors themselves—those solitary geniuses of earlier narratives. Peter Miller has reconstructed how one seventeenth-century intellectual, the French antiquary Nicolas-Claude Fabri de Peiresc (despite not publishing his own work) maintained a voluminous correspondence not only with famous figures like Hugo Grotius and Peter Paul Rubens but also with countless merchants, now forgotten, who traveled throughout the Mediterranean and Levant. Elman's examinees, Grafton's chronologers, Quantin's theologians, Blair's scribes, and Miller's antiquaries are not the typical actors one might have found in the history of ideas as it was once practiced.

Likewise crucial has been the effort to take a much broader view of the past. How to explain the long afterlife of books, ideas, and even disciplines once they are no longer considered to be at the cutting edge of intellectual history? As long as historians only focus on "firsts," they cannot make sense of the interleaving of different intellectual traditions that our textbooks treat as successive. As Ann Blair provocatively asks, "How about looking into 'lasts' instead?" Whether Aristotelian natural philosophy in the Renaissance or Scholastic argument in the seventeenth century, the long lives of intellectual traditions once considered moribund force us to rethink how to write the master narrative of intellectual history. Indeed, making sense of all these new contributions in a more than accretive manner—rewriting the history of human thought from the ground up—is a project still in progress, to which we hope that the conversations recorded here will prove stimulating.

These revisions and reconceptualizations have emerged in a number of domains. The practice of intellectual history has taken hold, with new energies and kindred approaches, in many distinct areas of inquiry. To name but a few, these include the late antique Mediterranean and Near East; Islamic intellectual history; the literary traditions of South Asia; modern Western philosophy; and many branches of the history of science.[12] Scholars in these and other areas approach their sources with similar aims and objectives to those discussed here, and the geneses of their approaches likewise deserve investigation. Indeed, it is our hope that scholars in these and many other areas of inquiry will produce their own oral histories of intellectual practice.[13]

Yet, as will be apparent from the names of the interviewees listed above, the historians who appear in this book all work on the period roughly between 1400 and 1800. This deliberate emphasis is arbitrary in

12. Below are just a few examples out of many from other fields: for late antiquity and the early Middle Ages, see, for instance, Peter Brown, *The World of Late Antiquity, AD 150–750* (New York, 1970); Rosamond McKitterick, *History and Memory in the Carolingian World* (Cambridge, 2004); for Islamic intellectual history, see Patricia Crone, *God's Rule: Government and Islam* (New York, 2004); Michael Cook, *Commanding Right and Forbidding Wrong in Islamic Thought* (Cambridge, 2000); Fred M. Donner, *Narratives of Islamic Origins: The Beginnings of Islamic Historical Writing* (Princeton, 1998); Khaled El-Rouayheb, *Islamic Intellectual History in the Seventeenth Century: Scholarly Currents in the Ottoman Empire and the Maghreb* (Cambridge, 2015); for the literature and culture of South Asia, see Sheldon I. Pollock, *The Language of the Gods in the World of Men: Sanskrit, Culture and Power in Premodern India* (Berkeley, 2006); for intellectual histories of twentieth-century philosophy and politics, see, for instance, Peter E. Gordon, *Continental Divide: Heidegger, Cassirer, Davos* (Cambridge, MA, 2012); Samuel Moyn, *Christian Human Rights* (Philadelphia, 2015); Daniel T. Rodgers, *Age of Fracture* (Cambridge, MA, 2012); for the history of science, Pamela H. Smith, *The Body of the Artisan: Art and Experience in the Scientific Revolution* (Chicago, 2004); Michael D. Gordin, *Scientific Babel: How Science Was Done before and after Global English* (Chicago, 2015).

13. Our undertaking has benefited from a number of precedents as models: Roger Adelson, ed., *Speaking of History: Conversations with Historians* (East Lansing, 1997); Maria Lúcia G. Pallares-Burke, ed., *The New History: Confessions and Conversations* (Cambridge, 2002); Natalie Zemon Davis, *A Passion for History: Conversations with Denis Crouzet*, ed. Michael Wolfe, trans. N. Z. Davis and M. Wolf (Kirksville, 2010), originally published as *L'histoire tout feu tout flamme* (Paris, 2010); Morten Haugaard Jeppesen, Frederik Stjernfelt, and Mikkel Thorup, eds., *Intellectual History: Five Questions* (Copenhagen, 2013).

the most literal sense of the term; it reflects a choice based upon our own areas of specialization and expertise. But it also bespeaks a particular liveliness that has animated the study of those centuries labeled early modern. This area of inquiry has been integral to the birth of some of the most influential historiographic developments of the last decades, developments that have proven consequential far beyond the confines of early modern studies. To name but a few, these include the contextualist history of political thought, the new history of classical scholarship, the rewriting of the narrative of the Scientific Revolution, new approaches to the study of religion and belief, the rise of the microhistory as a genre, and the genesis of the history of the book and of reading.[14]

Why has the early modern period, as it is known, been so productive for recent scholarship? These interviews are, among other things, an attempt at an answer. Three main themes emerge.

First, the early modern era was undoubtedly, on its own terms, an era of great changes: it witnessed renewals and transformations of religion, increased global interactions, and new technological and scientific pursuits. In the early twentieth century, the French scholar Paul Hazard argued that four innovations brought about a new way of thinking in Europe, which sparked what he termed the "crisis of the European mind:" the printing press, the revival of the classics, the discovery of the

---

14. Examples from these vast fields include J. G. A. Pocock, *Barbarism and Religion*, 6 vols. (Cambridge, 1999–2015); Richard Tuck, *Philosophy and Government, 1572–1651* (Cambridge, 1993); Noel Malcolm, *Aspects of Hobbes* (Oxford, 2002); Bernard Bailyn, *The Ideological Origins of the American Revolution* (Cambridge, MA, 1967); David Armitage, *The Ideological Origins of the British Empire* (Cambridge, 2000); David Armitage, *Civil Wars: A History in Ideas* (New York, 2017); Donald R. Kelley, *Foundations of Modern Historical Scholarship: Language, Law, and History in the French Renaissance* (New York, 1970); Constantin Fasolt, *The Limits of History* (Chicago, 2004); James Hankins, *Plato in the Italian Renaissance*, 2 vols. (Leiden, 1991); Steven Shapin and Simon Schaffer, *Leviathan and the Air-Pump: Hobbes, Boyle, and the Experimental Life* (Princeton, 1985); Mordechai Feingold, *The Mathematicians' Apprenticeship: Science, Universities and Society in England, 1560–1640* (Cambridge, 1984); Paula Findlen, *Possessing Nature: Museums, Collecting, and Scientific Culture in Early Modern Italy* (Berkeley, 1994); Brian W. Ogilvie, *The Science of Describing: Natural History in Renaissance Europe* (Chicago, 2006); Martin Mulsow, *Enlightenment Underground: Radical Germany, 1680–1720*, trans. H. C. E. Midelfort (Hamburg, 2002; Charlottesville, 2015); Jonathan Sheehan, *The Enlightenment Bible: Translation, Scholarship, Culture* (Princeton, 2005); Keith Thomas, *Religion and the Decline of Magic: Studies in Popular Beliefs in Sixteenth and Seventeenth-Century England* (London, 1971); Carlo Ginzburg, *The Cheese and the Worms: The Cosmos of a Sixteenth-Century Miller*, trans. J. and A. Tedeschi (Turin, 1976; Baltimore, 1980); Natalie Zemon Davis, *The Return of Martin Guerre* (Cambridge, MA, 1983); Roger Chartier, *The Order of Books: Readers, Authors, and Libraries in Europe between the Fourteenth and Eighteenth Centuries*, trans. Lydia G. Cochrane (Aix-en-Provence, 1992; Stanford, 1994); Robert Darnton, *The Business of Enlightenment: A Publishing History of the "Encyclopédie," 1775–1800* (Cambridge, MA, 1979); Jacob Soll, *Publishing "The Prince": History, Reading, and the Birth of Political Criticism* (Ann Arbor, 2005); Lisa Jardine, *Erasmus, Man of Letters: The Construction of Charisma in Print* (Princeton, 1993); William Sherman, *John Dee: The Politics of Reading and Writing in the English Renaissance* (Amherst, 1995).

Americas, and the new philosophy.[15] Without denying the transformative nature of these developments, we would emphasize that the early modern period was also a time when people—not just in Europe but in other intellectual traditions as well—looked to the past for guidance in understanding their changing world. The interplay between intellectual tradition and change is present in all historical contexts but was particularly pronounced between the fifteenth and eighteenth centuries. During these centuries, inherited intellectual cultures—the Greco-Roman past, visions of early Christianity and the primitive church, the classical Chinese tradition, the classical Islamic tradition—still seemed deeply compelling; innovation was often framed as renovation or renaissance. Later, the discourse of Western modernity would fatally diminish the prestige of traditional intellectual cultures, not just in Europe but all over the world. The intellectual history of the early modern period, then, remains enduringly rich and thought-provoking on account of the intellectual drama that then played out between adherence to the authority of the past and the challenges posed by new empirical realities and intellectual possibilities.

Early modernity thus has formed something of a laboratory for scholars of our day, who can examine how new ideas, practices, technologies, and institutions coexisted and conflicted with very old ones, including those inherited from distant pasts that early modern people labeled "ancient."[16] Our interviewees have shown that innovation often took place through recuperation, rather than radical rejection, of some aspect of the past. Change and continuity did not stand in simple opposition to one another but were facets of a continuously rediscovered and renegotiated relationship with one's intellectual inheritance. This poses difficult dilemmas for historians. In early modern Europe, for instance, which should receive more emphasis: the long history of Scholasticism, which persisted into the eighteenth century, or the breaks represented first by humanism and later by the new philosophy? The innovations introduced by the invention of print or the many features of writing and reading continuous with the manuscript culture of the Middle Ages? The seemingly alien facets of newly rediscovered classical texts or the manner in which such texts were harnessed to defend preexisting customs and norms?

---

15. Paul Hazard, *The Crisis of the European Mind, 1680–1715* (Paris, 1935; New York, 2013).

16. Sheldon Pollock, Benjamin A. Elman, and Ku-ming Kevin Chang, eds., *World Philology* (Cambridge, MA, 2015); Anthony Grafton and Glenn Most, eds., *Canonical Texts and Scholarly Practices: A Global Comparative Approach* (Cambridge, 2016).

Second, another reason for the usefulness of "thinking with" the early modern period is the fluidity of intellectual culture in those centuries. Intellectual agents then did all kinds of things—wrote poetry, collected antiquities, pursued astronomy and philology, studied numismatics and epigraphy. They did not see the boundaries and distinctions that hold us back; restoring their full intellectual range continues to stretch and challenge historians of our time. Looking back to an era before the disciplinary compartmentalization that emerged in the late eighteenth and nineteenth centuries can be fruitful for questioning what constitutes an intellectual tradition or a discipline or even a collection of disciplines such as the humanities, as well as for probing the supposed distinction between the two cultures, scientific and humanistic. Flux, in other words, is productive.

Third, early modernity deserves attention for the special role that it plays in our own era's genealogy of its origins. The early modern period's name expresses at once a teleology and a need to distinguish its referent from modernity proper. We still look, however ambivalently, to early modern traditions both to measure the distance that separates us from the world brought together by early modern people and to identify a prologue or harbinger of modernity proper. This ambivalence manifests itself in ongoing debates about just how much "we" people of the twenty-first century are heirs to the Renaissance, the Reformation, and the Enlightenment (whether for good or for ill is a separate debate). Early modernity is modernity but not quite, and hence our era claims ownership of its intellectual products through a simultaneous act of distancing. Precisely because of the unique place that early modernity occupies in modern perceptions of the relationship of past to present, it has proven fertile ground for meditations on the nature of intellectual traditions and historical change.

When we began work on this book, we had some notion of themes upon which our interlocutors might touch. Many others, however, emerged without our prompting, and we often encountered unanticipated echoes and resonances between interviews. Some intellectual inspirations, like Thomas Kuhn's *Structure of Scientific Revolutions*, are perhaps no great surprise.[17] So too is the method of study associated with the Warburg Library, especially its founder Aby Warburg's studies of the afterlife of antiquity in Renaissance culture.[18] The oeuvre of John G. A. Pocock

17. Thomas S. Kuhn, *The Structure of Scientific Revolutions* (Chicago, 1962).
18. Aby Warburg, *The Renewal of Pagan Antiquity: Contributions to the Cultural History of the European Renaissance*, trans. D. Britt (Leipzig, 1932; Los Angeles, 1999).

and in particular his *Ancient Constitution and the Feudal Law* of 1957 is one of the most persistent threads to join our historians—thanks especially to its investigation of the relationship between historiography and politics in the early modern world.[19] To some degree, our interlocutors also built upon the midcentury synthesis of intellectual history with literary analysis of genre and topoi practiced by the medievalists Erich Auerbach and Ernst Robert Curtius, themselves important figures in the emergence of comparative literature as an academic discipline.[20] The later eclectic cultural history of Carl Schorske, which embraced everything from musicology to psychoanalysis, also proved a key inspiration.[21] At the same time, the Italian classicist Arnaldo Momigliano offered a model for the history of scholarly inquiry by combining classical studies with investigation of the postclassical fortunes of the classical tradition.[22] For Lorraine Daston, the work of Ian Hacking proved an early influence.[23] In the history of Renaissance philosophy, Paul Oskar Kristeller looms large.[24] Further afield, the work of the anthropologist Clifford Geertz influenced two of our interviewees who were active already in the 1970s—Quentin Skinner and Anthony Grafton.[25] In sum, many of our interviewees voice their debts to sources far beyond the discipline of history and the study of early modernity.

Other common threads include the importance of intellectual collaboration, the difficulty of constructing canons of authors and the challenge of deciding where to start a project. "Following your nose" has been a metaphor repeatedly chosen to explain the process of historical inquiry; it offers encouragement to pursue interests even before they can be fully articulated. Indeed, many of our practitioners recount taking significant scholarly or professional risks—changing topics or even areas of study or determining to undertake a project without yet possessing all the technical skills required to complete it.

Our varied group is linked by what we might term elective affinity. Though their source material differs considerably, many of our scholars

19. J. G. A. Pocock, *The Ancient Constitution and the Feudal Law: A Study of English Historical Thought in the Seventeenth Century* (Cambridge, 1957).

20. Erich Auerbach, *Mimesis: The Representation of Reality in Western Literature*, trans. Willard R. Trask (Princeton, 1953); Ernst Robert Curtius, *European Literature and the Latin Middle Ages*, trans. Willard R. Trask (New York, 1953).

21. Carl Schorske, *Fin-de-siècle Vienna: Politics and Culture* (New York, 1981).

22. Arnaldo Momigliano, *Studies in Historiography* (London, 1966); Momigliano, *The Classical Foundations of Modern Historiography* (Berkeley, 1990).

23. Ian Hacking, *The Emergence of Probability: A Philosophical Study of Early Ideas about Probability, Induction, and Statistical Inference* (Cambridge, 1975).

24. Paul Oskar Kristeller, *The Philosophy of Marsilio Ficino* (New York, 1943).

25. Clifford Geertz, *Negara: The Theatre State in Nineteenth-Century Bali* (Princeton, 1981).

share a set of thematic interests. We will cast a spotlight on only three of them here. First, many interviewees have dealt with different aspects of the legacy of the classical past in early modern European culture. The Renaissance movement known as humanism, which recovered the classical Latin and Greek literary heritage, has long played a prominent role in grand narratives about early modern intellectual life. It once figured in a triumphalist tale: humanists used new methods of critical philology to recover the classics, supposedly neglected throughout the so-called Middle Ages. And, having reanimated antiquity, humanists helped to forge modernity, at least before the rationalism of the new philosophy replaced a culture that hitherto ascribed authority to transmitted texts. More recent scholarship (including that of several of our interviewees) has challenged not only the teleological nature of this narrative but also what it presupposed about early modern scholarly methods. Recent research has also shown that humanism, far from strutting its hour upon the stage and then being heard no more, informed the cultural outlook of European elites well into the eighteenth century and beyond. The tremendous endurance of certain traditions—whether those of Latin antiquity in Europe or the classical Chinese disciplines in East Asia—raises the challenging question of what exactly changes when a vocabulary, genre, or discipline endures across centuries.

Second, many of our historians are as concerned with knowledge making as they are with ideas. Questions about knowledge betray the influence of the history of science but also of the history of humanistic scholarship (lately sometimes described as the history of the humanities).[26] Historians have not only probed the interactions between new knowledge and ideas but also sought to establish how new knowledge was made and how it was translated from one domain to another, for example from the oral sphere to the written one or from the artisan's laboratory to the theoretical treatise. Indeed, craftspeople have newly come into view as knowledge makers, as the recent study of early modern knowledge making has erased a neat line between the learned and the unlearned.[27]

---

26. See Lorraine Daston and Glenn W. Most, "History of Science and History of Philologies," *Isis* 106 (2015): 378–90; and Rens Bod, *A New History of the Humanities: The Search for Principles and Patterns from Antiquity to the Present* (Oxford, 2013).

27. See, for instance, Pamela H. Smith and Benjamin Schmidt, eds., *Making Knowledge in Early Modern Europe: Practices, Objects, and Texts, 1400–1800* (Chicago, 2008); Paula Findlen, ed., *Early Modern Things: Objects and Their Histories, 1500–1800* (London, 2012); and Pamela O. Long, *Artisan/Practitioners and the Rise of the New Sciences, 1400–1600* (Corvallis, 2011).

Third, many of our scholars share an emphasis on overcoming heroic narratives about individual thinkers in order to recover a multiplicity of intellectual actors' practical interactions with available intellectual traditions. Taken together, their historical revisions offer an antidote to the falsifications of historical narrative, which all too often unfolds around the lone intellectual hero and his innovations. By refusing to take claims of novelty at face value, these scholars have carefully but relentlessly interrogated the stories that past intellectuals have told about themselves. In an age that remains wedded to the figure of the great thinker and his achievements, this form of inquiry offers no less than a fresh vision of intellectual history, and, more broadly, of how traditions of thought evolve and flourish.

By stressing these convergences, we do not mean to understate the differences between our interviewees, or assign them to a monolithic "school." Intellectual history is a broad tent. Distinct questions have directed our scholars to disparate kinds of sources, which have in turn required different methods of study. We do not mean to blur these distinctions, but neither do we find them troublesome. A division of labor, and methodological eclecticism, strike us as all to the good—not only healthy but desirable.

At the margins of these discussions, mostly of European intellectual history, unfolds another question, namely the future of the European past. In an age in which global approaches to intellectual history begin to become reality, the future of European history in US college curricula—and in a global research program—remains uncertain. Even as they welcome a broader vision of the past, our historians do not want to see the eclipse of European intellectual history, which has been such a productive and sustaining branch of inquiry. In his interview, Benjamin Elman suggests that intellectual history across the world faces kindred challenges. At the same time, a growing body of literature (including some contributions from our interviewees) has explored the global dimensions of early modernity itself. Early modernity marked a moment of unprecedented interaction between European and non-European cultures, and these interactions themselves transformed how European and non-European intellectuals viewed their respective pasts. We can no longer study the European tradition in isolation from others, and early modern studies has proven a fruitful site for the connective as well as the comparative study of intellectual practices and traditions.[28] We hope

28. See, inter alia, Anthony Grafton with April Shelford and Nancy Siraisi, *New Worlds, Ancient Texts: The Power of Tradition and the Shock of Discovery* (Cambridge, MA, 1995); Sanjay Subrahman-

that this volume can contribute to the large and urgent enterprise of defining and advancing the global study of intellectual and scholarly traditions.

In the meantime, a new generation of intellectual historians is forging its own paths forward. Current work builds upon the methodological contributions of our interviewees, and we expect that future work will do so as well. Where is this all headed? Any generalization would be reductive and, moreover, premature. To paraphrase Lorraine Daston in the interview below: watch this space; check back in five years.

---

yam, "Turning the Stones Over: Sixteenth-Century Millenarianism from the Tagus to the Ganges," *Indian Economic and Social History Review* 40 (2003): 129–61; Alastair Hamilton and Francis Richard, *André du Ryer and Oriental Studies in Seventeenth-Century France* (London, 2004); Urs App, *The Birth of Orientalism* (Philadelphia, 2010); Jan Loop, *Johann Heinrich Hottinger: Arabic and Islamic Studies in the Seventeenth Century* (Oxford, 2013); John-Paul Ghobrial, "The Archive of Orientalism and Its Keepers: Re-Imagining the Histories of Arabic Manuscripts in Early Modern Europe," *Past and Present* (2016): supplement 11, 90–111.

Ann M. Blair

ANN M. BLAIR is the Carl H. Pforzheimer University Professor at Harvard University.

What were your early intellectual interests?

In retrospect, a life might seem to follow a pattern, but at each moment along the way, you just go forward with what seems like the best decision. In other words, I never had a grand plan. I arrived at Harvard as a freshman in 1980, with two suitcases, from Switzerland. Within the first week, I decided I should take sophomore standing, based on my thirteenth year of school typical of the Swiss system, and in order to do that, I had to choose a concentration. I chose History and Science, partly because it was a hedge against having to make a decision. The concentration called for courses in history, the science of one's choice, and history of science. My science was math, and I thought of my history as medieval. My goal as an undergraduate was to read about all the schools of thought that I didn't know much about. I perceived, rightly or wrongly, that the History Department at that time wasn't very oriented toward the study of ideas. Therefore, history of science appealed to me as a way of approaching intellectual history. So I had an orientation toward intellectual history from early on.

One factor that influenced my interest in an earlier period of history was surely that I grew up in Geneva, where the Reformation was always perceived as an especially exciting period. During a number of summers, I worked as an official tour guide of the city of Geneva—my languages were French, German, and English. I would climb on a bus of people taking an organized tour that included Geneva, and we'd drive around the city for a couple of hours while I'd rattle off the sights, and then I'd get off that tour bus and onto another one [*laughs*]. I think growing up in Geneva pulled me naturally toward the sixteenth century.

What was it about intellectual history that drew you to the field? Were there particular questions or themes that interested you?

Because I was studying the history of science, science became a theme. I've never been particularly keen on political thought, which has dominated intellectual history. Other than that, as an undergraduate I didn't think of myself as focused on particular themes but rather on an encyclopedic desire to understand the sweep of intellectual history. Naturally I had in mind the European tradition, though I also took Donald Fleming's course on American intellectual history. But global perspectives were not prominent then. Even so, I enjoyed and pursued a lot of variety. I wrote my senior thesis on the French anti-Aristotelian Petrus Ramus, a sixteenth-century pedagogue who got flak in his time for turning every problem into a dichotomous diagram. That was my first introduction to reading early modern Latin treatises and to the sense of responsibility—both frightening and exhilarating—that comes from reading a text that has not been translated or commented on before.

Within the Harvard years, I also spent one year at the University of Geneva in 1981–82. That year was an important one, because at Geneva you chose one field as your principal focus along with two minor fields. I chose history, then philosophy of science, and in third place Sanskrit, from which I'm sorry to say I haven't managed to retain anything! Focusing on history at the University of Geneva (or elsewhere in Europe, I suspect) was to join a discipline with a strong sense of identity. The way students were introduced to history generated a real esprit de corps around the phrase "we historians!" By contrast, my experience at Harvard didn't have rousing moments of disciplinary identity formation.

After graduating I went to Cambridge, England, for a one-year MPhil in History and Philosophy of Science. That was my first introduction to the "strong programme" in the social history of science. I became especially interested in the principle of symmetry—of attending to the "failed" developments in science on the same terms as the ones that had a longer legacy. I took a bit of philosophy of science (with Mary Hesse no less) and concluded that I would stick with history! I was called a "keen American" for attending more lectures than was the norm. I wrote my MPhil thesis with Simon Schaffer, on the seventeenth-century mathematician Isaac Barrow. It was a wonderful year, living like an undergraduate and working like a graduate student. But the crucial formative phase for me was graduate school at Princeton.

What are some key intellectual moments that stand out from your time at Princeton?

I realized only in retrospect that the late 1980s were an exceptionally good time for early modern European history at Princeton, with five terrific faculty members in the History Department and John H. Elliott at the Institute for Advanced Study. We also had a large cohort of grad students in early modern Europe, many of whom focused on France. Natalie Z. Davis's seminar on France in the sixteenth century was delightfully memorable. She would combine readings, primary and secondary, that seemed puzzling when they were assigned but then came together brilliantly in the discussion. We sometimes met at her house. At one such meeting, she printed out copies of a handout for all ten of us on her printer, bypassing the photocopier—in the era of the dot-matrix printer this was a first! Robert Darnton was finishing up *The Forbidden Bestsellers of Pre-revolutionary France* at the time, and his seminar introduced us to some of his research and sources for that project among many other topics, which was great fun.[1]

Ted Rabb offered an excellent wide-ranging seminar for which I wrote a paper on historiography in seventeenth-century France. I remember coming up with a real argument only as I was writing the conclusion just hours before the paper was due and then frantically revising it. I am still grateful today for hard deadlines because they concentrate the mind; I find oral presentations—lectures or conference papers—useful in that way, in addition to the pleasure of getting immediate feedback. I also took a seminar with Lawrence Stone on the causes of the English Civil War and experienced vividly the point that coursework in graduate school is often about historiography more than history. I did not know much about what happened in the English Civil War, and we were plunging right into complex layers of historiographic debate. At

---

1. Robert Darnton, *The Forbidden Bestsellers of Pre-revolutionary France* (New York, 1995).

some point—embarrassingly far into the semester—it dawned on me that it might help if I read a nice encyclopedia article on the Civil War [*laughs*]! It was a good seminar in which we were encouraged to argue back and forth across different interpretive positions. Tony Grafton offered a graduate seminar on the Holy Roman Empire only when I was in my fifth year, but I attended for the fun of encountering a remarkable reading list full of primary sources I had never read.

After generals I taught for a semester in Bill Jordan's medieval history course. I had not taken a single medieval history course at Princeton, and I was very grateful for the existence of the *Dictionary of the Middle Ages*, which sadly wasn't complete at the time. It only went to letter *P* or so. So my challenge was to prepare for teaching based only on looking up terms that occurred before *P* in the alphabet [*laughs*]!

***Your first book was on the French Renaissance philosopher
Jean Bodin's treatise* Universae naturae theatrum *(1596).[2]
How did you choose Bodin's natural philosophy as your
topic of research?***

Bodin's *Theatrum* was Tony Grafton's suggestion. I had various practical criteria in mind: I wanted a French topic because I hoped to be in Paris for my research, and I was very interested in encyclopedism in the sixteenth century. I don't know whether Tony got the idea from noticing a copy of Bodin's book for sale, but in any case he suggested the topic just as a copy of Bodin's *Universae naturae theatrum* (the 1597 second edition) was available from William Poole in London. I bought it, though it seemed shocking at the time to spend 250 pounds on a book! The opportunity to buy the book was a wonderful stroke of luck. For the following ten years until *The Theater of Nature* came out, that book traveled with me wherever I went for any length of time, complete with a velvet cover that I sewed for it (putting to use the skills that girls acquired in sewing class in Swiss primary school and which I have hardly ever exercised since).

It seemed like a providential moment, soon followed by another. Bodin's *Theatrum*, an octavo book of 630 pages in Latin, was printed in three editions, but the French translation appeared in just one edition of 1597, so it is harder to find. Princeton did not have a copy, and it was not

---

2. Ann Blair, *The Theater of Nature: Jean Bodin and Renaissance Science* (Princeton, 1997).

easy to sustain day trips to study the copy held at Columbia. While visiting my soon-to-be in-laws in San Francisco that summer, I went to Stanford and out of curiosity checked their library catalog, which claimed that the stacks held a copy of Bodin's 1597 French *Théâtre*. This seemed hard to believe, but I went to look. In the stacks was a bound set of photocopies of the 1597 French translation. So I got myself a copy card and photocopied the photocopy [*laughs*]! As a result I had my main corpus easily at hand: the Latin in rare book form and the French through two layers of photocopying. At the time this was a rare privilege, though now almost all of Bodin's works are available in PDF format.[3]

Did some intellectual inclination of your own lead you to the Theatrum? *Many historians are interested in the first this, or the first that. Were you more interested in the persistence and longevity of certain traditions?*

I've mostly been interested in the long persistence of ideas and practices rather than the firsts—firsts are hard to ascertain, though they get so much more attention. How about looking into "lasts" instead? Bodin's *Theatrum* was more innovative than I realized initially, but I was especially interested in using it to learn more about what I called "ordinary" science—the lesser-known works that hadn't been hailed as forward-looking, even if they weren't "normal" in Thomas Kuhn's sense of being widely accepted. I got a little pushback from some people about this choice of dissertation topic: why would I write on an obscure book of natural philosophy by someone who's famous for being a political philosopher—what was going to be of interest in this? My reaction was, well, I'm a historian, and my job is to make it interesting. I suppose my naïve assumption was I could make anything interesting!

I had no idea then of the surprising things that I ended up learning about, such as the German popularization of the text or the work's strong reception among German university philosophers. The work's anti-Aristotelianism was also not clear to me until well into the research. On that point I deeply benefited from studying annotated copies. Upon first reading the text I was struck by how Aristotelian Bodin seemed—for instance, in his discussions of causes, matter and form, passive and agent intellects. What first alerted me to the fact that Bodin was hostile

3. For a portal to primary and secondary sources relating to Bodin, see http://projects.iq.harvard.edu/bodinproject/home.

to Aristotle on many specific points was a heavily annotated copy that I was able to study in Paris. One of the most common annotations in that copy was the marginal note "Aristotle criticized" (*Aristoteles reprehensus*), which appeared 160 times in the 630 pages.[4] These annotations made me pay closer attention to the many places where Bodin was indeed critical of Aristotle and offered a new causal explanation or (in another specialty of his) a "confession of ignorance." The latter occurred when Bodin rejected Aristotle's explanation but did not suggest an alternative, concluding that it was better to acknowledge the mystery of nature. Another annotator flagged some of those confessions of ignorance with the note "Bodin's piety." I realized from these annotations that historians can learn a great deal from the assessments of contemporary readers, who are better placed than we are to appreciate what was striking about a text at the time it was written. For scholars who study texts, contemporary responses help to develop what Michael Baxandall called the "period eye" for art historians.[5]

How did you track down that privately owned annotated copy of Bodin's Theatrum?

When I headed for Paris in my fourth year of graduate school, Natalie Davis gave me a number of names of people to contact. One was Jean Céard, a tremendous scholar of sixteenth-century French literature who had published a massive *thèse d'état* on monsters.[6] I wrote to him before traveling to Paris but didn't hear back. Once in Paris, I wrote again and again didn't hear back. But then I met with someone else from Natalie Davis's list who invited me to dinner with him. At the dinner, when I described my dissertation topic Jean said, "Oh, I think I might have a copy of that book. You should come to my house, and we'll look at it." When I went to his house soon after I realized why he hadn't answered my letters: his house was full of stacks of mail—on every surface, both opened and unopened [*laughs*]! There were books everywhere, too, but the piles

---

4. A transcription of these annotations is available from Ann Blair's Harvard website under Publications at http://projects.iq.harvard.edu/ablair/publications-0.

5. Michael Baxandall, *Painting and Experience in Fifteenth-Century Italy: A Primer in the Social History of Pictorial Style* (Oxford, 1972).

6. Jean Céard, *La nature et les prodiges: L'insolite au XVIe siècle* (Geneva, 1977). For a bibliography of Céard's wide-ranging publications to 2008, see Jean Dupèbe, Franco Giacone, Emmanuel Naya, and Anne-Pascale Pouey-Mounou, eds., *Esculape et Dionysos: Mélanges en l'honneur de Jean Céard* (Geneva, 2008).

of mail were especially remarkable. Obviously, he was in incredibly high demand, and massively overworked.

But he was also extremely generous. I went to his home once a week for a number of months that year, and while he went off to teach, I would make progress through the heavily annotated copy of Bodin's *Theatrum* that he had bought years before. I transcribed and translated every note, keying it to the text. At the end of the day, when Céard came home, I would have a long list of questions for him about the notes and also the text itself. He could answer many of them, recognizing allusions from memory, which was an incredibly valuable skill in the days before Google. But, in a more transferable fashion, he taught me how to find answers in early modern reference works. In his home he owned essential reference tools like Ambrogio Calepino's dictionary, where I could find not only definitions of words but also their sixteenth-century cultural connotations, which helped make sense of statements by Bodin and his annotator. For example, Calepino reported the ancient view that cabbage had an antipathy to the vine, citing Cicero, which explained Bodin's claim that cabbage juice dispelled drunkenness![7] Or when the annotator glossed Bodin's term *larus* [seabird or mew] saying, "this is Greek for the Latin *fulicae*, [which are] aquatic birds,"[8] I could see that that definition was available in Calepino and therefore not unusual at the time, even though both terms were new to me. Céard also introduced me to Caelius Rhodiginus's *Lectiones antiquae*, a wonderfully rich collection of ancient lore miscellaneously ordered, so that you have to use the alphabetical index to find things. The annotator (whom we never identified) cited Rhodiginus explicitly to gloss the term *Taraxippos* in Bodin's text and even did so accurately, so that reference was not hard to find.[9] But other times the entry in the index was wrong, so Jean would try to reconstruct the error involved (which digit of the page number might be different, for example) to track down a passage that was clearly in there somewhere. It was a thrill to find it finally, although sometimes we had to give up too.

7. See Jean Bodin, *Universae naturae theatrum* (Frankfurt, 1597), 294; and Ambrogio Calepino, *Dictionarium septem linguarum* (Basel, 1570), 174.

8. "Graece dicuntur, quae Latine fulicae, aves aquaticae," annotations in the copy of Bodin, *Theatrum* (1597), owned by Jean Céard, 115, line 27, keyed to "laros." Cf. Calepino, *Dictionarium*, 832.

9. At "Taraxippe": "de quo vide Caelium l.13.c.17," in the copy of Bodin's *Theatrum* owned by Jean Céard, 407, line 4. Cf. Caelius Rhodiginus, *Lectionum antiquarum libri xxx*, XIII, ch. 17 (Basel, 1550), 485, on the Olympic games: "In propinquo tumulus visebatur Ischeni gigantis Mercurio et Hieria geniti. Eum nuncupabant Taraxippum, quod illuc adventantes equi ratione occulta mire exterrerentur."

I learned a tremendous amount from Céard, not only about Bodin and this annotator, but especially about the value of using resources from the period as guides to understanding a Renaissance text—including near-contemporary annotations and reference works and classical texts that were available at the time rather than modern ones. It's also true that in the libraries of Paris like the BN (now BnF, Bibliothèque nationale de France), it was actually easier to call up a sixteenth-century edition of Aristotle than a twentieth-century one, which might be already in use or not even available in the collection. And I think the experience of looking for answers to my questions in Rhodiginus's *Lectiones antiquae* and other reference books from the Renaissance first seeded my interest in reference books, which is evident in my book *Too Much to Know*.

At this point, in what format were you taking your notes?

At Harvard in 1984, I was cutting edge. My father, who has always been a gadget person, lent me what was called a portable (later "luggable") Kaypro computer, which weighed twenty-nine pounds and had a tiny green screen and two drives for 5¼-inch floppy disks: one for the software, the other for the text you were writing. I wrote my senior thesis on that computer and continued to use it in graduate school, but only for writing papers, never for taking notes. I started composing at the computer at that point. Before then I had written my papers in longhand and then typed them up. But I wrote my senior thesis on the Kaypro and printed it out; I must have had a printer, too, because there was no common computer infrastructure. When I was done I lent my computer to someone in my dorm who reported that he had not yet started writing his thesis and managed to write it in the space of a weekend, thanks to word processing [*laughs*]! I also took the Kaypro to England for the following year and was stopped at customs and asked if I had any commercial goods. The customs officers were clearly eyeing my strange computer, but I said, "No commercial goods," and they let the Kaypro in and then out again when I came back to the United States.

By the time I went to Paris in 1988–89, I had a Toshiba laptop with 500K of RAM. It therefore needed only one 3.5-inch floppy disk drive to store one's texts, because the RAM could contain the software. At the old BN, the key thing was to find access to electricity, because my Toshiba did not have much battery life (about ninety minutes as I recall) [*laughs*]. A section at the back of the main reading room called the *Hémicycle* was used for semirare printed items such as pamphlets or unbound materials, and for some reason it had plugs at many of the seats. I made a point of always having something on hold at the *Hémicycle*, whether or not that's what I was actually reading, in order to be able to plug in.

How did your time in Paris inform your intellectual growth?

That time in Paris was crucial. I attended Roger Chartier's seminar in book history at the École des Hautes Études en Sciences Sociales. I went back to it in subsequent years when I was in Paris, and each time it was an anchor for one of my communities there. Céard was another strong influence, and through him I met other intellectual historians trained in French literature, like Frank Lestringant and Isabelle Pantin. Pantin is a historian of astronomy who, along with Annie Charon of the École des Chartes, the French institution that trains archivist-paleographers, gave me the idea and coached me through the process of running a mail survey of surviving copies of the *Theatrum*.

It was a real boon that Jean Bodin was such a famous author. The Séminaire de Bibliographie Historique of the University of Mons, in Belgium, had devoted a multiyear project to him, involving a gigantic worldwide survey of the locations of surviving copies of all Bodin's works.[10] In Mons, I learned of the existence of the German popularization of Bodin, which I might never have known about otherwise, since most editions of it were printed with the *Problemata Aristotelis* and often not cataloged separately. Hence the work, which was rare in any case, showed up in just a few library catalogs. At Mons, I was generously allowed to use a machine—at the time very special—which made paper copies from the Mons microfilm of the *Problemata Bodini*. I came away with a printout of that rare German work, in addition to a list of the libraries throughout the world that had reported that they owned a copy of the *Theatrum*. Whereas the Séminaire de Bibliographie Historique had contacted about 900 libraries, they had whittled the list down for me to about 250 that reported a copy of the *Theatrum*.

I wrote to those libraries with a questionnaire, which asked whether they had any copies of the *Theatrum* and requested details about them—which edition and which issue of the first edition (which appeared both with and without the dedication) and any copy-specific features, such as

---

10. See Roland Crahay, Marie-Thérèse Isaac, and Marie-Thérèse Lenger, *Bibliographie critique des éditions anciennes de Jean Bodin* (Brussels, 1992). Available online from the Bodin Project at Harvard: http://projects.iq.harvard.edu/bodinproject/bibliography.

annotations, ex libris markings, and works bound with Bodin's. I did not contact the major libraries that I visited myself but received very generous results from libraries all over Europe. My questionnaire also turned up other annotated copies, though none as thoroughly annotated as Céard's. Still, I traveled to see a number of interesting copies, including some censored ones.

In some cases, I never saw the copies themselves, notably those in Eastern Europe and the Soviet Union, which were very difficult to access in 1988–89. I was especially grateful for the answers I received from librarians in Poland and Czechoslovakia. Even if I couldn't see those particular copies, the answers I got about which texts were bound with Bodin's *Theatrum* turned out to be sufficient, because I was able to find a copy of those titles in Paris.

The books with which Bodin's *Theatrum* was bound introduced me to a number of texts I wouldn't have thought to study and in which I found multiple printed references to Bodin's *Theatrum*. I was interested in the reception of the *Theatrum*, but looking for citations of the book in French works of natural philosophy was like looking for a needle in a haystack, especially since there were almost no needles to be found: French authors of the seventeenth century generally ignored the *Theatrum*. Instead, its greatest uptake was in German natural philosophical academic books, and I was led to those titles by the books with which owners in the German academic world had bound their copies of the *Theatrum*. Again, the period eye proved crucial: the owners who made the decision to bind the *Theatrum* with something else were careful to do so thoughtfully, placing the *Theatrum* with another text that belonged with it thematically. Their judgment was so sound that those "bound-with" texts often mentioned Bodin's natural philosophy explicitly. By and large, bound-with texts proved valuable to my ability to track Bodin's reception, even though I had no inkling of that result when I started the mail survey.

At what point did you realize you were writing a "total history" of the Theatrum? *Where did that concept come from?*

That concept came out of Annales school readings that I had done for my field with Natalie Davis. I was very impressed by Pierre Goubert's *Beauvais et le Beauvaisis*, a two-volume *histoire totale* of a city and its region, starting from the climate, the geography, the demographics, and moving on to the social and the economic conditions.[11] I was quite taken with the Annales idea that history comprises multiple strands of change that run concurrently at different rhythms: from the slow pace of geographic change to the moderate speed of economic change and the fast pace of political events. The job of the historian is to try to keep in view the whole bundle (*faisceau*) of different strands even while focusing on a particular one. I took that to mean that intellectual historians should also think of themselves as historians tout court, who have knowledge about and interest in the broader context of the texts they study. Natalie Davis practiced that approach from the other point of departure, as a social historian who also studied texts, and Robert Darnton wrote explicitly on connecting social and intellectual history through the social history of ideas. I'm sure I absorbed those principles from them. But more broadly I liked the ideal of an *histoire totale* that tries to bring all the strands together, even though it's impossible to carry out.

The other model underpinning *The Theater of Nature* is the idea of following the life cycle of book, from birth to death. The book is born in the authoring of it and the author's methods of reading and composition; then it is printed and circulated and read and received. I suppose that death would be the end of the active use of the book, although books often have a rich afterlife, through survival down to the present in libraries and the antiquarian book trade. I only later learned about the chart in which Thomas Adams and Nicolas Barker map out the stages of a book's existence, which I use regularly now in my teaching.[12]

The argument that frames The Theater of Nature *is that traditional natural philosophy has a longer afterlife than we think. To what extent did you seek to correct the triumphalist narrative of the emergence of the new sciences in the seventeenth century?*

That was definitely my main message at the time. I didn't become aware of the book-historical aspect of my work until later, once I started teaching book history. Instead I couched my work on Bodin in terms of my

---

11. Pierre Goubert, *Beauvais et le Beauvaisis de 1600 à 1730: Contribution à l'histoire sociale de la France du XVIIe siècle* (Paris, 1960).

12. Thomas R. Adams and Nicolas Barker, "A New Model for the Study of the Book," in *A Potencie of Life: Books in Society*, ed. Nicolas Barker (London, 1993), 5–43, here 14. For some discussion of this chart as compared to his own earlier one that inspired it, see Robert Darnton, "'What Is the History of Books?' Revisited," *Modern Intellectual History* 4, no. 3 (2007): 495–508, esp. 502–5.

experience in the history of science and of the principle of symmetry: that it was just as important to look at the lesser-known, "ordinary" thinkers as it was to study the figures who have been canonized as "great men." In doing so you tend to find more continuity than revolution, but continuity with variations and transformations. For example, Bodin introduced anti-Aristotelianism into his traditional natural philosophy, but it was not the anti-Aristotelianism that led to Descartes or to Bacon, on which so much modern work had been focused. My main intervention was to show the long persistence and creativity of traditional natural philosophy.

For my second book project, my plan was to study traditional natural philosophy as it continued into the first half of the seventeenth century, at the University of Paris. I spent the first year after finishing my dissertation in Paris again, on an NSF-NATO fellowship. During that year I read a lot of textbooks by authors more obscure than Bodin—French university philosophers. I worked especially on Jean Cécile Frey, who, although he was explicitly Aristotelian, often strayed from Aristotle's positions. Comparing him to Bodin made me realize how the ways these authors portrayed themselves (as Aristotelian or anti-Aristotelian) had less to do with their actual positions than with the impact they wished to have on their contemporaries.[13] But, much as I enjoyed that foray into Frey, I realized that others were better qualified and more interested than I was in examining the precise mixture of philosophical sources and new positions in each of those traditional natural philosophers.[14]

When did you first begin to consider yourself a historian of the book?

My early teaching was on the Scientific Revolution, on encyclopedias from the Middle Ages to the Enlightenment, on science and religion, and early modern France. I first taught book history in spring 1998. I had just been hired in the History Department at Harvard as an assistant professor.

---

13. Ann M. Blair, "The Teaching of Natural Philosophy in Early Seventeenth-Century Paris: The Case of Jean Cécile Frey," *History of Universities* 12 (1993): 95–158 and "Tradition and Innovation in Early Modern Natural Philosophy: Jean Bodin and Jean Cécile Frey," *Perspectives on Science* 2 no. 4 (1994): 428–54.

14. See, for example, the work of Roger Ariew and Daniel Garber, including Roger Ariew, *Descartes and the First Cartesians* (Oxford, 2014) and, more generally, Daniel Garber and Michael Ayers with the assistance of Roger Ariew and Alan Gabbey, eds., *The Cambridge History of Seventeenth-Century Philosophy* (Cambridge, 1998).

Attending Harvard's seminar in book history (which still exists today, now at the Mahindra Humanities Center) helped me identify with book history as a distinct subfield. Some invitations to speak did too.

I was offering two lecture courses at Harvard and felt I needed a third, so I developed a course called History of the Book and of Reading. Originally, I arranged the course chronologically, in a long sequence from antiquity to the present, with a bulge around the early modern period. But I am very pleased with how I have recently restructured it. I start with a five-week sequence that provides a chronology of technologies from the scroll to the mechanization of printing. The following six weeks are arranged thematically, with one week each on publication, authorship, regulations (censorship and licensing), distribution and trade, reception and reading, libraries and survival. I wrap up in the last two or three weeks by considering the impact of digital techniques on these themes. This way students have time during the first few weeks to select a book to study for their final paper. In each of the thematic weeks I ask them to investigate how that week's theme applies to the source they have chosen. The relevant secondary literature has also exploded in the years between each iteration, so I constantly need to update the course, which is a great pleasure.

How did you first begin to explore the topics of information overload and information management, which would lead you, eventually, to writing your book Too Much to Know?

It happened slowly, that's for sure! My first book came out in 1997, and *Too Much to Know* in 2010.[15] That's a long time. Along the way I wrote a lot of articles, often completely unrelated to my second book project. But these proved helpful to broadening my knowledge and understanding, particularly articles I was asked to contribute to handbooks—for example, on natural philosophy for the *Cambridge History of Early Modern Science*; on science and religion for the *Cambridge History of Christianity*; on the organization of knowledge for the *Cambridge Companion to Renaissance Philosophy*.[16] Writing those helped me focus on the bigger

15. Ann Blair, *Too Much to Know: Managing Scholarly Information before the Modern Age* (New Haven, 2010).

16. Ann Blair, "Natural Philosophy," in *The Cambridge History of Science*, vol. 3, *Early Modern Science*, ed. Katharine Park and Lorraine Daston (Cambridge, 2006), 365–405; "Science and Religion," in *The Cambridge History of Christianity*, vol. 6, *Reform and Expansion, 1500–1660*, ed. Ronnie Po-Chia

picture and introduce some of my teaching experience into my scholarly writing.

Remember that my original interest in Bodin's *Theatrum* had been to study its encyclopedic character. But I found that in studying one encyclopedia of natural philosophy, I could not talk effectively about encyclopedism more broadly. Although I discussed Bodin's principles of organization (and the chain of being, for example), I didn't feel I had learned much that was new about encyclopedism as a broader phenomenon.

In redefining my second book project away from traditional natural philosophy, I set out to understand Renaissance encyclopedism more broadly. I enjoyed, for example, tracking down all the works that Johann Heinrich Alsted hailed as models for his *Encyclopaedia* of 1630—seventeen of them, including one, by Joannes Colle, which also named twenty-three of his predecessors. I tracked a corpus of about three dozen books (given a few overlaps between the two lists) that these two contemporaries felt were encyclopedic and which ranged widely from the thin and diagrammatic to the large and disorganized.[17] It wasn't easy to find all those books—some of them stayed for years on a "to find" list that I would try to whittle down in each new library I visited. That research didn't lead to any publication directly, but I learned a lot from it and returned to some of that material much later.[18] But I got frustrated with the concept of "encyclopedia." A turning point came when after a talk I had given someone asked, "Are you going to include Don Quixote, because it's an encyclopedic novel?" I just thought, Oh, no [*laughs*]! I can't be responsible for every single work. I have to abandon this term, which can be applied so broadly that I cannot set any reasonable boundaries on the category.

That's when I decided to define my topic around books that invited a certain way of reading—reference reading or reading for consultation. Even though one could, of course, read a reference book from cover to cover, some books were designed to be consulted rather than read through, given the presence of finding devices and even explicit advice to that effect (offered by the sixteenth-century Swiss encyclopedist Conrad Gessner for example).[19] I also remember how useful I had found early modern

---

Hsia (Cambridge, 2007), 427–45; "Organizations of Knowledge," in *The Cambridge Companion to Renaissance Philosophy*, ed. James Hankins (Cambridge, 2007), 287–303.

17. Johann Heinrich Alsted, *Encyclopedia*, 4 vols. (Herborn, 1630; Stuttgart-Bad Cannstatt, 1989) and Joannes Colle, *De idea, et theatro imitatricium et imitabilium ad omnes intellectus, facultates, scientias et artes* (Pesaro, 1618).

18. Ann Blair, "Revisiting Renaissance Encyclopaedism," in *Encyclopaedism from Antiquity to the Renaissance*, ed. Jason König and Greg Woolf (Cambridge, 2013), 377–97.

19. Conrad Gessner, *Bibliotheca universalis* (Zurich, 1545).

reference works in studying the annotations in Bodin's *Theatrum*. I still haven't written that paean to the utility of early modern reference books for historical research that I have in mind—maybe I'll get to it someday! But using early modern reference books is part of my larger commitment to use not only the mental categories but also the books and editions that were available at the time as I work through a text, its sources, and its context. So I abandoned encyclopedias and moved on to reference books.

The concept of information overload came from a comment Dan Rosenberg made at the History of Science Society meeting in 2000. Rosenberg offered a powerful point that has stuck with me ever since: information overload is a feeling that you can have regardless of the scale of the overload; it's quite widespread, but like all feelings it is experienced as if it were new time and time again. That whole session ended up being a set of articles in the *Journal of the History of Ideas*.[20]

In writing *Too Much to Know*, I had a false start when I wrote a chapter on the Swiss polymath Theodor Zwinger, who is indeed a major player in the book. But the chapter didn't break out of the pattern I had followed in *The Theater of Nature*—of taking one work and unpacking it, trying to be encyclopedic about it. I realized, this is dull, and I've done this kind of thing before. So I started over and made a conscious effort to incorporate the broader themes that I had been broaching in my various oral presentations of my work, in which I emphasized parallels with current digital tools and concerns. Realizing that I could use those themes to shape my book was a breakthrough.

Managing the notes for *Too Much to Know* was the biggest challenge. I spent a whole summer just going over my notes and trying to figure out what would fit where, and what I was going to use and not use. The other big challenge, as I was working through that material that I'd laid out for myself, was to stop constantly questioning my plan all over again and saying, "Oh, I should rearrange everything." [*laughs*] I was deeply tempted many times to do that! At some point, though, you have to realize that you could revise your work indefinitely. There are many perfectly good ways of presenting a complex body of material, so ultimately you

---

20. See the following articles in *Journal of the History of Ideas* 64, no. 1 (2003): Daniel Rosenberg, "Early Modern Information Overload," 1–9; Ann Blair, "Reading Strategies for Coping with Information Overload ca. 1550–1700," 11–28; Brian Ogilvie, "The Many Books of Nature: Renaissance Naturalists and Information Overload," 29–40; Jonathan Sheehan, "From Philology to Fossils: The Biblical Encyclopedia in Early Modern Europe," 41–60; Richard Yeo, "A Solution to the Multitude of Books: Ephraim Chambers's *Cyclopaedia* (1728) as 'the Best Book in the Universe,'" 61–72.

just have to carry on with the one that you started with, because you do need to finish.

How do you manage your own information?

I ran into my Geneva professor Bronislaw Baczko many years later in the Paris archives and asked what he was working on. He said, "Vous savez, on ne travaille jamais que sur soi-même" (You know, you only ever work on yourself). In other words, you only ever work on your own problems. And, in a way, my interest in note-taking, in organization, I think, is a sign of my own sense of inadequacy in tackling this problem.

I do have a system, but it's far from perfect. The notes from classes I took and from my reading for general exams were all in ink on paper, and I hardly ever consult them. I'm envious of today's graduate students to whom I recommend taking notes on computer right away. It's a great privilege to create your professional stock from the beginning, in a medium that's searchable and portable, among other valuable features. In Paris I started taking notes on computer, but I also used notebooks to keep track of my research plans and tasks and because there were times when I couldn't use the computer. I was told I couldn't use a nearby plug at the Bodleian in 1991, until a more senior American scholar also using a laptop offered to pay them for the electricity with the equivalent of a sarcasm emoticon, and they relented. I was also told that my computer was making too much noise at the library of the University of Geneva, on a day when the reading room was almost empty. The reader, I suspect, objected to what was a new way of working at the time; I was told to turn off my computer, and I did, so I was grateful that I had a notebook with me too.

I still take notes on paper during talks and meetings, although, if I do not transfer them into the computer, I don't expect to consult them again. I find that I have become more careless about keeping track of notes on paper even though they are especially precious, because they exist only in one copy. By contrast my electronic notes seem to me better organized, and I have them backed up in multiple ways. So I'm a fan of electronic note-taking, even though I realize it's not optimal. I mostly take notes in Word documents. At first, I created one file per book or author and now more commonly I use larger files that cluster multiple sources on a given theme. I keep track of my notes in two ways, because I've never had confidence in the functions for searching within files on my computer, and I started my files before such search tools existed. The first is a bibliography of items that I've read that also lists the file and folder in which the relevant notes are stored. The other, inspired by early modern note-taking, is called Places: it's a very large file containing thematic rubrics in which I remind myself briefly of passages or authors of interest on that theme, with a reference to the full notes stored somewhere else. I go through phases of simple accumulation (e.g., during the semester while I'm teaching), interspersed with periodic organizing sprees when I take stock of what I have and improve the rubrics by consolidating some and subdividing others. Some of the headings became too large to be part of the Places file, so I spin them off into separate files on "note-taking," "readers," or "libraries," for example. These files contain cross-references to or excerpts from relevant notes in another file, or I'll just take notes on something directly in that file. It's still vital to enter the items into the bibliography to keep track of where the main corpus of notes on each item is. And the Places file is useful for headings that I don't use very often, where the material doesn't get excessively large.

After I finished *Too Much to Know*, I wrapped up the bibliography and the Places files I had created for those ten years. I closed them and opened new sets of files! I can go back to consult the old ones, but I'm not adding to them anymore. By now the new files are getting unwieldy and messy. So I need to finish my current book project in order to start all over again.

When it's time to write I like to use the program Scrivener as an intermediate place in which to organize and rearrange material taken from the notes files. Then I draw from the organization I formed in Scrivener when I start to write. But I write in a separate Word file and refer back to the original note files and whenever possible to the sources themselves. One thing I haven't been good at is keeping together different kinds of media, like photos and PDFs. I know there are other software programs that let you cluster these in one place, but I rely on notes to myself to look in my folders of photos or PDFs. I'm also conscious of the risks of using software programs that will not prove durable—it's impossible to tell today which ones will be around tomorrow, let alone in a couple of decades.

What are your thoughts on the connections between the digital transition that we've lived through and the changes that early modern scholars experienced?

One interesting impact of the changes we've all been living through is that they have made us more aware of note-taking. Note-taking was rarely discussed in classes when I was a student. Everyone took notes according to habits they formed whether from a teacher in high school or on their own, but no one talked about it. Now we're all more attentive to our working methods because technology is changing them. There are also studies about the effectiveness of taking notes by handwriting versus on computer, etc. It strikes me that those studies may prove limited to the experience of a particular point in time or generation and that they might not carry over to another context. I'm not sure that handwriting will always be associated with better retention, as some current studies have argued is the case now—especially since new generations may be less and less comfortable with writing by hand and reading the results (which presents its own challenges).

I see a lot of basic continuities between early modern methods of note-taking and what we do today to select and summarize what we want to retain from our reading. The techniques and tools of note-taking have changed a lot in recent decades, but there were also variations and innovations in the early modern period, foremost among them the gradual rise of the movable slip or index card equivalent. We feel we have lived through a unique transition to digital tools, but change is not unique to our period. However, I'm delighted that our heightened awareness of change in media and ways of reading has generated an increased interest in the history of books and of working methods!

So much of your work has focused on compilation as a practice and as an art. Can the history of compilation also provide insights and lessons for us today?

Absolutely. When you do a Google search, what are you doing but using Google to select things from the web in a kind of compilation? Google uses algorithms that it keeps top secret but which are now and then the object of discussion. When we criticize the search function and the software behind it we are paying attention to a process of compiling that was performed for centuries by people copying from books. The compiler has usually been treated as a "little guy" and passed over by historians on the hunt for noteworthy thinkers, but the compiler's decisions and judgment were crucial—just as Google's searching algorithms are today—to the material that was readily available, notably in reference works, which were and still are widely distributed, and read, and used. Reference works and their compilers have in most cases been left out of intellectual history.

The history of compilation offers examples of large projects that were finished just as a new technology appeared that would have made them so much easier. The *Isis Cumulative Bibliography* of secondary sources in the history of science issued its first cumulative indexes in 1965 and 1975, just before computers became commercially available.[21] We should realize that we, too, are caught in this difficulty; in any large project we use methods that we know will soon be superseded. Yet we have to complete them now with the tools we have available.

Too Much to Know *begins with a chapter comparing information management in the Islamic world, Europe, and China. How did you come to that comparison, and what did you learn from it?*

In some sense that comparison has roots in the nineteenth-century historiography on encyclopedias, when European scholars started applying the term *encyclopedia* to Arabic and Chinese works. Since I don't read Arabic or Chinese, that European historiography that extends down to the present was my point of departure. But the book-historical approach added new possibilities for me to examine these works, even without understanding the text. I was very fortunate to learn from generous colleagues and graduate students who gave me tutorials in Chinese rare books at Yenching Library and Ottoman manuscripts in Houghton Library. I've tried to make a record of some of that expertise in the module I contributed to the HarvardX course titled The Book: Print and Manuscript in Western Europe, Asia, and the Middle East (1450–1650) (HUM1.3x), featuring Dr. Lianbin Dai on East Asian materials and Dr. Meredith Quinn on Ottoman manuscripts. Conferences were also valuable ways to gain some understanding of these fields. I was invited to a conference at the Aga Khan Institute in London on Islamic encyclopedias in 2003 and learned a tremendous amount.[22] I have engaged with specialists of China on encyclopedias and book history, which is a rapidly growing field among East Asianists.[23]

21. The *Isis Cumulative Bibliography* is available online with some discussion at http://cumulative.isiscb.org/about.html.

22. Ann Blair, "A Europeanist's Perspective," in *Organizing Knowledge: Encyclopaedic Activities in the Pre-Eighteenth-Century Islamic World*, ed. Gerhard Endress (Leiden, 2006), 201–15.

23. "Le florilège latin comme point de comparaison," in *Qu'était-ce qu'écrire une encyclopédie en Chine? What did it mean to write an encyclopedia in China?*, ed. Florence Bretelle-Establet and Karine Chemla, *Extrême-Orient, Extrême-Occident*, special issue (2007), 185–204.

These comparisons have helped me reflect on the impact of print-ing in Europe—an area that has generated much interest and debate, especially since Elizabeth Eisenstein's 1979 *The Printing Press as an Agent of Change*.[24] A comparative perspective highlights, first, the fact that the single term *printing* is used to describe two different types of technol-ogy with distinct constraints and advantages. Xylography or wood block printing, on the one hand, along with its modern counterpart of lithog-raphy, enables you to keep and reuse the source of the printed page, offering the potential for a kind of "print on demand." On the other hand, typography or printing with movable metal type requires you to print a certain number of copies at one time because you will need to reuse the type from the sheet you just printed to compose the next one. As a result of these technical differences, East Asian printing did not require as much initial investment or financial speculation as typogra-phy, and the distinctions that European bibliographers make between editions, issues, and reprintings do not apply as clearly. In comparing the development of book production in different places like Europe, the Islamic world, and China (among many other interesting comparisons that could be studied), we can appreciate how culture plays an impor-tant role in shaping the impact of technology.

These comparisons have helped me appreciate what's unique about the European case: it isn't so much the birth of printing but the specific ways in which printing was applied. And I have focused on Europe not because it's inherently more interesting but just because I'm a European-ist, so I focused the comparison in that direction. But the comparison works just as well in the other directions, and I'm delighted to see seri-ous comparative work of that kind in print now.[25] Comparative work requires collaboration across the different kinds of linguistic and his-torical expertise that are needed. I benefit tremendously from working with graduate students with many different specialties (from the manu-scripts of Timbuktu to Manchu writing) who have prepared an exam field with me in book history and/or on whose dissertation committee I have served. Wherever there is text, there can be book history—which focuses on the surviving material texts to shed light on a whole range of

---

24. Elizabeth L. Eisenstein, *The Printing Press as an Agent of Change: Communications and Cultural Transformations in Early Modern Europe* (Cambridge, 1979). For two different kinds of critiques see Anthony Grafton, "The Importance of Being Printed," *Journal of Interdisciplinary History* 11, no. 2 (Autumn 1980): 265–86 and the forum featuring Elizabeth Eisenstein and Adrian Johns, "How Revo-lutionary Was the Print Revolution?" *American Historical Review* 107, no. 1 (2002): 84–128.

25. Joseph R. McDermott and Peter Burke, eds., *The Book Worlds of East Asia and Europe, 1450–1850: Connections and Comparisons* (Hong Kong, 2015).

topics, including authorship and authority, transmission and distribution, reading, commentary, canon formation, loss and survival.

A theme that runs through a lot of your work concerns attempts at universality or comprehensiveness, to be able to know everything, or to catalog everything. What can we gain from studying that idea of universalism, or the polymathic impulse?

A lot of historians work on very grim topics—violence and abuses of power of many kinds. But I've gravitated toward rather upbeat, optimistic ones. I study dreamers, idealists who had ambitions of bringing all knowledge into harmony, and who often harbored an implicit irenicism, which they strove toward despite the religious and national conflicts they lived through. It's hard not to feel sympathy for them, despite the fact that they did not succeed in their ambitions and that they were embedded in the hierarchical social and political structures of their time. I'm conscious, when I look around at my colleagues who are working on war and slavery, that I have focused on the happy topics of history. Intellectual history may offer more such opportunities than other fields, but it's also a matter of what you look for in your research. A student recently reminded me of an inspiring formulation by Natalie Davis: "I have wanted to be a historian of hope."[26]

You mentioned earlier your piety toward the little person in intellectual history. What would an intellectual history be like in which all of those anonymous collaborators were given their due?

That's a great question—and I'm trying to answer that "so what?" question in the book I'm writing now on amanuenses or the hidden helpers of intellectual work in early modern Europe.[27] First of all, my purpose is not to debunk the great men but to add to our understanding of how they worked and wrote the texts that made them significant and famous. Helpers of many kinds made much greater contributions than they've

26. Natalie Zemon Davis, "How the FBI Turned Me On to Rare Books," NYR Daily, *New York Review of Books*, July 30, 2013, http://www.nybooks.com/daily/2013/07/30/fbi-turned-me-on-to-rare-books/.

27. Ann Blair, "Hidden Hands: Amanuenses and Authorship in Early Modern Europe," A. S. W. Rosenbach Lectures in Bibliography, University of Pennsylvania, March 2014, and "Early Modern Attitudes toward the Delegation of Copying and Note-Taking," in *Forgetting Machines: Knowledge Management Evolution in Early Modern Europe*, ed. Alberto Cevolini (Leiden, 2016), 265–85.

been credited for—since they get zero credit at the moment, that's not saying much [*laughs*]! I'm not trying to argue that someone other than Montaigne wrote the *Essays*, for example. But I doubt that many prolific early modern authors worked alone. They had help from people whom they hired—servants with more or less specialized roles—but also from students (who not infrequently boarded in their teacher's house) and family members, typically sons, wives, and daughters. What kind of work these helpers contributed varied a lot. Some of it we might consider mechanical, constrained by very clear guidelines (e.g., alphabetizing, or exact copying or proofreading), and in performing those tasks helpers freed up the author's time. But in other tasks (e.g., making corrections, indexing, taking notes, or arranging material) helpers used their judgment and made an intellectual contribution to the work even though no one acknowledged that at the time. So I hope my research on this topic will give us a better sense of the communities on which people drew when they composed books in the early modern period. I also hope that the study of the past can make us more aware of our own practices and of the helpers on which we rely, both human and electronic. Early modern helpers are hard to ferret out but are sometimes more visible in especially large books. For example, I've come across a unique "amanuensis to the reader" in a large edition of medieval English manuscripts printed in 1652.[28] So it seems that I'm still working with polymathic megabibliomaniacs [*laughs*].

Have the kinds of questions that can be asked, or that are asked, changed since you were a graduate student? What role, if any, has technology played in this change?

The first change I remember noticing was the power of the online library catalog that you can consult in your office and now pretty much anywhere. When I was a student, it was a challenge to try to follow up on a reference that a professor would give you in office hours by mentioning an approximate name, title, and date for a book—what I had scribbled down on a note card from an oral conversation was often hard to find at the next opportunity to consult the card catalog in the library. Now I try to find the book I have in mind in the catalog while the student is with me, so I can fiddle with my memory or other sources until I can email the precise library record. The multiplicity of online library catalogs and the

---

28. Roger Twysden, *Historiae Anglicanae scriptores X* (London, 1652), following column 2,768.

portals that combine them (like the Universal Short Title Catalogue for books printed before 1600) offer searching power that was unthinkable before the web. And just in the last few years the quality and quantity of PDFs available (e.g., on E-rara and the Staatsbibliothek in Munich) has changed my conception of a viable project. For example I just finished a series of articles on the publication strategies of Conrad Gessner, in which I studied the dedications and other paratexts of all sixty-five of Gessner's publications, almost all of which I found in full text online.[29] I still make a point of viewing copies of the books themselves whenever possible, and in a few cases that direct contact has been crucial to identifying a cancel (visible in the PDF but only once you know to look for it) or a foldout table that was not reproduced in the PDF, whether because it went unnoticed or posed too much complication because of the larger format involved. But some of these books are so rare that no one library owns them all, so digitization makes it possible to bring together in a virtual library books that once were together but are now dispersed. Similarly, comparisons between different editions or between a manuscript and a printed book held in different locations have become easily feasible now when one of the two items has been digitized. The prospect of trying to negotiate comparing a manuscript and a printed book at the BnF was so daunting that I never tried; now those two reading rooms are a few arrondissements apart, but digitizations have come to the rescue. I know that I have only scratched the surface of the many new kinds of research that are possible now and which will hopefully become increasingly possible if we continue to make progress with optical character recognition for unusual fonts and ligatures.

Are technologies like Google Books, with its snippet view and keyword searches, changing reading practices and scholarly practices?

I'm sure they are changing our practices. At this point I can barely remember how exactly to consult printed annual bibliographies to find recent articles, and it's hard to mourn that particular ritual. There are of course risks involved in the ease of a Google search: the risk that people

29. See, for example, Ann Blair, "Printing and Humanism in the Work of Conrad Gessner," *Renaissance Quarterly* 70, no. 1 (2017), 1–43, and Ann Blair, "The Capacious Bibliographical Practice of Conrad Gessner," *Papers of the Bibliographical Society of America* 111, no. 4 (2017): 445–68 and other articles cited there.

looking for a quick fix can just settle for the snippet view, finish their footnote, and be unaware of the larger context of the snippet they used. And it's very sad that Google Books often has weak metadata, so to really understand the text you are using it is valuable to consult a library catalog or the book itself to grasp fully the nature of the digitization. On the other hand, the quick searching at our disposal also makes it easier to contextualize what we read if we choose to do so. For example, it's much easier now to scan book reviews to see if the book we're citing is well regarded. A Google search can also rapidly cast doubt on something we thought we knew. When you look at the attributions of a quotation, for example, you might find one attribution and assume it's correct, but if you search online you'll find multiple different attributions and realize that the problem is more complicated. So the technology isn't inherently a negative. We need to explain to students and remind ourselves why it's important to be thorough in thinking through our questions and the answers we offer for them, regardless of the technology we use.

What do you think that you have unlearned, as well as learned, in the course of your career? Has what seemed true or significant to you changed over time?

Perhaps not surprisingly given my predilections as a historian I think of my intellectual trajectory in terms of steady accretion and gradual rather than sharp turns. I have never had in mind a grand plan and have thoroughly enjoyed the unexpected directions (which one might call detours) I've taken, which were often born from conversations with and invitations from others. I started out with a desire to learn about famous thinkers, and I've ended up attending increasingly to the "little guys." But the most unexpected thing I've learned is the importance of attending to one's intellectual community—realizing what a central role it can play as a source of feedback and inspiration and taking the time to contribute to it and perhaps undertaking some initiatives to improve it. I started out with an idea of academic work as rather solitary, and certainly some aspects of it are—the writing process in particular. But we all also operate as members of multiple communities; some, defined intellectually by a discipline and one or more subfields, span the globe, while others are formed locally through institutions and places—and people. Tony Grafton, for example, has fostered a vibrant community of scholars working across many areas and themes through his teaching, advising, and mentorship of scores of students and colleagues who have come into his ambit at some point.

I have always been grateful for his exceptional generosity as dissertation adviser and mentor during and long after my years of graduate study. And Tony has sustained similar relationships with so many others! The conference held at Princeton for his sixty-fifth birthday in May 2015 allowed us all to appreciate the remarkable scope and strength of the "Graftonian" community.[30] Technology has also wonderfully facilitated interactions within intellectual communities at every level, but we are of course only extending the practices of a republic of letters that has for centuries relied on scholarly exchange carried out both in person and remotely, using multiple media. I trust that this republic of learning, with its many provinces, will live long into the future too!

What do you see as the future of intellectual history? Where is it going, and where would you like it to go? What role might it play in the wider historical profession? And in what ways might it continue to influence other disciplines and enterprises?

Intellectual history seems to me more visible in the profession and certainly in the Harvard History Department than when I was an undergraduate. Nevertheless, it is far from central to the discipline of history viewed as a whole, in which the dominant emphases are economics, politics, international relations, and empire. But I think it's healthy for intellectual historians to engage with colleagues with these quite different foci, even while they also interact with colleagues in neighboring fields like the literatures, philosophy, or the history of science or of art. I'm delighted that intellectual history now embraces a wider range of themes than political thought, which was long the main focus of study, and that it includes attention to working methods and practices of textual production.[31] Although the questions that have motivated me are not at the core of intellectual history, I expect that they will continue to generate productive new perspectives on how ideas have been written, interpreted, and disseminated.

30. For a digital record of the conference and updated lists of Grafton's students and publications, see https://graftoniana.princeton.edu/.

31. For a recent overview of intellectual history see Peter E. Gordon, "What Is Intellectual History? A Frankly Partisan Introduction to a Frequently Misunderstood Field," Harvard Colloquium in Intellectual History, March 2012, http://projects.iq.harvard.edu/files/history/files/what_is_intell _history_pgordon_mar2012.pdf.

Lorraine Daston

LORRAINE DASTON is director at the Max Planck Institute for the History of Science in Berlin and visiting professor in the Committee on the Conceptual and Historical Studies of Science and the Committee on Social Thought at the University of Chicago.

How did you begin?

I'm very typical of many historians of science: we are people who could never make up our minds. I went to college thinking that I would be an astronomer, which was a kind of *nomen est omen* fantasy. My family is Greek, and I was actually christened Urania. And because Urania was the muse of astronomy, I had an idée fixe that I was going to study astronomy. I ended up studying math, history, and philosophy, but I had the good luck, because of this idée fixe, to take in my freshman year a course that was then called NatSci 9. I think it was originally NatSci 3, taught by Thomas Kuhn, among others. It originated in James Bryant Conant's attempt to educate Harvard students in science in the age of the atomic bomb. In my day it was taught by an astronomer and historian of astronomy, Owen Gingerich, who was a mesmerizing teacher. To this day I remember his experimental demonstrations of Newton's laws.

This was my first encounter with something called the history of science. And like many, many other students of Owen's, I was utterly beguiled by it. But I still didn't think that you could make a career of this kind of thing, and so I zigzagged between math courses, history courses, and philosophy courses. After college, I at first tried philosophy of science and went to Cambridge to study with Mary Hesse, who had written on models and analogies in what is still, I think, an extremely original way.[1] I soon realized that my idea of philosophy, a hybrid of metaphysics and science fiction rather like Leibniz's *Monadologie*, had gone out of fashion sometime toward the end of the seventeenth century. It was certainly not what was on offer at Cambridge in those years. So I ended up going back to Harvard and doing a PhD in the history of science, still thinking that if it didn't work out, well, what about Egyptology? What about crystallography? I think it's very typical of historians of science that they remain in a state of suspended commitment with regard to their intellectual direction. It's a reluctance to hear the doors of possibility slamming behind you.

What was the question that led you to the history of mathematics?

I pursued the history of mathematics first and foremost because I liked math, but my choice was also a reflection of how history of science was structured in the late 1970s: in a disciplinary fashion. Many historians of science will still identify themselves as historians of a specific modern scientific discipline, such as physics or psychology or chemistry. Early modernists know this makes very little sense for the sixteenth and seventeenth centuries, or for classifications of knowledge even in the Western world pre-1900. But, at the time, the organization of the history of science was mimetic: it mirrored contemporary classifications of science. It also mirrored contemporary definitions of what science was, especially in the Anglophone or Francophone world. So, since you had to choose a discipline, I chose history of mathematics.

The history of mathematics also seemed a gauntlet thrown down. This was the period when there was a war raging within the history, sociology, and philosophy of science, a war in many ways triggered unintentionally by Thomas Kuhn's *Structure of Scientific Revolutions*.[2] The two warring factions were the internalists and the externalists, and mathematics was seen as the hard case for externalism. The very terms now

---

1. Mary B. Hesse, *Models and Analogies in Science* (New York, 1963).
2. Thomas S. Kuhn, *The Structure of Scientific Revolutions* (Chicago, 1962).

seem absurd—I can see you looking at me with the indulgent look of the young, thinking to yourselves, "How very quaint." But in the 1970s and '80s, people got red in the face when they argued over such matters: voices rose, blood pressure soared. Mathematics seemed the hard case for a more contextual, historicized version of the history of science. In many ways it still is; the history of mathematics has largely remained an island within the history of science, which otherwise became more assimilated to general history in the 1990s and thereafter. For a graduate student in the 1970s, it was a welcome challenge to try to historicize an episode in the history of mathematics. I wrote my Cambridge thesis on projective geometry in early nineteenth-century France, in the context of the French Revolution, the Napoleonic recruitment of savants, and worker education. For my Harvard dissertation, I ended up writing on the early history of probability theory in the seventeenth and eighteenth centuries, also within a broader context or at least broader intellectual context—but also, I realized in retrospect, within an economic context. It proved very hard to remain in the history of mathematics, partly because I was an early modernist. You cannot be an early modernist for very long without having deep doubts about the projection of the classifications of late twentieth-century knowledge back upon the sixteenth and seventeenth, and in many cases, the eighteenth and nineteenth centuries. In contrast, the history of mathematics was presentist in a strong and quite interesting sense: many of its practitioners believed that all premodern mathematics could be translated into modern terms without significant loss of conceptual content (e.g., turning book 2 of Euclid's *Elements* into algebra). So it just became untenable, intellectually, to define oneself in that way.

And when did you come to that realization?

I think by then I was at Princeton as an assistant professor, so circa 1984. After finishing my dissertation in 1979 I was a member of the Columbia Society of Fellows, quartered in the Philosophy Department, and then went back to Harvard as an assistant professor. The latter was really just slipping back into the role of an aggrandized graduate student. It was completely continuous with my life as a graduate student [*laughs*], so there was no reason to change anything. Between Harvard and Princeton, I spent a year (1982–83), really such a pivotal year for me in every way, in Bielefeld, here in Germany, at the Zentrum für interdisziplinäre Forschung, as part of a research group organized by Ian Hacking, Nancy Cartwright, and Lorenz Krüger on the probabilistic revolution.

Everything about that year was transformative for me. First, there was the novel idea of working in a group, which was led by such remarkable intellectual personalities. I'll give you just one example. This group consisted of people who were luminaries, including Ian Hacking and Nancy Cartwright. I had heard Nancy lecture on the philosophy of quantum mechanics while still at Cambridge, and I knew Ian's work on the basis of having picked up his 1975 book *The Emergence of Probability* in Widener Library at Harvard. That book completely changed my mind about my dissertation topic and, more generally, how to write the history of science. So he was a demigod, as far as I was concerned! Lorenz, also a philosopher of remarkably broad range, immediately commanded respect as a thinker and person. There were people of that level of seniority in the group, and then there were people who were one or two years past their PhD: Ted Porter, Mary Morgan, and I.

After the first group meeting, somebody said, "Well, it would be a very good idea if somebody took minutes." Mary, Ted, and I exchanged glances; we were sure that we would be handed this job as the most junior people in the room. Ian raised his hand and said, "I'll do it this time, and then we'll just take turns." The magnanimity of that gesture, of effectively saying, "I'm not too good for this," elevated the task and transformed the dynamic of the group. It taught me the importance of a charismatic personality with a sense of egalitarianism but also an approach to the history of science and mathematics that was deeply infused with a philosophical sensibility. The Bielefeld seminar repositioned my interest in the history of probability theory in a much broader context, a more philosophical one, because of the strength of the philosophers in that group, especially Nancy, Lorenz, and Ian.

Yet my experience in the Bielefeld group also oriented me toward a different kind of history, focused on practices as well as ideas—in the case of early probability theory, practices having to do with insurance and legal doctrines of evidence. This shift was reinforced with emphasis by my colleagues at Princeton, especially Gerry Geison and Michael Mahoney, when I moved there after the Bielefeld year. Because the Princeton Program in the History of Science was embedded in the History Department, I also had the benefit of a crash course in new trends in cultural and intellectual history, which Princeton historians such as Natalie Davis and Anthony Grafton had pioneered.

What drew you to the study of probability as an intellectual project?

Ian Hacking's *Emergence of Probability*.[3] This is one of those rare moments that are permanently etched in memory, a moment when life pivots. In the mid-1970s, Widener Library had a new books table. I was going to go babysitting that night and wanted to grab something to read. This was a thin book [*laughs*], and I probably thought, Why not? I checked it out. I read it all in one sitting, as Descartes said you're supposed to read the *Meditations*. I don't remember the poor kid I was supposed to be looking after [*laughs*]. It was not just the topic that gripped me, it was the way of doing history. It was a way of doing history that, first of all, asserted radical novelty: Ian was given to writing apodictic sentences of the form, "Before November 1654, the idea of probability as quantitative evidence was strictly unthinkable," albeit seasoned with a soupçon of self-irony. But he also asserted radical historicization: ideas, such as *evidence*, that might seem part of the eternal intellectual equipment of human thought in fact become thinkable only under certain circumstances. That model of radical historicization of the self-evident washed over me like a wave. From that night on I knew what I would be writing my dissertation on, and I abandoned projective geometry without a regret.

Did you have other interlocutors at Harvard? Who were your other role models or influences from that period?

At Harvard at that time, the policy toward graduate students was basically one of benign neglect. I italicize *benign*: we were given freedom to explore and wander in ways that must seem luxurious by today's current careerist standards. I had a wonderful adviser, Erwin Hiebert, who didn't know, I think, very much about what I was working on, but he believed in me. He was a model for me as a person as well as a scholar: a model, when I think back retrospectively, for a kind of ecumenicism with regard to intellectual topics and also with regard to fostering young women scholars. It is not an accident that Erwin's women students were among the first women historians of science to remain in academia even after they had families. I don't want to exaggerate; history of science has always had a strong con-

---

3. Ian Hacking, *The Emergence of Probability: A Philosophical Study of Early Ideas about Probability, Induction and Statistical Inference* (Cambridge, 1975).

tingent of women scholars. For example, Thomas Kuhn, in the introduction to *The Structure of Scientific Revolutions*, names four scholars to whose work he felt particularly indebted: the French historian of chemistry Hélène Metzger, the German medievalist Anneliese Maier, the British Renaissance historian Frances Yates, and the Russian-French historian of science and philosophy Alexandre Koyré. I do not think that the fact that three out of the four scholars named were women implies that Thomas Kuhn was a feminist; I just think they were scholars of extraordinary originality.

So I don't want to exaggerate; there was always a strong minority presence of women in the history of science. But Erwin's commitment to supporting his women students was also rooted in personal factors. His wife, Elfrieda, was a PhD in musicology, and his daughters, who were about our age, were also in graduate school. Also, Erwin came from a Mennonite background and held a deeply egalitarian view of marriage and the treatment of women. I really felt those convictions in his advising, in ways that I can only now articulate. But when I listen to the experiences of other women my age in the history of science (including those who studied with Kuhn, or at least tried to), what a difference!

In terms of intellectual stimulation, it came mostly from the other graduate students. And they were wonderful, absolutely wonderful! My friend Joan Richards, then writing a dissertation on geometry in Victorian Britain, was a comrade-in-arms in trying to rethink the history of mathematics as genuinely historical. Katy Park, writing a dissertation that took a social-historical approach to medieval and Renaissance medicine, became a coconspirator in a clandestine project: she was supposed to be writing about the plague in Renaissance Florence, and I was supposed to be writing about the history of probability theory, but there we were in Houghton [Harvard's rare books library] reading books with titles like *The Hog-Faced Woman* and *A Thousand Notable Things* for an article we wrote together about monsters in early modern Europe [*laughs*].[4]

Collaboration is a theme that runs throughout your whole career. What does one get from it?

Well, one thing to say is, it's great fun [*laughs*]! Katy Park and I came perilously close on many occasions to being thrown out of Houghton and other rare books libraries for laughing too loudly—for example, over that *Hog-Faced*

4. Katharine Park and Lorraine Daston, "Unnatural Conceptions: The Study of Monsters in 16th and 17th Century France and England," *Past and Present*, no. 92 (August 1981): 20–54.

Woman broadside. There is also an element of *folie à deux*, which can rein-
force biases but which also gave me the courage to tackle a topic that neither of us would have dared to have ventured upon alone—monsters were
certainly such an outlandish topic when Katy and I were in graduate school.

We both took a seminar on seventeenth-century metaphysics in the
Philosophy Department, which I will never forget. We were the only historians among the philosophers, who approached the canon of Bacon,
Descartes, Locke, Leibniz, and others from the standpoint of the validity
of their arguments *sub specie aeternitatis*. Just to give you a sense of how
unhistorical this seminar was, the student assigned to report on Locke's
Essay on Human Understanding couldn't remember whether it had been
first published in 1689 or 1789. For historians used to thinking in terms
of sequence and context, such disorientation concerning dates seemed
the equivalent of not knowing left from right. For their part, the philosophers in the seminar thought we were just as odd. While everyone else
was analyzing arguments pro and contra innate ideas and the like, Katy
and I were asking, "Did you notice that Bacon mentions monsters, and
that Leibniz *also* mentions monsters?" There was a kind of camaraderie
of the loony; that's how our project got started.

So the origins of your and Katharine Park's coauthored book,
Wonders and the Order of Nature, *go all the way back to that
moment?* [5]

It does indeed go back to that seventeenth-century metaphysics seminar. But to answer your question more seriously, the other great thing
is that collaboration gives you a *longue durée* periodization as well as a
different analytical perspective. Katy and I were complementary in obvious ways. She's a medievalist/Renaissance specialist; I'm early modern/
Enlightenment. The historiography of the latter turns on the belief (very
much that of the historical actors themselves) that the sixteenth through
the eighteenth centuries in Europe were periods of radical rupture with
all that preceded them. This illusion can only be sustained if one
reads nothing written before 1500. I now never begin a sentence in
Katy's presence, "For the first time in the sixteenth century . . . ," because she'll reply, "Honey, have you looked at the thirteenth century
recently?" That was a necessary and helpful corrective of early modern-

5. Lorraine Daston and Katharine Park, *Wonders and the Order of Nature, 1150–1750* (Cambridge, MA, 1998).

ist chutzpah, very strong in a discipline that still views the Scientific Revolution as the big bang of modernity. The very name *early modern* says it all. In terms of analytical perspective, Katy was trained as a social historian as well as in intellectual history of a Warburgian sort. I had been trained in intellectual history and philosophy. That, too, was an illuminating clash of perspectives, in which both of us had to come to terms with the other's position and, moreover, convince each other.

Is there a similar temporal dynamic, but in the opposite direction, in your work with Peter Galison that culminated in Objectivity?[6]

Yes, exactly. Peter does have strong seventeenth-century interests, but the center of gravity of his work lies in the twentieth and twenty-first centuries. He is much more interested in things, in the material. I'm more interested in ideas. Both of us have had to figure out how to translate the insights that you can get from both approaches into a common language. In this case, it's been a help that both of us have philosophical interests or, rather, interests in how philosophy and history can mutually enrich each other.

As someone who has worked on many collaborative writing projects, how do you find the experience of merging your voice with another's?

It's the hardest question. I can remember vigorous (and invigorating) discussions with both Katy and Peter about how to get an argument right. In my mind's ear, I can hear Katy's voice say, "If I don't understand it, no one else is going to understand it. Say it again, more clearly." Those discussions went well, with gusto. I also remember when Katy and I had to cut one hundred pages one summer from the manuscript of *Wonders*; mindful that every word counted, Katy would shorten my sentences [*laughs*]. At that point our friendship was really on the line [*laughs*]. But over the years we've reached a stylistic equilibrium: Katy's sentences are a bit longer, and mine are shorter. And now, because with Katy I've written quite a few things, we have a modus operandi. First, we read a whole lot of stuff, mostly with a division of labor but with some overlap for key texts. Then we sit down

---

6. Lorraine Daston and Peter Galison, *Objectivity* (Cambridge, MA, 2007).

together in the late afternoon over a cup of tea and start exchanging notes (we are both demon notetakers) on our reading: "Have you read this? What do you think of this? What do you think of that?" We are basically taking inventory of what we think are the most interesting items and groping toward an argument. Then we break for dinner and go to bed. (This latter is an essential step in the incubation of ideas.) I usually wake up early in the morning, so I sit down at the computer and start writing. When Katy gets up, she takes over at the keyboard. And then I take over, and so forth. As a result, we no longer know, in many cases, who wrote which sentence.

And is the style of collaboration different with each collaboration?

It is, of course, because there are different personalities, rhythms, and writing routines. It's also the case that in almost every chapter of *Objectivity* there are passages that both Peter and I wrote. We were present in all the chapters. But I should say how much I've learned, obviously substantively but also stylistically, by working with two such different styles, each strong and vivid in its way, at a word-by-word level. That's been world-opening in many ways, second only to learning a new language.

As you diversified and worked on very different kinds of topics, did you feel that there was a common thread among them? Was this part of one single larger question that you were asking? What was driving you?

The answer I'm going to give you is a retrospective answer and should therefore be taken *cum grano salis.* This is a rational reconstruction, as they say in the philosophy of science biz. At the time I had absolutely no notion of any overarching program except, "That sounds interesting." And so much seemed interesting to me. I was quite indiscriminate in my choice of topics. This is simply a continuation of the indecisiveness that I mentioned earlier, which is: I have very little discipline with regard to disciplines. I just follow my nose.

In retrospect, however, I do think that there are some threads, and one of them is surely the idea—born on that epiphany evening of reading Ian Hacking's *Emergence of Probability*—that there can be a history of the self-evident. A great deal of the work that I've done, histories of observation, histories of reason in the guise of probability theory, histories of order as defined by breaches of order, histories of the cognitive passions of wonder and curiosity, objectivity—much can be seen as histories of the self-evident, of ways of thinking and feeling that seem too fundamental to have histories. I also have an enduring interest in writing a history of rationality without thereby debunking rationality. Historicism does not corrode all that it touches; to historicize is not to relativize. I see rationality as an achievement, a historical achievement, much as science is a historical achievement, both of them still ongoing pursuits.

It's more difficult for me to pinpoint when I began to think in these terms. Sometime in the 1990s I realized that you could bring together ideas of daunting abstraction, like objectivity, with very concrete practices, like making a measurement or making an image. I am greatly indebted to the history of scientific practices that has remade the field in the past twenty-five years (and which buried the hatchet in the internalism-externalism dispute I mentioned earlier). The realization that one isn't obliged to choose between being an intellectual historian versus a historian of practices also became a leitmotif. One could turn up the amplitude on both of them to high and see what happens, in terms of the concords and the discords of that approach.

Another distinct and formative memory dates from my stay as a fellow at the Wissenschaftskolleg zu Berlin; it was, I think, '87 or '88, the year before the Berlin Wall came down. About such world-historical events we fellows in the Grunewald were clueless. But so was everyone else. Instead of anticipating the impending collapse of the Soviet bloc, we historians of science at the Wissenschaftskolleg that year were still fighting the internalism-externalism battle. But there were already glimmers of things to come at least on that parochial front. I remember that Simon Schaffer visited from Cambridge, and we discussed his paper that became "Astronomers Mark Time," about how, prior to the introduction of the personal equation by the astronomer Friedrich Wilhelm Bessel, astronomical observation had been highly moralized.[7] I remembered that in 1827 when the Bremen physician and astronomer Heinrich Wilhelm Olbers reported to the Göttingen mathematician and astronomer Carl Friedrich Gauss that Bessel and his assistant Walbeck systematically diverged by one second of arc in their observations for the same astronomical objects over the period of a month, Gauss replied, "between us, Walbeck (whom I consider otherwise to be quite intelligent) seems to me still somewhat

---

7. Simon Schaffer, "Astronomers Mark Time: Discipline and the Personal Equation," *Science in Context* 2, no. 1 (1988): 115–45.

unpracticed in observation."[8] For Gauss, accurate observation was a matter of voluntary effort; practice would make perfect. Every act of will, including the will to be attentive, can be moralized. That was also a moment when I realized how difficult it was to disentangle the moral and epistemic dimensions of science. This difficulty became a recurring theme in my work, starting with my article on the moral economy of science, again very much influenced by Simon's article and the discussions at the Wissenschaftskolleg.[9]

As a historian, you have attended to a large time scale. How do you define the domain, whether temporal or otherwise, of history of science?

I think that all historians, especially historians of science, are in the process of rethinking the way in which we divide up not only the continents of time, but also the continents in a more literal sense. There has been a salutary shaking up of our geography and periodization, occasioned by recent work on non-Western traditions (and on whether "the West" is a coherent analytical category). Traditionally, the history of science has thought about non-Western traditions in diffusionist terms: modern science originates in Europe and gradually spreads to the rest of the world. The history of science is not just *a* Eurocentric narrative; we are *the* Eurocentric narrative. There is good reason to think that we invented Eurocentrism. The narrative begins in the mid-eighteenth century, starting with Jean Le Rond d'Alembert's *Discours préliminaire* of the *Encyclopédie*, and runs roughly like this: yes, Europe has had a very difficult time, languishing in darkness from the fall of the Rome until the seventeenth century. Even the best and the brightest made terrible mistakes, embracing Ptolemaic astronomy and Aristotelian natural philosophy. But then [*laughs*], starting with Bacon and Descartes, we Europeans finally found the path to truth and progress, and this is what will distinguish us from the rest of the world—or so d'Alembert, Turgot, and other Enlightenment thinkers argued.

Because some variant of this Enlightenment narrative justifies the existence of the history of science as a discipline, global history has been much more of a shock for us than for other historians. The old diffusion-

---

8. C. F. Gauss to H. W. Olbers, Göttingen, 3 May 1827, in Gauss, *Werke, Ergänzungsreihe IV: Briefwechsel C. F. Gauss—H. W. M. F. Olbers*, ed. C. Schilling (Hildesheim, [1909] 1976), letter number 613, 2:480.

9. Lorraine Daston, "The Moral Economy of Science," *Osiris* 10 (1995): 2–24.

ist model posited a supernova, the Scientific Revolution, from which light gradually diffuses via the Jesuits to China, and Japan, and Peru, et cetera. This model is no longer tenable, as recent detailed research has shown. But as yet we have nothing to put in its place.

I think that the very structure of the narrative is also going to change, because periodization and geography are also being redrawn. The movement toward contextualization, in many ways a most welcome development of the history of science within the last twenty-five years, has tempted historians of science to adopt the periodization of their historian colleagues rather uncritically. For example, "Victorian science" seems like a perfectly natural unit of inquiry under that dispensation. So does "early modern European science."

But such rubrics make no sense at all if you are looking not just at the trade routes between the Far East and Europe from a very early period but also at the people who move along those trade routes. There's a great project to be done on a kind of atlas of scholarly travel through the ages. We had a project of the Max Planck Institute for the History of Science (MPIWG) called *Before Copernicus* (organized by Rivka Feldhay and Jamil Ragep), which was about astronomy and its context in the fifteenth century: just looking at the trajectories of the dramatis personae of that project exploded any notion of intellectual communities narrowly defined by a place or a language or a religion.[10] They were traveling all over the place. Long before the invention of the jet plane, long before David Lodge's *Small World*, scholars were highly mobile, and their ideas traveled as well. Just a map of their perambulations (and those of their works) would undermine many assumptions about late medieval intellectual life—for example, the increasingly bizarre-sounding divisions between "Latin," "Islamic," and "Byzantine" science during this period, divisions that still define specialties within the history of science.

I think everything is up for grabs, including the definition of our subject matter. The impetus for redefinition has come from at least two directions. Thanks to the work of Anthony Grafton, Ann Blair, Gianna Pomata, and other scholars, historians of science—at least we early modernists—have gotten used to thinking of the history of scholarship as part of our bailiwick. I recently wrote an article with Glenn Most about why it might be worthwhile to carry this combined approach to the history of science and scholarship into the nineteenth century, at least for the history of philology and astronomy.[11]

10. *Before Copernicus: The Cultures and Contexts of Scientific Learning in the Fifteenth Century*, ed. Rivka Feldhay and F. Jamil Ragep (Montreal, 2017).

11. Lorraine Daston and Glenn W. Most, "History of Science and History of Philologies," *Isis* 106, no. 2 (2015): 378–90.

That's one source of pressure on the mimetic definition of the history of science's subject matter, which has implicitly taken present science as its guide to what science is and who is a scientist. The move to expand the history of science to include at least some aspects of the history of scholarship has implications for the geography and periodization of the history of science. If there's one science cultivated by canonical literary traditions in many parts of the world, it's some version of philology. The recent collection on world philology edited by Sheldon Pollock, Benjamin Elman, and Kevin Chang pays tribute to these traditions.[12] Glenn Most and Anthony Grafton's edited volume on the scholarly practices applied to canonical texts in multiple traditions—including Hebrew, classical Chinese, Sanskrit, Arabic, Greek, Latin, Assyrian—applies the methods of the history of scientific practices to learned philologies.[13]

The other source of pressure on the subject matter of the history of science comes from forms of knowledge whose study used to be the province of the anthropologist—ethnobotany, for example. Recent historical studies of what is now called bioprospecting show that there was a brisk exchange between learned naturalists and laypeople on the medicinal properties and other uses of animals, vegetables, and minerals—not only within Europe but also in other cultures and, above all, between cultures. This has also exerted enormous pressure on the subject matter by blurring the line between local and universal knowledge, between pure and applied science, and between learned and lay inquirers. So, *panta rhei*, everything flows. Stay tuned. Come back in five years [*laughs*].

You mentioned earlier that when it comes to choosing topics you follow your nose, and I wanted to ask more about that process. Do the topics choose you?

I fear the answer lies buried in the murky subconscious and has to be dredged up with all of the mud adhering to it. I suppose the one common denominator is being ambushed by surprise: the moments when I stumble while reading, when I simply cannot parse the sentence because it seems at first nonsensical. I remember reading a deservedly obscure mid-seventeenth-century treatise by the son of the great classical philol-

---

12. Sheldon Pollock, Benjamin A. Elman, and Ku-ming Kevin Chang, eds., *World Philology* (Cambridge, MA, 2015).
13. Anthony T. Grafton and Glenn W. Most, eds., *Canonical Texts and Scholarly Practices: A Global Comparative Approach* (Cambridge, 2016).

ogist Isaac Casaubon, Meric Casaubon, also a classical scholar and Anglican clergyman. Meric Casaubon (I have always wondered whether Meric was actually George Eliot's inspiration for the pedant in *Middlemarch*) was trying to combat incredulity among learned and laypersons alike. Of the latter, he cited the unreasonable skepticism of country bumpkins who balked at tales of flying cats, just because there didn't happen to be any in their village—after all, they had no trouble crediting stories about flying mice (i.e., bats). Well-traveled sophisticates, Casaubon thought, might credit such strange-but-true marvels, but they even more culpably denied the existence of witches. To Casaubon, it was simply impossible that wise judges could have willfully condemned the innocent, or have been deceived into doing so.[14] There is Casaubon, poised on the edge of the cliff, about to realize that twelve thousand innocent people have been wrongly condemned to a horrible death—and he averts his eyes. It's moments like that when the inner antennae go up.

So the process involves casting a wide net and reading all kinds of things?

Right! That indeed is the great joy of being a historian of science, as opposed to being a more disciplined (in every sense of the word) historian. We cover the waterfront. If historians were to announce to the people who write them letters of recommendation, "I've had it with the seventeenth century. I think I'm going to go back to the twelfth, or forward to the twenty-first," eyebrows would be raised. But historians of science do it all the time. We are insouciant about this kind of leapfrogging time travel and the wide, some might say indiscriminate, reading that goes with it.

So you have to take joy in the alien and disparate nature of different corners of the past?

Yes. Katy Park calls it the Ursula Le Guin sensibility [*laughs*].

---

14. Meric Casaubon, *Of Credulity and Incredulity in Things Natural and Civil* (London, 1668), 38; "That so many [judges], wise and discreet, well versed in that subject, could be so horribly deceived, against their wills; or so impious, so cruel, as willfully to have a hand in the condemnation of so many Innocents: . . . what man can believe." Casaubon's tract was reprinted in London in 1672 as *A Treatise Proving Spirits, Witches, and Supernatural Operations*.

So how do you define a question and frame a book? How do you break off a manageable chunk of all the historical raw material you encounter?

There are two different answers to that, depending on whether I'm working alone or in a group. I should explain that in addition to my collaborative projects with Katy Park and Peter Galison, and the multiauthored books I've published, such as *The Empire of Chance* and *How Reason Almost Lost Its Mind*, I've also done a lot of organizing, especially since arriving in Berlin in 1995, of working groups of scholars. These groups have produced edited volumes on various topics such as *The Moral Authority of Nature* and *Histories of Scientific Observation*.[15]

If I'm working alone, a crucial first step is to figure out what my sources are. What kind of sources can I use to answer these questions? Second, how can I render a rather ethereal intellectual topic concrete? How can I make it granular, give it texture, and anchor it to specific historical contexts? At the moment I'm struggling with another one of those ethereal categories: rules. I gave the Davis Lectures at Princeton in 2014 and am now writing a short book on this vast topic, truly one of those graveyard-of-scholars topics. I've been looking at cookbooks and reading sumptuary laws, because those are among the most detailed rules I can find in the late Middle Ages. I collect lots and lots and lots of examples and then stand back to see if patterns and trends emerge. That's the kind of Hoovering reading I do alone.

If I'm working with a group, then the first and most important step is to recruit its members, usually to represent as many periods, cultures, and disciplines as possible, given the constraints of the subject matter and availability of people. One of the rewarding aspects of working in a country where what I'm doing is called *Wissenschaftsgeschichte*, instead of the history of science, is that *Wissenschaft* is much closer to the medieval term *scientia* in all its amplitude than to the Anglo- or Francophone "science" as used since the late nineteenth century. Most of the working groups that I've organized at the MPIWG have taken advantage of the capacious German *Wissenschaft*, embracing both the human and the natural sciences—as in the *Histories of Scientific Observation* volume, for example.

15. Gerd Gigerenzer, Zeno Swijtink, Theodore Porter, Lorraine Daston, John Beatty, and Lorenz Krüger, *The Empire of Chance: How Probability Changed Science and Everyday Life* (Cambridge, 1989); Paul Erickson, Judy L. Klein, Lorraine Daston, Rebecca Lemov, Thomas Sturm, and Michael D. Gordin, *How Reason Almost Lost Its Mind: The Strange Career of Cold War Rationality* (Chicago, 2013); Lorraine Daston and Fernando Vidal, eds., *The Moral Authority of Nature* (Chicago, 2004); Lorraine Daston and Elizabeth Lunbeck, eds., *Histories of Scientific Observation* (Chicago, 2011).

Once the working group is constituted, we have to strike a balance between individual case studies and some overarching chronology and framework that makes the volume cohere. That is done through hours and hours of discussion, writing, rewriting, writing, rewriting.

What was the intellectual impact of moving to Berlin? How has it changed your perspective?

Wissenschaft is one way. Another is my discovery of how productive a working group of humanists can be. This is another discovery I owe to the Bielefeld year and its inspiring organizers. Collaboration need not be the exclusive way we humanists work; I do not mean in any way to suggest that. But I think most people find such collective work enormously stimulating once they have been exposed to it. That possibility of organizing such collaborations, which would never have been a possibility in an ordinary university context, reconfigured the way I work.

More generally, working in the German language; it always opens up another world to inhabit another language. And German is a language of fabled precision and inventiveness.

Also the possibility of bringing people together whose paths would otherwise not have crossed: that's the freedom of a Max Planck Institute, in which I can bring together junior and senior scholars. I can bring together scholars from different intellectual traditions. That's a great privilege—to listen to alternative views of how the continents of learning should be carved up.

You've mentioned the new geographies of the history of science. Have the kinds of questions that can be asked, or that are asked, in the history of science changed as well?

What's changed since I was a graduate student? First of all, if you would now utter the words *internal* and *external* to graduate students in the history of science, they would look at you as if you had horns. You really could be a visitor from the nineteenth century, as far as they're concerned. What had been the structuring principle, not to say the battle line, in the history of science has completely evaporated.

The reason for that has been the new focus on practices and contextualization. This was done brilliantly in Steven Shapin and Simon Schaffer's book *Leviathan and the Air-Pump*, which focused on a practice that was undeniably scientific, experiment.[16] Other historians of science, such as Pamela Smith, have followed the practice back to artisanal workshops; others have pointed out the prominence of the kitchen as an early modern site of chemical transformations, long before there was a dedicated space known as a laboratory.[17] An undeniably "internal" practice like experiment could be traced back to people, places, and procedures that seemed "external" by most standard criteria—thereby making a hash of the distinction. So the study of practices resulted in an enormous reconfiguration.

If the pre- and postdocs at the MPIWG are any indication, I think that we are on the verge of a turn to decontextualization, in part occasioned by their own practices, which I'll try to describe neutrally. First of all, we are in the midst of a revolution in reading practices. Reading practices, in part because of the web and hyperlinks, are now far more granular. The unit of analysis is now no longer the book or even the chapter. If you're lucky, it's the paragraph. It's a reading pattern that the up-and-coming generation of scholars has mastered in ways that I never will, in which readers of a text are constantly clicking and associating to something else. When I teach I notice that students fixate upon a word that glows to them and juxtapose it to others in often quite brilliant ways.

This is a very different form of reading than the close reading techniques taught to the previous generation, and I think it's led to a kind of pulverization of texts, which has its uses. The implicit assumption of my generation of intellectual historians, or historians of science, was that you read a text holistically. In fact, you read an oeuvre holistically. So if you studied the seventeenth-century English Orientalist Edward Pococke, for example, you did not read just one of his books; you tried to read his oeuvre. You researched the Oxford of his day, his ties to Archbishop Laud and his travels to Constantinople, and the context of mid-seventeenth-century biblical studies in England. Ideally, all the parts could be made to fit together into a coherent picture, like a jigsaw puzzle. That holistic reflex, and it really became a reflex, a matter of unexamined assumptions, is no longer self-evident to the new generation of historians. I think reading practices are key to this shift in assumptions. Scholars trained to read in a certain way will produce convergent effects in their analyses. Because we are undergoing a revolution of read-

16. Steven Shapin and Simon Schaffer, *Leviathan and the Air-Pump: Hobbes, Boyle, and the Experimental Life* (Princeton, 1985).

17. Pamela H. Smith, *The Body of the Artisan: Art and Experience in the Scientific Revolution* (Chicago, 2004).

ing practices, I expect a revolution also in units of analysis and forms of analysis. A new kind of logic is emerging, comparable to that of a museum exhibition. If the curator of the exhibition succeeds in the juxtaposition of objects, a spark jumps between them. And that's what a new generation of scholars seems to be looking for, not a holistic, thickly textured, contextual account or the analysis of book-length arguments.

What are the limits of the discipline? Are we missing something by privileging certain kinds of explanations over others?

I would love to see a history of our own categories of history. Why do we parse history into the categories of intellectual, social, economic, cultural? If my departure point were the eighteenth century, this would be a nonsensical division. At some point, the clan of historians decided to divide up the world in this way for reasons that escape me. So I suppose my short answer to your question is another question: why do we have such a thing as intellectual history? I don't in any way doubt the importance of intellectual history, only that it constitutes a natural kind. Intellectual history is perhaps a special case because it has been under fire from all sides: from the perspective of social history, it's a form of mystification, a history of the superstructure; from that of cultural history, it's elitist. Finally, to argue for the importance of intellectual history seemed vaguely narcissistic, as if scholars were asserting the centrality of their own tribe. But I think intellectual historians must take unpopular stances. First, they must argue for the causal efficacy of ideas, disputed by many, and, second, they must argue that some ideas are meatier and mightier than other ideas and are therefore more worthy of historical inquiry.

Does the same thing apply to history and history of science? That is, is the distinction between the two an artificial boundary that we have constructed?

I think many, if not the majority, of my colleagues would now say yes. I'm not so sure. I think it's undeniably the case that historians of science have profited enormously from being trained as proper historians, especially when I think now of the standards that reigned when I was in graduate school! Archives? What are archives? Or even the elementary precept that primary sources should be read in the original language, not in translation. This is how bad it was. There's no question but that our association with historians has elevated professional competence. Also, we have learned and profited from contextualization, a form of history that was quite alien to the history of science some forty years ago. The gifted practitioners of this brand of the history of science, for example Jim and Anne Secord, have produced extraordinary work.[18]

On the other hand, what the history of science always had, which history rarely had, was a high level of theorization. We felt licensed to ask big questions about the history of reason. We had alliances with, on the one hand, philosophy, on the other, sociology and anthropology. But that connection has waned as the bond with the historians has waxed. I'm ambivalent about losing that freedom to ask epoch-spanning questions, which I think most well-trained historians consider unintelligible or irresponsible [*laughs*]. Not to mention the irresponsibility, the unruliness that I described earlier, of leaping from the seventeenth to the twentieth century, with all of the risks attendant thereupon.

What do you see as the relationship between the history of science and scientific enterprises with living practitioners? What can historians communicate to those who work in scientific disciplines?

For the history of science there is an obvious answer to that, which is, we can't do what the scientists most want us to do. Recently I gave a talk to the Max Planck Gesellschaft, which is composed mostly of scientists, and what they wanted to know was, What's going to be the next breakthrough? Their idea of the history of science is extrapolation from past to future. Could you please tell us what the next Nobel Prize will be awarded for? Of course my answer disappointed them: "No, I'm sorry, I can't. And you don't want us historians of science to be able to do that. If we could extrapolate in that fashion, it would mean that your science is no longer capable of creative innovation." What I think the history of science can provide for scientists, especially in today's high-pressure, accelerated world of scientific research, is orientation and overview: where do the scientists' current research questions come from, and what are the alternatives? For practitioners immersed in a research program, the questions

18. James A. Secord, *Victorian Sensation: The Extraordinary Publication, Reception, and Secret Authorship of "Vestiges of the Natural History of Creation"* (Chicago, 2000); Anne Secord, "Science in the Pub: Artisan Botanists in Early Nineteenth-Century Lancashire," *History of Science* 32, no. 97 (1994): 269–315.

great gift to be with young people. For them, the world is fluid, it is full of possibilities; it is full of decisions that may be made this way or that way. Their life is still open-ended. I'm sorry if that sounds trite and saccharine, but it's a strongly felt truth to me.

In Objectivity *you offered a thought-provoking alternative model of historical narration, an alternative to rupture, or even gradualist development: reconfiguration. Do you consider this to be a model that could be more widely used to think about intellectual history at large?*

I think it can be applied in many cases, especially in the history of learning. Think about the commentary tradition, for example. The commentary tradition still has left its traces in the scientific article. The way in which every scientific article effectively begins by positioning itself within a publication sequence: "The literature says *X*." This is a commentary, however brief, however polemical, on the literature. There's always a bow, however perfunctory, in the direction of the past. That's always a reconfiguration of the past in the terms of the present and in terms of all the intervening commentaries, sometimes to the point of dismemberment. But I think that's the inbuilt structure of traditions. Even the most conservative imitate the children's game of Simon Says, in which the players try to advance stealthily while Simon's back is turned, only to freeze into position when Simon whirls around to face them. There is always change masked by continuity.

Of course, it is not to deny that there are moments of world-changing originality—except that these usually become evident only in twenty-twenty hindsight. Rarely is a book published—Darwin's *On the Origin of Species* (1859), which sold out on the first day, may be an exception—that immediately is hailed (and remembered) as a watershed. Even *Origin of Species* was foreshadowed by the anonymously published succès de scandale, *Vestiges of the Natural History of Creation* (1844). And neither book would have been conceivable without the tradition of natural history and geology that preceded it. A tradition builds upon itself. It's a process of continual rethinking of what we already know in light of now. This is most dramatic in the humanities, centered on textual canons, but such reconfiguration is also at work in the sciences, albeit with a shorter time line. Scientists seldom cite anything that goes back more than five years, an occasion for melancholy reflection among those who wonder how, or rather if, their contributions will be remembered a generation from now.

There are moments in science of startling continuity. This is most evident in sciences that investigate phenomena that unfold on a superhuman time-scale, such as astronomy, which is still indebted to ancient Babylonian and Chinese observations. But other sciences also occasionally reach across the centuries to long-dead predecessors: the great French naturalist Georges Cuvier, who was also proficient in ancient Greek, vindicated several of Aristotle's observations of animals and pronounced him a genius of classification at a time when the ancient Greek philosopher's scientific reputation was at lowest ebb. That impulse to embrace one's past is particularly vigorous in philosophy but not unknown in the modern sciences: "You, my colleagues across the vast expanses of time, my colleagues, I hold out my hands to you." There's something enormously moving in that expression of a community that defies time and space. It's a moral as well as an intellectual impulse.

How do you decide when to end your books?

I'm tempted to answer exhaustion [*laughs*]. But that would be too facile. I think that I know the end has come when I can write a coda that surveys the trajectory of the book and shows how so much has changed that its point of departure is no longer comprehensible without the help of a historian. The historical actors at the beginning and end of the book have come to live in different worlds, but we the historians can explain the migration. In the *Wonders* book, that coda is the late Enlightenment, which, looking back at the early sixteenth century, can only giggle at the preoccupations of its predecessors. There has been a sea change, which has thrown a veil between some historical period and another.

How do you feel the historical narrative taking shape when you are working on a project?

We're back in the murky subconscious—it just comes out of your fingers. I have no idea, really, how to answer this question. I'm one of those people who doesn't know what she thinks until she writes.

Is it a chemical process, really?

I'm not sure. I think dream work, or at least sleep work, has a lot to do with it. There's a reason why, even when I'm not working with a coauthor and talking intensively together about all we've read, I nonetheless read and reread all my notes. I'm still very old-fashioned and take notes by hand in little notebooks (a habit I began in graduate school; I now have dozens of such little notebooks). I then thematically index my notes, the moment when patterns begin to crystallize. I then go to bed, and in the morning I almost always wake up with the first sentence fully formed in my head—and off I go. This is such an inadequate answer to your question, but that is the phenomenology.

We've talked about current trends in the history of science. What do you wish for the future of the field?

I'm fortunate to be at an institution that rewards audacity, including audacity with respect to choice of research topics. One sterling example is the research of my new colleague at the MPIWG, the historian of Chinese technology Dagmar Schäfer. Her interests in the history of rational planning are terra incognita for the history of science, at first hardly recognizable as part of the field.[19] From the Han through the Qing dynasties, China had an extraordinary history of rational planning in a broad range of areas, from sericulture to architecture to military campaigns. Moreover, because planning and administration were bureaucratized and bureaucratized in a scholarly fashion, they left a paper trail—an archive of a longevity and thoroughness that is the envy of historians working on other periods and places. A history of planning combines the history of science and technology with the history of rationality more broadly. It is a history of the understanding not only of cause and effect but also of risk and uncertainty. Turning to what for me is terra cognita, early modern Europe, I realize how many of the figures dear to historians of science—Bacon, Leibniz, Newton, almost the entire Paris Académie Royale des Sciences—were involved in exactly such rationalizing planning enterprises. That is just one example of the fruits of working with people from other cultural traditions, and I expect that the newly enlarged geography and chronology of the history of science will yield many more such examples in the next decade.

More generally, rethinking geography and periodization will, I believe, force historians of science to rethink the ways in which the foundational narratives of the discipline have been yoked to the concept of modernity. I mentioned earlier that this concept, which does so much

19. Dagmar Schäfer, *The Crafting of the 10,000 Things: Knowledge and Technology in Seventeenth-Century China* (Chicago, 2011).

heavy lifting in history and the humanities, dissolves like a mirage under scrutiny. One obvious problem is that it's a hodgepodge: no two historians or social scientists can agree on when modernity was (I've gotten answers ranging from 1492 to 1945), much less what it was. The Scientific Revolution? The Industrial Revolution? The French Revolution? The demographic transition? Secularization? Global historians have begun to talk about "multiple modernities" in an attempt to expunge the Western taint of the concept, but no one seems willing to give it up altogether. There's a good reason for this reluctance: there's no alternative narrative of comparable sweep and drama. Historians of science in particular are in urgent need of a new narrative—an area that invites a collective effort.

The third growth area is the history of philology. I think philology is the *Urwissenschaft*. It's not an accident that in Medieval Latin, the only two disciplines in which the word *lex* (law) is applied to regularities are grammar and astronomy. Grammar especially is one of the earliest sciences to be formalized and methodized. Along with astronomy, grammar is one of the first areas in which scholars detect iron regularities, where they first have the idea of cumulative knowledge. I expect breaking news there.

To return to your comments about the persistence of modernity, do you fear the harmful effects of presentism upon the historical investigation either of other cultures or of the deep past?

Yes, I think that is a very acute observation. I think that it does explain how the premodern has expanded enormously (some historians would now describe everything that happened prior to 1914 as premodern) [*laughs*], thereby contracting the frame of reference allegedly relevant for understanding ourselves now to the point of claustrophobia.

What would a historical investigation of irrational or extrarational phenomena look like?

I'm in the business of making the apparently irrational rational without becoming irrational myself. So you really have to push me very hard before I'll admit an example of irrationality. But I do admit to its bare existence, indeed to the existence of willful irrationality: cp. Meric Casaubon on witches. Especially in the history of science, which many scientists regard as a history of error if not of irrationality, one must repeat to oneself like a mantra, "These people aren't lunatics. There is a way of making sense of this belief in terms of their knowledge and experience without embracing it." Historians of science must also acknowledge the possibility that rationality itself has a history, so the criteria by which we judge the rationality or irrationality of historical actors are themselves in flux. The ground is always moving under our feet, and the trick is not to lose our balance.

Benjamin Elman

BENJAMIN ELMAN is the Gordon Wu '58 Professor of Chinese Studies, Emeritus, at Princeton University.

How did you start out? What were your early interests?

People often ask me, "How did you know that China and East Asia would be so important in the future?" Well, the truth is I didn't. Growing up during the "Cold War," I was caught up in a world in which science was everything and inseparable from global politics in American life. The Soviet Union launched Sputnik on October 4, 1957, and thereby threw our free press and public media into a tizzy. I remember entering the eighth grade in September 1959, when our science and mathematics "aptitudes" were tested, and we were selected for special "science preparation" sections in junior high school. In these classes, science teachers presented the cutting edge of the "new" sciences in the 1950s. These subjects were now required of us if we were to keep pace in the space race with the communists. Some of us as high school seniors were sent to universities as bogus freshmen, so that we could get the training in the calculus and higher mathematics that our high school could not offer.

The brouhaha that greeted Thomas Kuhn's claims that science was historically contingent and grounded in its time and place occurred because the Cold War was a time when science was proclaimed universal. As a trained scientist, Kuhn had seen through the scientism of his peers;

as a trained historian, he saw through the allure of the philosophy of science, which allegedly explained the universal "logic" of scientific discoveries. Instead of "conjectures versus refutations" à la Karl Popper, the claims of science were, Kuhn argued, always tied to some sort of zeitgeist or weltanschauung that he defined in terms of a "paradigm," a bloated concept that he later regretted coining and retracted.[1]

As a philosophy major at Hamilton College in upstate New York in 1966, I became interested in historical arguments about the nature of science. At that time I was trying to figure out what to do; I had thought I would be in the sciences, possibly at Cornell, and perhaps go into engineering. Out of nowhere, my Hamilton teacher told me about the University of Hawaii's East-West Center, which had just been established. If your school didn't offer Chinese or Japanese, and most small colleges didn't, you could get a US government fellowship to spend a year in Hawaii studying one of those "critical" languages. And the program treated undergraduate students the same as graduate students.

I received an undergraduate fellowship and spent my junior year there. I enjoyed living like a graduate student. We had separate intensive programs in either Chinese or Japanese and served as guinea pigs for the eventual University of Hawaii language textbooks for first-, second-, and third-year Chinese. In addition, I also studied Confucianism and neo-Confucianism. I grew fascinated with Hawaii, which was enthralling, the beginning of the grand Oriental parade of foreigners going to Asia and back. There were very few East Asian figures, except for Zen masters, on the West Coast in the 1960s or even in the '70s and certainly none on the East Coast. Hawaii was an introduction to the Pacific world, but I still did not think it would become a career, academic or otherwise.

My family came to New York from Europe in 1947. I was born in 1946 in Munich, Germany, in a Displaced Persons camp after the war. There wasn't a sense in my family that Europe was great and wonderful. Rather a deep-seated feeling remained that Europe was appalling. It was an apocalyptic period of time, and clashes between Eastern and Western Europe were the norm. The mess out of which I came was in the end something of a creative chaos: I was trying to make my way and decided I didn't want to be an engineer, a doctor, or a lawyer. But I enjoyed learning Chinese.

Then the Vietnam War hit, so I couldn't go to graduate school in 1968 because the local draft board wouldn't approve my alternative

---

1. See Thomas S. Kuhn, *The Structure of Scientific Revolutions* (Chicago, 1962); Karl Popper, *Conjectures and Refutations: The Growth of Scientific Knowledge* (London, 1963).

schooling interests in East Asia. I wound up joining the Peace Corps instead, serving in Thailand and Southeast Asia, and working for three years in public health, specifically on malaria epidemiology as part of the World Health Organization's eradication efforts. I learned a lot about Buddhism, but also about reality. After my philosophical education, I began to see what Thai monks actually did and what the vastly different peoples there really did with their lives. In that sense, I received the cutting edge of an education in social, political, and economic history—not through book learning but through observation of my own small arena of "area studies" or "field studies."

I tried to go to graduate school again after two years in the Peace Corps, but there was a lottery for the draft beginning that year, and I drew the "unlucky" number six, so I stayed in Thailand for another year. Eventually, after failing my military draft physical at the Army Fifth Field Hospital in Bangkok in 1971, I returned to attend American University and George Washington University in Washington, DC, as an MA student, and then joined the PhD program in Oriental Studies at the University of Pennsylvania. It was an interesting struggle to find your way in East Asian studies at that time. People still couldn't understand why you would study Chinese or Japanese. I didn't come from an academic family. I chose to be somewhat unorthodox just out of curiosity and because I wasn't that interested in the history of Europe, given what I knew about it.

In essence, I chose Chinese because it was completely unfamiliar to me. I learned a little, began to learn more and more, and grew fascinated. I was very fortunate to spend one undergraduate year in Hawaii and discover in the process that I liked studying Chinese. With hindsight I could say I always knew, but we all know hindsight doesn't explain the beginnings of such things. At the time, who knew which were the inauspicious and which were the good decisions? My father thought I would never get a job.

What was the process of learning Chinese like? And how did you learn to tackle the different genres with which you've worked?

It takes time, effort, and experience. Our native Chinese students here at Princeton have advantages because both in China and in Taiwan they have already studied classical texts, with punctuation. When my generation was starting out, we didn't even have punctuation, and we had to start from scratch. Sometimes we read transliterations into the Roman alphabet before we started to read Chinese characters themselves.

Thanks to one year in Hawaii, including a 1967 summer session in Taiwan, I had the equivalent of several years of intensive Chinese language study under my belt. I could speak and read modern vernacular Chinese based on the Beijing (Peking) "dialect." I could also read classical Chinese texts that had been translated into the modern Chinese vernacular language. In graduate school, however, as I increasingly specialized in the original classical texts, I also realized that the entire written language, even the classical novels, had not been strictly vernacular; until comprehensive vernacular language reform took hold after 1911, it was all encompassed by classical Chinese. I started reading these pre-1911 genres and then reached the test of having to read unpunctuated primary classical sources themselves and to see how they were used in written and spoken vernacular discourses as well.

Since then, wherever I worked, I read texts with students, and we figured them out together. We also tried to find texts that were not punctuated, because the great writers and thinkers did not punctuate their texts; they just gave them to you and you had to be smart enough to know how to read them. The arrogance of the reader was that he believed he knew how to read because he had been trained, and the author didn't have to tell him how to do it. In terms of classical Chinese, our advantage as foreigners was that we didn't know anything, so we didn't realize that the punctuation was problematic. We took it for granted that the punctuation was always right, whereas the Chinese have fought long battles over the presentation and punctuation of classical texts, and we had to catch up with them.

Eventually, I started to go to Japan as part of my graduate program. They had classes at Tokyo University where they just read classical texts nonstop and translated them into modern Japanese. To make them easier to read, they changed the order of the Chinese characters and moved them to different places: the subject in the beginning, the verb in the middle, and endings at the end. For example, if they gave you a text by Zhu Xi (a twelfth-century Confucian scholar), they gave it to you in Japanese form. The Japanese have been doing that to classical Chinese texts since the eleventh and twelfth centuries. They've produced marked up, postclassical texts, ready for everybody to read—they're a lot easier to read than the originals. You may think that my colleagues and I are great linguists, but we're standing on the shoulders of the Japanese! In some ways we recapitulated their achievements.

Going to Taiwan and to Hong Kong has shown me how other dialects that are called "Chinese" fit in with all of this and how remarkable the Chinese system was: the Chinese didn't care so much what you said;

they cared what you wrote. Cantonese people outside Hong Kong spoke the language completely differently from people in Shanghai or from people in the north, but, from 1400 to 1900, they all could gather as civilian candidates and take the civil service examinations to become officials. The examiner might laugh and say, "Oh, you have a very bad accent from the south." But they still passed the exam if their writing was superb. The lingua franca was a written language, and everyone memorized it, but they still pronounced it differently.

Did particular seminars or mentors influence you during your graduate education?

One of my teachers at Penn, Philip Rieff, had written a famous book on Sigmund Freud.[2] In his course, a group of twenty graduate students read Paul's Letter to the Romans, for example. We got through just two pages of the English version over one semester. Everything led to everything else, and we discussed all the ramifications. He was teaching exegetically, almost religious reading and understanding, because he believed nobody knew how to read anymore. Zhu Xi had a fear of printing, precisely because people would just rush through the texts. You wouldn't savor the language reading this way. And Rieff understood this.

Every semester we got through about two pages of one book. The second semester we tackled Freud's theory of repression. Rieff had edited Freud's professional papers, and there was one essay on repression.[3] It's only about seven or eight pages, but try getting through it, and try to understand what Freud was doing. It took us a semester and a half. I remember how petrified we used to be in the class; we were terrified of Rieff. It was like being in kindergarten [*laughs*] and knowing that the master would scold you.

Rieff made a big difference in what I did. He was curious about China because he felt that if his own ideas regarding the "triumph of the therapeutic" in modern times were going to work, they had to work in a global sociocultural context; he had to understand the great ideas of other places as well.[4] For the sake of the health of contemporary culture, had the hospital superseded the church everywhere? To test this theory, he had to understand the great ideas of other places as well, not just

2. Philip Rieff, *Freud: The Mind of the Moralist* (New York, 1959).
3. Sigmund Freud, *Collected Papers*, ed. Philip Rieff, 10 vols. (New York, 1963).
4. Philip Rieff, *The Triumph of the Therapeutic: Uses of Faith after Freud* (New York, 1966).

those of the West. Occasionally, he assigned works in translation by Chinese figures. Once we read Lu Xun (1881–1936), the great radical writer of the early twentieth century whom Rieff and others had discussed in light of their notions of living in "unhealthy" cultures. But Rieff didn't treat Chinese authors with the same degree of nuance he applied to Western authors, because he didn't know their work very well.

How did you come to the history of Chinese science?

I'd inadvertently studied a lot of science and a lot of math in high school. Thomas Kuhn had taken the narrative away from the philosophers and said, "It's the practitioners of science who have to tell us what we're really doing." I learned a great deal in that transition from philosophy to history. Kuhn was a physicist reacting against the philosophers declaring what science is and is not, what is good and bad science.[5] I became appreciative of what Kuhn was trying to do, but Kuhn, of course, didn't know anything about Asia. Slowly but surely, I began to see there was space to develop this new area.

Ultimately, in the Euro-American "West," we began to understand the role of science in our macrohistorical narratives. I got interested in the history of science after I came to see that the narratives about science in Asia were similarly problematic. Joseph Needham, the great scholar of Chinese science, had set up the paradigm for the study of Chinese science in the 1950s and '60s, when he published his massive *Science and Civilisation in China* series. He and Nathan Sivin at Penn, with whom I later worked, had established certain different lines of inquiry about science in imperial China. These lines of inquiry are illustrated by Sivin's short biographies of the polymath Shen Kuo (1031–95) and the herbalist Li Shizhen (1518–93) (included in encyclopedias such as the *Dictionary of Scientific Biography*).[6] But their "Europe versus China" perspective was too broad and overarching, and so they weren't getting to the heart of the real issues. Joseph Needham was a great embryologist who met Chinese scientists in the 1940s in China during the war. He and other Western scholars who had been involved in wartime China absorbed the narrative of the failure of China. They thought that such a poor country,

5. Kuhn, *The Structure of Scientific Revolutions*.
6. Joseph Needham, *Science and Civilisation in China* (Cambridge, 1954); Charles Gillespie, ed., *Dictionary of Scientific Biography*, 16 vols. (New York, 1980).

which had been so promising in ancient times, had suddenly become a failure in the present.

The Chinese, in the midst of the Communist Revolution, thought everything about China was bad: it had an awful government, an awful economy, awful languages, awful cultures; Confucianism was awful, foot binding was awful. The revolutionaries needed a failed China to succeed, and who provided that failed China? The Japanese. They not only won the modern wars; they provided the historical narratives. It took me a long time to unravel the narrative that had been written up after the 1894–95 Sino-Japanese War: it claimed that China was a failure and Japan a success. War matters. It's a cultural event, and the narrative transformed during that war. The Japanese began to argue, "Our art, our literature, our culture are all better than Chinese art, literature, and culture."

Slowly but surely, I began to unpack the Japanese material. I went to Japan several times, and also Taiwan. Because of the political situation, we Americans couldn't yet go to China. Europeans could start going in 1975, but Americans couldn't until about 1984. I spent a lot of time in Japan and learned the Japanese canon about China. Sinology as we knew it, in Japan, Europe, and the United States, depended on Japanese expertise; they were the leading scholars. A lot of these Japanese scholarly works had been translated into Western languages, but many of us also had to become fluent in Japanese in addition to Chinese in order to grasp what the Japanese were doing.

We learned appreciation for Japanese scholarship; over the long run we also began to see its limitations. The Japanese were interested in China not because they loved China but because they wanted to supersede it. Particularly in the early twentieth century, Europe became the new model, and Japanese scholars began to say, "China's clearly falling apart. It's lost these wars. We've defeated them. We are now the key country of Asia." In my lifetime we had to unravel exactly what the Chinese thought about themselves and to learn how to no longer accept those Japanese arguments. My colleagues and I had to be very sharp with our tools, or we'd be taken in easily. The beginnings of this process of unlearning were very complicated but also inspiring for me. I began to gain access to the information that the Japanese, who had the necessary toolkits, had compiled. They read the Chinese materials, and they had practiced six hundred, seven hundred years of sinology before the Europeans came on the scene. They were a remarkable think tank for us to use and learn from, at first.

Initially, most of us accepted the narrative of China's failure. I used to give lectures on the "sixteen reasons" why China failed to have science;

I misled a generation of graduate students and undergraduates. Now I teach it as a joke, and everybody fortunately laughs. The failure narrative is so dense that initially you can't see through it. It took a lot of unlearning to get rid of its explanatory power. It's very hard to force yourself to unlearn things. You have to doubt almost everything, and sometimes you overstep and doubt too much. Needham, for example, was wrong about almost everything—he was very much responsible for the narrative that my generation had to deconstruct—but at the same time he was absolutely essential for us; he provided us with a "scientific" starting point.

Needham saw the rise of Chinese science as a unique story only up to the coming of the Jesuits around 1600; he called what came after that "ecumenical science." The term implied that, whereas starting in 1200, China had independently led the world in science and technology, by 1600 China was no longer cutting edge. That wasn't quite true, as I eventually found. Chinese science retained differences from European science for much longer, and we have to deal with these differences "on their own terms," as I wrote.[7] The Chinese stuck to their guns, quite literally, for a long period of time. What used to be the narrative of failure is now best told as a dialogue between the different groups: at what point did the Chinese adopt Japanese and European scientific terminology? And why? What were the politics of those linguistic choices? It's much more complicated than it once seemed. But Needham, to his credit, saw that Chinese science was interesting. He understood that ancient, medieval, and early modern China had done amazing things.

How has the history of Chinese science been rewritten in recent decades?

The Jesuits had such an impact, not just on Chinese science but also on how the history of Chinese science has been told—they were like the Japanese in that respect. Moreover, they had an agenda. The Italian Jesuit missionary Matteo Ricci and others made grandiose claims about Chinese civilization beyond what they actually knew; had they known more, they would likely have been more cautious. They portrayed a triumphal late Ming China (1368–1644), and they recommended it as a model state and society from which Europeans had much to learn.

7. Benjamin A. Elman, *On Their Own Terms: Science in China, 1550–1900* (Cambridge, MA, 2005).

Similarly, in the nineteenth century, many Protestant missionaries, had they known more, would have been more careful. However, rather than expressing excessive enthusiasm about China as the Jesuits had, the Protestants emphasized the irredeemable weaknesses of China in a time of civil wars and demographic catastrophe after 1850. All of which is to say that we should be extremely cautious ourselves. At one time we said China had no word for science. Then we discovered the terms *gewu* ("to investigate things") and *gewu zhizhi* ("to investigate and extend knowledge"). This was one of Zhu Xi's greatest sayings, and it became very prominent during the medieval Song dynasty and thereafter. Later on people used it in medicine, astronomy, and mathematics; they all professed to investigate things and extend knowledge. To be clear, I'm not arguing that this word meant science across the board from, say, the eleventh or twelfth century to 1900. But by the sixteenth and seventeenth centuries, and undoubtedly by the eighteenth and nineteenth, it was a Chinese term for natural studies.

We also believed that, in the nineteenth century, Chinese scholars abandoned that tradition. But that's not what happened at all. In the nineteenth century, Chinese scholars took the term for "investigating things and extending knowledge" and applied it to the new sciences. Shanghai Polytechnic was called in Chinese the "Academy for the Extension of Knowledge and the Investigation of Things." The classical terminology was translated into a modern term. We misunderstood that for a long time and claimed they had no such term.

When the Japanese won the war with China in 1894–95, the Chinese adopted the Japanese term for science, *kagaku*. It is still the term for science in China and Japan today. This obscured the fact that the classical meaning of the Chinese word had already encompassed science. We stopped looking for that earlier moment, in part because scholars were fixated on a particular historical vision in which there was no science in China.

We used to study Chinese science only up to the time of the Jesuits. Then a new and different set of scholars studied Chinese science from the Opium War in 1840 until the twentieth century. The intermediate period was neglected. Now we have realized, or at least I have tried to clarify, that you cannot just study one or the other; you have to study the whole span of Chinese intellectual history. We must overcome the urge to study Chinese science in relation to just the Jesuits after 1600 or just the Protestants after 1840.

Let me give you an example. For the longest time, the Chinese started learning algebra and calculus in new organizations like naval yards and machinery-producing factories, because algebra and the other mathematics were important to engineering. They used traditional Chinese mathematics as a stepping stone to early modern Western mathematics. That was criticized as backward, because they could have gone right to Western mathematics and avoided Chinese math altogether. But Chinese mathematics had been very sophisticated, and around 1800 or so it was still based upon the tradition that had come into China from exchange with the Mongols and the Islamic world. When the Chinese said, "We're going to do the calculus, but we have our own kind of text that's pretty close to the calculus. Let's use that first as an introduction," they were standing on the shoulders of their own predecessors and using their own tradition to learn the new math that came from the Protestant translators. But the tendency among my predecessors was to just ignore that. Why study backward mathematics? And thus a false picture of the history of Chinese mathematics was born.

In many ways, what we're trying to do now is to redress the earlier narrative of Chinese "failure." We now are going through that door and looking for other things, seeing other things, and reinterpreting them. The notion of the deficiency of Chinese science is, I think, an old game.

What questions led to your book From Philosophy to Philology, *which explores an intellectual transition in late imperial/early modern China by reconstructing a massive scholarly effort to recover and study authentic ancient Chinese writings?* [8]

I started off in Hawaii studying what we then called neo-Confucianism, a term in vogue via the teachings of Wm. Theodore de Bary at Columbia.[9] Like de Bary, my teacher in Hawaii, Chung-ying Cheng, also represented both Confucianism and neo-Confucianism as a unified "black box" of moralistic theories. They tended to interpret such theoretical terms philosophically, thus favoring the term "neo-Confucian." But the American scholars didn't question technical terms very much or query texts as much as Chinese classical philologists themselves had. Chinese scholars had a term for "paleography" already by the second century CE. The Chinese approach favored philology. By way of contrast, the

---

8. Benjamin A. Elman, *From Philosophy to Philology: Intellectual and Social Aspects of Change in Late Imperial China* (Cambridge, MA, 1984).

9. See, for example, *The Unfolding of Neo-Confucianism*, ed. Wm. Theodore de Bary (New York, 1975).

Europeans didn't have the Latin word *paleography* until much later, in the early modern period.

The discourses of Chinese classical scholars during the eighteenth century reinforced a shift from Song-Ming rationalism to a more skeptical and secular empiricism, derived from research into the classical tradition. By making precise scholarship the source of acceptable knowledge, Qing classicists contended that the legitimate reach of ancient ideals should be reevaluated through comparative delineation of the textual sources from which all such knowledge derived. This turn to empirically based classical inquiry meant that abstract ideas and rational argumentation gave way as the primary objects of elite discussion to concrete facts, verifiable institutions, ancient natural studies, and historical events. In general, Qing classicists regarded Song and Ming "learning of the way" (i.e., neo-Confucianism) as an obstacle to verifiable truth, because it discouraged further inquiry along empirical lines.

The empirical approach to knowledge they advocated placed proof and verification at the heart of analysis of the classical tradition. During this time, scholars and critics also applied historical analysis to the official classics. Commentary yielded to textual criticism and a "search for evidence" to refortify the ancient canon. Representing a late imperial movement in Confucian letters, Qing classicists still sought to restore the classical vision. But the work of these early modern Chinese philologists ended up promoting a process of decanonization, even if this isn't what they had originally intended.

The Chinese were dealing with different explanations for why the classical texts were created the way they were, and why they were spoken the way they were. A range of issues related to the pronunciation and formation of characters promoted a paleographic or linguistic orientation to their scholarship. Like the German theorist Hans-Georg Gadamer's critical readings of Western philology, the more philological scholars in China stressed the glossing and exegesis of entire texts. These "evidential scholars" had three rules: (1) you had to know the phonology of the language; (2) you had to know the paleography of the system, and (3) you also had to master the exegetical approaches to the texts. Those were their three cornerstones. One of the texts I worked on came from Tang period China (618–907). It was later lost in China and brought back from Japan in the mid-eighteenth century.[10] In the 1780s the Chinese transformed this eighth-century text, which is a preface for Confucius's *Analects*, into

10. Benjamin Elman, "One Classic and Two Classical Traditions: The Recovery and Transmission of a Lost Edition of the *Analects*," *Monumenta Nipponica* 64, no. 1 (2009): 53–82.

an account about paleography, phonology, and comparative ideas. I've argued that the preface to this recovered classic was a forgery. It was also a hoax perpetrated by the Japanese on the Chinese, who unwittingly published the Japanese version. Because I've spent so many years studying the eighteenth century, I was able to see how the Japanese were deceiving the Chinese about their own texts. The Japanese claimed that this source was by a medieval Chinese philologist who had precociously pioneered a seemingly modern philology in ancient times. In fact, however, they had invented him in early modern Japan. Even the name of the Chinese author in the Japanese version wasn't the same name. The names were wrong because the pronunciations were written with different writing forms and conventions. The Japanese pronounced the text differently.

Also, the Chinese Empire had a huge examination system. One of the reasons I got interested in the examination system was its scale. When people took exams, over time an orthodoxy emerged. The examiners did not tolerate dissent for very long. For instance, Zhu Xi remained the main orthodox voice of the Confucians. But in the sixteenth century, during the late Ming period, the followers of the scholar-official and military leader Wang Yangming (1472–1529) were major dissenters. Some of Wang's students at that time were able to get answers based on his views counted as acceptable orthodoxy, but their dissent didn't last very long. We get dissenting interpretations from other people and read them accordingly, but the orthodox response to the dissent was set in cement. Emperors didn't just fight wars; they also destroyed texts that they did not like. Over time the loss of these texts was covered up.

Recovering accurate intellectual history is a very rocky road through these texts and materials. It's very easy to be taken in. What I tried to do with the history of classical Chinese philology was ask, What were the rules of philology? Different kinds of philology exist historically. The Chinese practiced a critical philology that tested the classical languages and argued for different forms; they debated whether a text was authentic or not, believable or not. They made an effort to be critical about meanings and not just take them for granted.

The Chinese, and later the Japanese and the Koreans, valued philology greatly. It became a lingua franca for them and one in which they competed. By the eighteenth century, the Japanese were claiming their versions of Chinese classical texts were better because they were more authentic. The texts had come to Japan in the sixth or seventh century and then survived in Japan when many of the texts that remained in mainland China were destroyed. In that sense, the Japanese had better texts and therefore better arguments.

There began an interesting East Asian give-and-take that we now are beginning to focus on and discuss more, though not as successfully as we should. Unfortunately, the scholars who study Japan still are somewhat distant from those who study China, and most of the people who study neo-Confucianism in China don't even know what was going on in Japan. They don't talk about it because we're bifurcated in the way we work. But the traditions and histories need to be integrated if we want to understand both sides.

Did libraries in the United States support your research? To what extent did you depend on travel to East Asia?

Without the Asian libraries that had come to the United States my generation could not have done what we tried to do. We were lucky to have the libraries that we did. American library collections of East Asian materials were mostly built in the twentieth century; what was achieved is quite remarkable. Some collections were started earlier: for example, Berkeley started collecting Chinese books after it founded the Agassiz Oriental Chair in 1872. The first holder, John Fryer, an English scholar who had been living in Shanghai, came to Berkeley from China with all of his materials. The Gest Collection at Princeton was started by an American businessman, Guion Moore Gest, who had gone to China in the early decades of the twentieth century. Because he had eye problems, he became interested in traditional Chinese medicine, acupuncture, and massage, and started buying books on those topics. Gest donated his collection to McGill in Montreal, Canada, in the 1920s; it opened in 1926. When McGill was going to sell the Chinese collection in pieces, Gest managed to buy it back. Robert Oppenheimer at the Institute for Advanced Studies in Princeton later heard about it, and the Institute wound up buying it. The first curator, Nancy Lee Swann, was never allowed to teach about the collection, however, because she was a woman.

The big boom in collecting happened right after World War II. Starting at the end of the war, people bought whole sections of collections in China and Japan and sent them to the United States. At Yale, for example, a very famous scholar, Mary C. Wright, wandered northern China in the years after World War II. Wherever she found books she bought them and was reimbursed by Yale. The Chinese had minilibraries already, collections of books, because they started printing in the twelfth century, and Western buyers could collect these minilibraries.

Books were cheap initially. You could buy Japanese books after the war for almost nothing; books that today would cost hundreds or thousands of dollars you could get for ten, fifteen dollars, just because the Japanese had lost the war, and many thought their culture was valueless. People were poor, and they got rid of these things.

Overall, we have too many sources for Chinese history; the Chinese kept records of everything. If you want to work on the examinations, for example, I can give you policy questions that show what the examiners were worried about from 1573 to 1630 under a single reign, with several hundred questions and answers. It's a bit mind-boggling. Sheldon Pollock, the Indologist, just looks at us and says, "It's not fair. It's not fair at all," because Indian sources are so hard to find [*laughs*]. But if you came from the United States, it was a challenge to gain access to lots of Chinese materials. To read the most important texts you had to travel. Nothing was online in those days, and you had to deal with the politics of getting access to materials in China.

Before, we were just happy to get the books in our hands, because it was very hard to gain access. It's been a difficult exchange. In European history, you probably don't have much trouble politically getting materials when you want to. In contrast, we have to do a political dance sometimes. A very enterprising woman who was writing a dissertation on porcelain in southeast China, for instance, posed as a tourist, because she knew that if she told the Chinese she was a scholar from the Academy of Social Sciences they wouldn't let her in.

The Chinese wondered why you'd want to see their books and why you should get to see them before their scholars did. Seeing them required a certain amount of finesse and diplomacy, and luck. When I first went to China in the early 1980s, I couldn't go to the library; they wouldn't let me in. The Shanghai Academy of Social Science gave me a room and the catalog list. I would say, "Can I see this?" They would bring the item to my office privately and let me take a look at it that way. In Beijing when the Chinese Social Science Academy library was closed to everybody, I just happened to have the support of one of the leaders of the library, who let me go through that entire library by myself. You had to be lucky to gain access to that kind of collection.

Nowadays, computers have transformed research, and we have a lot of texts and materials online, both in China and in Taiwan. It's much easier to go through the Royal Library, the Imperial Library in the eighteenth century, online. In addition, the graduate students have devised their own programs and put together their own search engines, which has made a big difference as well.

How did you come to one of your major topics of research, the
examination system of late imperial China, which lasted
from the Song Dynasty (960–1279) until 1905? [11]

For a long time I would stay away from examination essays. Who would read examination essays? Why bother with them? They're only the so-called eight-legged essays, which conformed to a balanced and predictable rhetoric of eight "parts" and were written in a phony prose that nobody takes seriously any longer. But, in fact, it turned out that there were contemporary policy questions on astronomy, science, and government at the end of the examinations. These dealt with the current relevance of the classics for state and society—very practical affairs. I started reading these and realizing this is quite revealing. Why, in 1525, for example, are they calling for calendar reform? Something must be wrong with the calendar that is being reformed. The Mongols had conquered China and used Arabic and Islamic materials for the Song-Ming calendars.

Thanks to the examination essays, you could see more clearly that in 1525 the Chinese had a particular interest in mathematics and science. They brought in Muslims and Sogdian Persians before the Jesuits arrived. If there was ever an international astronomy bureau, it was in China. The Chinese were in one building, the Persians/Sogdians in another, and later the Jesuits in a third. The Chinese said, "We have three different buildings. Give us the right answers." Whoever gave them the right answers— and it increasingly became the Jesuits—would be honored even more.

More broadly, you could say that we do certain things once we take them for granted. The examination system was taken for granted, and people just kept it going. Eventually people said, "Well, the examination system is bad," so the system ended. But when I began working on this topic, no one had really figured out the long-term story about how the exam system operated. It turns out that the long-term story was devastating for those who failed the exams, because only five percent of examinees were passing. And you had some twenty thousand men taking each of the seventeen highest provincial examinations every year. What happened to the other nineteen thousand men at each venue who failed? What careers were they going on to? Can you imagine Harvard, if only five percent of the undergraduates passed and graduated? What would happen?

---

11. Benjamin A. Elman, *A Cultural History of Civil Examinations in Late Imperial China* (Berkeley, 2000); Elman, *Civil Examinations and Meritocracy in Late Imperial China* (Cambridge, MA, 2013).

The 95 percent pursued anything that involved literacy. They became Buddhist monks, printers, all kinds of different things. Moreover, elite women could read relatively well, and, when they became mothers, their sons benefited from smart mothers who knew the classics that informed the canon. I tried to understand why in the Ming Dynasty the examinations mattered so much. Why were all of these people PhDs? What was going on when everyone in the civil service had PhDs? What were their majors? What were they doing? And what were they being trained for?

Scholars of early modern Europe have long argued about whether and how early modernity is distinctive. What, if anything, do you find distinctive about the period 1500–1800 from a Chinese perspective?

What to call the period is a hard debate for sinology. Initially I called everything after 1600 "late imperial," and then the younger people started using "early modern." I was somewhat resistant to that term and what it implies. In many ways, the newly emerging "evidential" scholars whose philology I studied were not trying to debunk the classical texts. During the early modern/late imperial transition, between 1600 and 1800, the evidential studies of the new Ming-Qing philologists began to buttress philological critiques of Song-Ming philosophy. These "evidential" scholars were similar to the Christians who approached the Bible not in order to debunk the Old Testament but to perpetuate it in a new form, to purify it. And so they tried to purify the Chinese classics and rectify them in many ways. That group was late imperial. They were believers.

From the sixteenth century to the nineteenth, even when Chinese scholars doubted their source materials, they didn't doubt their entire enterprise. They said, "This text is a forgery. We have to replace it. We have to do something else." But the upper echelon of the government would not replace it. Government officials would respond, "No, we don't want people to lose faith in the canon." Not even the scholars could be that successful.

We call the period "early modern" because it's not quite modern yet, but we also have to be careful not to overemphasize its modernity. I prefer to call the period "late imperial/early modern" just to emphasize, with my use of the term "late imperial," that intellectually people were still part of the old tradition. The "early modern" aspect refers to the emergence of doubt and questioning. At some point in the nineteenth century, the more revolutionary positions took over: doubt about the canon began to outweigh belief in the minds of those generations. People were willing to go from the fact that one text was false to the conclusion that they all were—in some instances even overstating the case.

In this sense, it seems better to call the period up to 1800 "late imperial," but, if you go beyond 1800, there are certainly strands of what we'll call "early modern" there. Yet these strands don't become manifest until later in the nineteenth century. I don't know what you would do in your field, but we've tried to have it both ways, to emphasize both tradition and transformation. "Late imperial" describes a mindset that looks back to the Ming and the Mongols, and all the dynasties that came before. Eventually, you get to that striking transition, and then we can use the term "early modern." In my opinion, describing the sixteenth and seventeenth centuries as early modern China is—in some cases—to use the term a little bit too early. It might be better to use "early modern" for the eighteenth and nineteenth centuries. It's a debate, however, and younger scholars are more likely to call everything early modern.

How do you go about formulating a question, and how does that question percolate into a research program?

Initially I was told by my advisers to pick a spot and go backward and then follow it up to the present. That is the pure teleology I was taught! It had its uses, because it created pockets of knowledge and of information. But, over time, I learned that these pockets didn't work quite the way everyone thought they did: to know what happened in 1895 and then to go back to 1865 and see the developments that led to 1895 was in many ways to miss other things that had happened in 1865.

My generation was brainwashed into teleology, namely the historiological assumption that knowing the results of past events enables you to know their beginnings. I have spent much time trying to undo this assumption. We need to appreciate "unintended consequences" to undo teleology properly. The civil service examinations, for example, weren't intended to flunk 95 percent of examinees; they were just supposed to select the best and the brightest. It turned out that many people wanted to hire scholars from among the 95 percent that failed. Then the question became, well, what did all of these people do? Did they rebel? Were they unhappy? No, some wrote novels in which they even mocked the examiners. They did all kinds of things. The unintended consequence of the examinations was the creation of a prodigious group of literate people who could do many different things. Even women were writing poetry quite widely in the fifteenth, sixteenth, and seventeenth centuries. We didn't think they did until we read their works.

Some scholarship on early modern European intellectual history focuses on how early modern Europeans understood the concept of the classical. How do you understand the notion of classicism in the Chinese context?

As with "early modern," the question becomes: is "classical" the term we want to use? What is a classic? That's a debate for Western historiography as much as it is for us. What is a *jing*? A *jing* is a patterning and mirroring of the true world and the true situation. The respect a classic gets is one way to define what a classic is—it's the book that everyone is required to study. In the Chinese tradition, classics became markers for truth, as they did for the European Renaissance. A classic stood out from all of the other texts and was reproduced over and over again; it was used in the examinations.

In sinology, we worked with the European notions of a classic and tried to bring them into a discussion with Chinese and Japanese materials as well. In East Asia, there's the belief that the text contains a certain transmission of truth. The Chinese traced this transmission back to Confucius or even further to the sage kings before that [i.e., legendary sovereigns of the third millennium BCE]. Yet at some point in the early modern period Chinese scholars began to debunk all of that, and they began to argue in toto that none of the sources really went back to Confucius, or, if some did, it was only a small amount. But the debunkers don't really triumph until the twentieth century.

We take for granted—perhaps too much—that a classic is, in European terms, the same thing as a classic in Chinese terms. We should look at what a classic means, starting from the European notions of a classic, and then compare them to what the East Asians meant by a classic and how their definitions operated.[12] In the end, we can't just dissolve the word classic and *jing* together and say they're exactly the same thing. They're not. You can make comparisons, but you must be careful.

12. See Frank Kermode, *The Classic: Literary Images of Permanence and Change* (Cambridge, MA, 1983) and T. S. Eliot, *What Is a Classic? An Address Delivered before the Virgil Society on the 16th of October, 1944* (London, 1945).

*How has recovering the forgotten history of Chinese science
changed the study of more traditionally humanistic or
philological pursuits?*

Over time we began to see that the philologists and the people interested
in science tended to overlap considerably. They were interested in mathematics, but they were engaged in all kinds of disciplines. Chinese scholars
used humanistic research to provide support for state ideology. It supplied
rhetoric to defend the government. Everyone who learned about science
did not become a scientist, but they had to be aware of why the calendar
was important, for example. They had to be wise about why the Jesuits kept
track of these things: "We may not do it ourselves, but certainly we can get
the Jesuits to do it for us." And then as the Jesuits become more and more
unreliable, they said, "We don't want to rely on them to do this. We want
to do this ourselves, and so we have to learn how to do this." The Manchu
state tried to get the Manchu bannermen to learn science. It was to no
avail for the warrior class. Who learned the sciences? The Chinese elites
did, because they were interested. It became part of their tradition to do
this. I think this tradition promoted the interests of statecraft. The sciences
were a practical means of dealing with the technical aspects of the imperial
state. Unexpectedly, Manchu military bannermen had failed to heed the
increasing marriage of traditional statecraft with the new mathematics and
sciences, leading ultimately to the birth of new technology. Ironically, the
Manchu state had no choice but to rely on avant-garde Chinese literati-
officials, who helped prioritize mathematics and natural studies in order to
normalize long-term astronomical, political, and economic realities.

What was it like to produce the volume World Philology, *which you
coedited?*[13] *And how does China fit into world philology comparatively?*

Although *World Philology* does not offer a narrative for the historical rise of
global "philologies," it presents multiple chapters that reveal the linguistic intensity and structural depth of philology worldwide. We canvassed
very widely among contemporary classicists to offer a global context for
their philological interests. The resulting book is chronological in some
ways and topical in other ways. Topically we depict each of the global

13. Sheldon Pollock, Benjamin A. Elman, and Ku-ming Kevin Chang, eds., *World Philology* (Cambridge, MA, 2015).

cases in the volume by including scholars from the five continents. We include a lot more so-called Islamic materials, some Indian materials, and some other materials associated with Latin and Greek. If we now bring in the Chinese and Japanese material, in the future we need to bring in Korean philology as well. There are different voices in *World Philology*, and we decided not to arbitrate between them, because disagreement is what philologists do. And what would be a volume on philology without some disagreement? Philologists were notorious for their animosities toward each other. You might consider *World Philology* as the beginning of a source book. It is a source book of essays about the topic, and we hope that there will be follow-ups as well; it's just a starting point.

My essay in *World Philology* is in many ways an effort to mediate the late imperial/early modern story I discussed earlier. Aspects of the "late imperial" and the "early modern" were present simultaneously in eighteenth-century China.[14] At the time it was unclear which narrative was going to prevail. We know with hindsight that one won out over the other, but we need to recreate the possibilities and uncertainties. I try to show that in the end the Chinese weren't trying to destroy their traditions, they were trying to purify them.

How has the geopolitical rise of contemporary China affected East Asian studies and East Asian intellectual history?

It used to be that everybody—not just in the West but also in East Asia—ran away from things Chinese, because Chinese was deemed a backward language and China a backward culture. They preferred to learn modern Japanese. Things have changed, of course. Now, increasingly, Koreans regret getting rid of Chinese characters. They'll probably begin to revive them in the future. The Japanese kept Chinese characters, but other groups who got rid of Chinese characters are starting to relearn Chinese. For instance, the Vietnamese got rid of Chinese characters and started using French, but now contemporary Chinese scholars are collecting Vietnamese materials from the Middle dynasty, roughly from 1750 until 1900. Scholars at Fudan University in Shanghai have recently put together twenty volumes of materials from Vietnam that were written in classical Chinese.

The Vietnamese are beginning to regret the jettisoning of their classical Chinese heritage. After the colonial period, French, English, and the other

---

14. Benjamin Elman, "Early Modern or Late Imperial? The Crisis of Classical Philology in Eighteenth-Century China," in Pollock, Elman, and Chang, *World Philology*.

Western languages became dominant in Vietnam. The Vietnamese cannot turn the clock back. The Koreans can't read anything in their own language from before 1900 because they got rid of classical Chinese. But, in general, as Chinese learning is gaining more respect, the classical texts are taken more seriously. The Chinese themselves are beginning to look at these texts and say, "What do they tell us about ourselves?" The people I work with at Fudan University, for example, are proposing, "Let's look at China from outside. If we look at China from outside, what can we learn about China?" I think they are offering useful comparisons.

What role has teaching played in your intellectual life?

I think teaching is very important. I try to stress how important teaching is for understanding the problems you teach. In other words, you may be so fixated on a small meaning that might be of relevance to your adviser or someone else that you completely overlook the larger picture that's going to appeal to a larger audience. But you need to address the larger audience.

It doesn't matter whether you are a great orator or have a presence or are a wonderful actor. Just being in front of students and interacting with them is essential. You learn what you take for granted when you try to tell them what's going on. In lectures, we love easy answers. Do I use the category of neo-Confucianism very much in my writing? Not very much. But if I were giving a lecture, neo-Confucianism would be all over the place, because it's simple, and the students absorb it very easily. At the same time, you also have to begin to problematize the material and get the students into the material—and explain, for example, why you can't always use neo-Confucianism. I think it's very important to expose students to the problems that scholars face. That way, you can draw students into your field. If the students can see the problems you're working with and the problems you're trying to deal with, they're more likely to think, "I'm not going to be a doctor. I'm not going to be a lawyer. This can be interesting, and it's something I can do."

Do we have more unlearning collectively ahead of us?

I think we need a lot more unlearning in the East Asian field if by that you mean questioning what we take for granted in order to find the right answers. We also need to understand that sometimes we must unlearn what the Chinese or the Japanese have said about themselves. We have always said we're the Orientalists, the people imposing a distorted vision of that part of the world. In an unexpected way, however, the Japanese were the Orientalists in their representation of Chinese culture and society. It took me about ten years to get over Japanese sinology. I still admire it and think a great deal of it, but I can show you Japanese quotations on Chinese art that are irresponsible—calling the Metropolitan Museum of Art the home of "indigent art" produced by the Chinese, for example. It was unnerving to realize that some Japanese scholars and scholars of Japan who were hired as art historians in the West—such as Ernest Fenollosa (1853–1908) and Okakura Tenjin (1862–1913), both at the Boston Museum of Fine Arts—put out arguments about the inferiority of Chinese art. You can say art is bad, art is good, but to put it on that metaphysical plane? No art historian should do that, as I stressed at the Reischauer Lectures in April 2011 at Harvard.[15]

Has your study of scholarly practice in the early modern period shaped your own practices as a scholar?

I try to distance myself from the people whom I study, so when I study the history of philology, I'm not a philologist. There are times when I use the techniques of a philologist, but I also want to approach the philologists themselves as objects of analysis, and to see what they're doing with philology, the claims they're making, what they're adding, what they're leaving out. In general, I am interested in thinking through intentions and consequences. We have to know when those intentions are put into place and when those consequences are realized, whether it's immediate or whether it's ten, fifteen, twenty years later. The examination system is an example of the growing distance between intentions and consequences over time. Very often people's intentions when they set up institutions prove very different from the actual results.

How has the rise of book history changed your field?

We used to focus on the rise of printing in the European Renaissance, and we forgot that the Chinese were doing printing on a wide scale two

15. Benjamin Elman, "The Great Reversal: The 'Rise of Japan' and the 'Fall of China' after 1895 as Historical Fables" (Reischauer Lecture, Harvard University, Cambridge, MA, April 13, 2011), https://www.youtube.com/watch?v=Pn4rI6JqSI4. See also Elman, *On Their Own Terms*.

centuries before the Germans. We've underestimated a good deal about early modernity by saying that print culture began in Europe and that the Chinese dealt with it only once the Jesuits came to China. India didn't produce a print culture per se, although it had lots of manuscript writing on certain topics. But the Chinese had widespread government printing in the eleventh and twelfth centuries, and then they had local merchant printers and other kinds of commercial printers in the fifteenth and sixteenth centuries. Remember Elizabeth Eisenstein writing about how wonderful printing was and how great a leap this was, and then Adrian Johns chimed in and said, "No, no, no, print culture was not an automatic achievement"?[16]

Susan Cherniak looked at printed material in China in the eleventh century and found many eleventh-century sources that argued, "Books are terrible, printing is leading away from learning, all of these printing mistakes are entering into the material."[17] Very few scholars of China bought into Eisenstein's narrative, because the Chinese were traditionally very critical of print. Print was dangerous, not so much politically but because it led to mistakes and then transmitted these errors. Lots of texts were lost, misplaced, or misinterpreted, and manuscripts disappeared once they were published. So some of those things can be compared with the print culture of the Europeans.

Indeed, arguments about print culture in some ways have to start with East Asia. If you're going to do a chronology it has to start there, and then we can see how aspects of German print culture compare.[18] The Jesuits didn't seem surprised that there were printed books all over the place in China in the sixteenth and seventeenth centuries. They bought books and published their own; they knew about them. They took it for granted that the Chinese printed them, just as they took it for granted that Europeans printed books. It's not about what they learned from us or we learned from them; everyone just took books for granted. Ricci even sold books; he wrote on friendship and gained a wide readership, and the Chinese printed the books for him.

16. Elizabeth L. Eisenstein, *The Printing Press as an Agent of Change: Communications and Cultural Transformations in Early Modern Europe* (Cambridge, 1979); Adrian Johns, *The Nature of the Book: Print and Knowledge in the Making* (Chicago, 1998).

17. Susan Cherniak, "Book Culture and Textual Transmission in Sung China," *Harvard Journal of Asiatic Studies* 54, no. 1 (1994): 5–125.

18. Lothar Ledderose, *Ten Thousand Things: Module and Mass Production in Chinese Art* (Princeton, 2000).

*What are the present directions that you find most interesting
in your field, and what things would you hope for its future,
for the next generation? What is on the to-do list?*

We've had a lot of additions. Try to think of a history that had no gender issues before. Scholars once claimed there were no sources for the
study of the history of gender in China. What kind of nonsense was that?
Would you believe that Europeans claimed that China historically had
no economic experience? In the nineteenth to early twentieth century,
European scholars claimed imperial China was a noncommercial or anti-
commercial environment. We now know that was nonsense. I think we
are breaking away from a lot of these false notions. Hopefully, that will
happen with things like *World Philology*. People will do what Tony Grafton did in an essay in 1985 when he compared his sources with mine and
tried to figure out the similarities and differences.[19] But we should also
do it in reverse: what does the European case say for China, as well? It's
useful to continue doing comparative projects in this manner.

I think we are more critical historically than we have ever been, but, at
the same time, academic history is not broadly influential in society. Universities produce historians, and we produce books about history, but most politicians and most people have their own views of history, and they have a different kind of history that they watch on TV. What we scholars think may or
may not matter. There are times when, as happened after 9/11 with respect
to the Islamic world, if you still have an open mind about certain things you
can be marched off the TV screen. History matters. People still believe in the
mythologies we debunk. The big picture still involves the limitations of research and scholarship that many of us have to put up with. As long as we're
in the academy and we can train our students, though, I think we are doing
well, but that could change. It could change more quickly in China than I
would have expected, when politicians get involved in academic life. The
uncertain future of Hong Kong as an intellectual center is a case in point.

As often as historians think they are right, they simultaneously learn
something that we must all unlearn. Unexpectedly, the global revival of
philology still has the power to unleash the forces of delegitimation. As
modernist trends pile up in globalized contexts, our collective mythologies and shared politics still reach beyond the intellectual limits we have
imposed on ourselves.

---

19. Anthony Grafton, "Renaissance Readers and Ancient Texts: Comments on Some Commentaries," *Renaissance Quarterly* 38, no. 4 (1985): 615–49.

Anthony Grafton

ANTHONY GRAFTON is the Henry Putnam University Professor of History at Princeton University.

How did you fall for the classics?

I was interested in the classics as a child, early enough that I was interviewed for one of the TV quiz shows. As I recall, my subject was Greek mythology, so I was interested in Greece when I was six or seven. I became fascinated with the idea of actually learning Greek. And here we were, sitting in Connecticut, to my parents' growing dismay. My parents found a young man from a local Jesuit college who was majoring in classics. He came and gave my mother and me a weekly lesson in Greek, using the old Jesuit curriculum, which to my delight started with Homer [*laughs*]. From when I was ten to when I was twelve, my mother and I did Greek together. She said she was going to have to be in the house when a stranger was there anyhow, so she might as well improve her mind.

Then we moved to New York, and I continued to be interested in languages; my school had very good Latin and taught excellent French. I knew I still wanted to learn more Greek, and so finally my parents talked to the school I was going to, and they said that I really needed a boarding school. The only school in New York that taught Greek was Regis, which was a Jesuit school, and you had to be Catholic to go there! So, I went off to boarding school and did Latin and Greek and French and not much else—a bit of American history. It was very nice, the old-fashioned private school that let you do what interested you. After that I ended up going to the University of Chicago, which turned out to be a great thing. I was just eighteen that spring. I started out planning to major in classics and discovered that I simply didn't fit anywhere. Chicago, unlike Harvard and Yale, didn't get many people from boarding schools or prep schools who had Greek. So there really wasn't much to do in the Classics Department if you could already read Latin and Greek. The undergraduate courses weren't so useful anymore, and the graduate courses were completely beyond me.

In the summer between my first and second years, I stayed in Chicago to be a techie for the summer theater, Court Theater, and used my salary to pay to take Western Civ. I'm not sure why I did that, but I really liked Western Civilization. Not the civilization, which was presented critically, but the course, which was all about trying to think in terms of context, in terms of close reading of texts, how a close reading could let you set a text in context.

It wasn't a tremendously sophisticated form of history, but it was a kind of cultural history centering on the issues that intellectual historians were fascinated by at the time: the rise of the Western individual, for example, who has since disappeared like a trace in the sand of a beach as Foucault predicted, or wished, the rise of historical sensibility, the development of new formal kinds of metaphysics in the early modern era, different kinds of education, history of social theory. That's been, of course, very durable; the others, perhaps less so. But every part of it seemed really congenial. And so, in my second year, I moved from classics to history, took a whole lot of history courses, and started German.

I also took Hanna H. Gray's course on the Renaissance, and while taking that I decided to write a term paper on Erasmus. At her suggestion, I took home the volumes of Allen's edition of Erasmus's letters and realized that I couldn't stick to the practices I'd learned in classics.[1] The thing to do was not to try to read forty lines a night of twelve volumes but to sit down and read. So I sat down and started reading and realized that I could read Erasmus's Latin. It was a lot of fun, and I learned a lot. I wrote a really terrible paper [*laughs*]. But I realized that humanism really interested me. We didn't think of it in terms of reception. We certainly weren't thinking yet in terms of the history of scholarship or anything like that. It was really just Renaissance humanism, the way that humanists interpreted and played with classical texts.

---

1. Erasmus, *Opus epistolarum*, ed. P. S. Allen et al. (Oxford, 1906–58).

The other thing that really educated me was the paperback revolution. All of those books that were translated in the forties and fifties by the Bollingen Series, paid for with money from the Mellon Foundation, with its wonderful combination of Jungian analysis and the classical tradition. There was a big interest in the Western tradition, and that meant we had cheap paperbacks of Erich Auerbach's *Mimesis*, E. R. Curtius's *European Literature and the Latin Middle Ages*, Jean Seznec's *Survival of the Pagan Gods*, A. O. Lovejoy's *Great Chain of Being*.[2] And those were the books that I was reading for fun, from the summer after my first year, through the summer after my second, and on into my third year.

I remember reading E. K. Rand's *Founders of the Middle Ages*, still an amazing book, reading about the classical tradition in mythology, reading a lot of Erwin Panofsky, reading Edgar Wind and Rudolf Wittkower, all of whom were available in paperback.[3] We couldn't read the echt Warburg tradition. Almost nothing by Aby Warburg had been translated even into Italian much less into English, and I don't think my German would have been up to it at that point. Though I was working hard on German, Warburg's German is really a *Ding an sich*. But we learned about the Warburg Institute from Panofsky, from Wittkower, from Wind, and from Frances Yates, of course, and D. P. Walker.[4] I remember the explosive excitement of reading Michael Baxandall's *Giotto and the Orators* when it came out just at the beginning of my graduate study and thinking, "Ah, this is new. This is why humanist Latinity mattered. It was a language in which they could talk critically about the new art of the fifteenth century."[5]

It was a tremendously exciting period to be thinking of being a historian, because new books kept exploding, most of them not so much about what I was doing; they were about other things but still utterly fascinating. So, new forms of intellectual history, like Peter Gay's two volumes on

2. Erich Auerbach, *Mimesis: The Representation of Reality in Western Literature*, trans. Willard R. Trask (New York, 1953); Ernst Robert Curtius, *European Literature and the Latin Middle Ages*, trans. Willard R. Trask (New York, 1953); Jean Seznec, *The Survival of the Pagan Gods: The Mythological Tradition and Its Place in Renaissance Humanism and Art*, trans. Barbara F. Sessions (New York, 1953); Arthur O. Lovejoy, *The Great Chain of Being: A Study of the History of an Idea* (Cambridge, MA, 1936).

3. Edward Kennard Rand, *Founders of the Middle Ages* (Cambridge, MA, 1928); Rudolf Wittkower, *Architectural Principles in the Age of Humanism* (London, 1949); Edgar Wind, *Pagan Mysteries in the Renaissance* (London, 1958).

4. Erwin Panofsky, *Renaissance and Renascences in Western Art* (New York, 1960); Frances A. Yates, *Giordano Bruno and the Hermetic Tradition* (Chicago, 1964); D. P. Walker, *Spiritual and Demonic Magic: From Ficino to Campanella* (London, 1958).

5. Michael Baxandall, *Giotto and the Orators: Humanist Observers of Painting in Italy and the Discovery of Pictorial Composition, 1350–1450* (Oxford, 1971).

the Enlightenment, and then the wonderful, sharp piece in which Robert Darnton mau-maued Peter Gay.[6] But just reading the bibliographical essays in Gay's volumes was an extraordinary revelation. There was the appearance in English of Braudel, though I actually tramped through the French Braudel for an undergraduate paper before the translation appeared.[7] Eugenio Garin was translated into English; I remember reading *Portraits from the Quattrocento* and *Italian Humanism*.[8] Some new books offered what seemed to be radically new ways of understanding and writing about the past. Ted Rosengarten's book *All God's Dangers* showed us, a few years before Carlo Ginzburg did, how rich and revelatory a history the life of a single person—a former tenant farmer—could make. John Demos's *A Little Commonwealth* offered a compelling model for thinking one's way into the life of past households—and made the material turn decades before it had a name. *Time on the Cross* claimed to transform the history of slavery—and though it failed it started a debate that ranged from the morality of history to the nature of data and that riveted the attention of historians in every field.[9] Other books had an explosive impact because they brought materials together that had previously been kept separate—and it turned out that those reached critical mass. J. H. Elliott's *The Old World and the New*, for example, showed that the ways in which scholars tried to understand and describe the Americas were deeply connected to classical models. Reynolds and Wilson's *Scribes and Scholars* told the story of the classical tradition through the lenses of scribal and scholarly practice—and made clear that those practices had a history.[10] Everything that was exciting came out in paperback after a few months, or at the latest a year, so you could buy it and take it home and make it yours.

6. Peter Gay, *The Enlightenment, an Interpretation*, 2 vols. (New York, 1966–69); Robert Darnton, "In Search of the Enlightenment: Recent Attempts to Create a Social History of Ideas," *Journal of Modern History* 43, no. 1 (1971): 113–32.

7. Fernand Braudel, *The Mediterranean and the Mediterranean World in the Age of Philip the Second*, 2 vols. (Paris, 1949; trans., Siân Reynolds; New York, 1972–73).

8. Eugenio Garin, *Portraits from the Quattrocento*, trans. Victor A. and Elizabeth Velen (New York, 1972); Garin, *Italian Humanism: Philosophy and Civic Life in Renaissance Italy*, trans. Peter Munz (New York, 1965).

9. Nate Shaw, *All God's Dangers: The Life of Nate Shaw*, comp. Theodore Rosengarten (Chicago, 1974); Robert William Fogel and Stanley Engerman, *Time on the Cross: The Economics of American Negro Slavery* (Boston, 1974).

10. J. H. Elliott, *The Old World and the New, 1492–1650* (Cambridge, 1970); John Demos, *A Little Commonwealth: Family Life in Plymouth Colony* (Oxford, 1970); L. D. Reynolds and N. G. Wilson, *Scribes and Scholars: A Guide to the Transmission of Greek and Latin Literature* (Oxford, 1968).

Do you remember any particular primary texts that spoke to you?

Always historiography. I wrote my Western Civ paper on Herodotus and Thucydides. It was always historiography. And I was fascinated by Augustine's *City of God*. In my third year I took Hanna Gray's two-term proseminar on Renaissance intellectual history, and I remember being caught by Theodore Mommsen's and Hans Baron's articles on Petrarch, all of which emphasized the nature of his views of history.[11] I was interested also in the history of scholarship, but it was hard to find books that went into much detail about the work that past scholars actually did.

Julian Franklin's book on Jean Bodin had come out in 1963.[12] Donald Kelley's articles were appearing in great numbers; his *Foundations of Modern Historical Scholarship* came out in 1970 as did George Huppert's *The Idea of Perfect History*.[13] So you could learn something about the historical approach to Roman law and its context that developed in early modern France. We all read John Pocock's *Ancient Constitution and the Feudal Law*, with its dazzling first chapter on the French prelude to modern historiography, which traced continuities that others missed between medieval jurisprudence, humanist legal scholarship, and the beginnings of historical thinking about medieval law and society. But it was also enigmatic: Pocock brilliantly described Bodin's work on history as a "strange, semi-ruinous mass" but did not help us climb Bodin's Watts Towers of texts and arguments.[14]

Another really exciting presence was Quentin Skinner, who had begun publishing articles. I recently found my notes from 1969 when in Hanna Gray's seminar we were reading the Yale edition of *Utopia* against Skinner's massive *Past and Present* review, which dramatically showed how editorial decisions had distorted the meaning of the text, especially in the accompanying translation—Latin mattered, again! With his *His-*

11. Theodore E. Mommsen, "Petrarch's Conception of the 'Dark Ages,'" *Speculum* 17, no. 2 (April 1942): 226–42; Hans Baron, *From Petrarch to Leonardo Bruni: Studies in Humanistic and Political Literature* (Chicago, 1968).

12. Julian H. Franklin, *Jean Bodin and the Sixteenth-Century Revolution in the Methodology of Law and History* (New York, 1963).

13. Donald Kelley, *Foundations of Modern Historical Scholarship: Language, Law, and History in the French Renaissance* (New York, 1970); George Huppert, *The Idea of Perfect History: Historical Erudition and Historical Philosophy in Renaissance France* (Urbana, 1970).

14. See J. G. A. Pocock, *The Ancient Constitution and the Feudal Law: A Study of English Historical Thought in the Seventeenth Century* (Cambridge, 1957), 11.

tory and Theory article, "Meaning and Understanding," he also made a powerful case against the study of sources and influences—one that anyone interested in humanists' uses of their sources, as I was, had to try to answer.[15] All kinds of things were happening. One of the big sources of excitement in the university then was analytical philosophy, so Skinner's early bridging of analytical philosophy and history to push his thesis home and reconfigure our notions of context seemed extremely exciting.

When did you first know that your particular field was going to be the history of scholarship?

Fairly early on I became interested in the history of science. I studied with Noel Swerdlow, a great historian of astronomy. I took the first course he ever gave, in 1968, when he was fresh from his PhD at Yale, and later had a course with him on late antique encyclopedias and grammars, which was a lot of fun. We read Isidore and Cassiodorus. In graduate school, since I stayed at Chicago, I did a field with him in the history of astronomy.

The way I came to thinking of history of scholarship was a bit roundabout. It was thinking about humanism through the history of science and asking if there was any way to apply some of the questions and tools of history of science to humanism, which hardly anybody seemed to do. Some echt classicists would look at a humanist from their current standpoint. They seemed to be asking, How well does the past scholar do this thing that we do? What mark does he deserve? There were also classicists who would push harder and give you a sense of how a great scholar in the past used his tools in a way no longer acceptable, thanks to a different set of assumptions. I can remember the excitement of reading Eduard Fraenkel's first volume of the edition of the *Agamemnon*, which includes a magnificent study of Isaac Casaubon's work as an annotator of Aeschylus.[16] Fraenkel shows that Casaubon understood and emended Aeschylus's text with great skill and learning but, still, as a staunch reformed Protestant, wanted to see Aeschylus as a monotheist. Historians didn't look at practices in that level of detail, and nobody was asking if the methods of history of science, the genetic histories of texts and analyses of technical sources that people were already doing for Newton's *Principia*,

---

15. Quentin Skinner, "More's *Utopia*," *Past and Present* 38, no. 1 (December 1967): 153–68; Skinner, "Meaning and Understanding in the History of Ideas," *History and Theory* 8, no. 1 (1969): 3–53.
16. Aeschylus, *Agamemnon*, ed. Eduard Fraenkel, 3 vols. (Oxford, 1950).

for example, could be applied to the history of scholarship. Noel was following Copernicus through the margins of the texts he worked from and the tables from which he took his data while I was studying with him. He was, I think, trying with great brilliance to understand how a technical text came into its final shape.[17]

I still had a love of Erasmus, and I thought Erasmus had a wonderful combination of interests in language and how it functions, social reform, ethics, and Christianity. So my plan was to work on Christian humanism, and that's what I applied to do in graduate school. I decided, after not very much thinking, to stay at Chicago. I was in love with somebody, whom I'm still living with, and I didn't want to leave.

I did my senior thesis on Erasmus's text *Lingua* with Eric Cochrane.[18] Eric was a fantastically engaged teacher who really cared about students and expressed his care in the classic, sharp way of the Lithuanian rabbi. I learned about getting rid of all kinds of self-indulgence. But I didn't immediately see a dissertation topic taking shape. What helped me figure out what I was doing was deciding that I really wanted to make humanism and history of science come together analytically. One day I asked Noel if this was possible, and he said, "Well, there's an early modern scholar called Joseph Scaliger. Nobody's written about him since Bernays in 1855, and he worked on historical chronology, which looks like the kind of thing you're interested in." I started reading what was on the shelves: Bernays, Scaliger's autobiography as translated by G. W. Robinson of Harvard, Reynolds and Wilson, a few other things, and found myself getting more and more interested in trying to do something with this scholar who had done all this textual criticism and chronology.[19]

I talked to Eric and Noel, and they said, "Well, it's a great subject. We know nothing about this, so you should go work with Arnaldo Momigliano," whose work on historiography they both knew very well. Eric had drawn on the Italian scholar Momigliano for his history of historiography in Renaissance Italy, and Noel had assigned his work in his seminar on Gibbon. I applied for a Fulbright, took my general exams early, and went off to London in the summer after my second year of graduate school, at the ripe age of twenty-three, to try to do something on Joseph Scaliger.

17. N. M. Swerdlow and O. Neugebauer, *Mathematical Astronomy in Copernicus's "De Revolutionibus,"* 2 vols. (New York, 1984).

18. Erasmus, *Lingua* (Antwerp, 1525).

19. Jacob Bernays, *Joseph Justus Scaliger* (Berlin, 1855); Joseph Scaliger, *Autobiography*, trans. George W. Robinson (Cambridge, MA, 1927).

What in particular attracted you not just to Scaliger but also to the field of historical chronology?

I don't really know. I thought that the modern scholars who'd worked on the history of the *ars historica* and on the French antiquaries had gone as far as you were going to go, doing what they did. That turned out later not to be true; there was a lot more to do in both fields. But I couldn't really see a reason to write another book about historical criticism or about sixteenth-century ways of judging sources.

What I wanted to do was see how criticism was applied in practice. It's always seemed to me that the interesting thing about historical method is what kind of history it yields, not just the method itself. For hermeneutics, similarly, the theory of interpretation, vital though it is, has to be judged by the kind of interpretation that it yields. That much already made sense to me, at this very tender age. I didn't really have a much better idea than that. I thought I was going to work on chronology, but I realized that Scaliger spent the first half of his life mostly editing texts. I didn't know anything about that, but I figured I'd better find out. Beyond that, nobody had much inkling of where such a dissertation might go.

Was there anything that drew you to intellectual biography as an enterprise, in particular?

That was connected, at first, with the history of science, though it probably looks in retrospect as if I patterned myself on Arnaldo Momigliano and the biographical profiles he wrote. In fact, the people who really influenced me were Alexandre Koyré and Frank Manuel, who were both masters of a combination of contextual and text-analytical writing. Two of the books that really made an impression on me were Manuel's *The Eighteenth Century Confronts the Gods* and *Isaac Newton, Historian*, which was one of the few books that said anything about chronology.[20] Both used biography not to write about the deeds of heroes but to set intellectual enterprises into their historical contexts.

One thing I knew was that it wasn't going to be possible to do scholarship in a single period. I was going to have to move up and down,

20. Frank E. Manuel, *The Eighteenth Century Confronts the Gods* (Cambridge, MA, 1959); Manuel, *Isaac Newton, Historian* (Cambridge, MA, 1963); Alexandre Koyré, *From the Closed World to the Infinite Universe* (Baltimore, 1957).

chronologically, to see what scholars had done with similar projects before my hero and what they might do with them now. Most people who
work on humanism choose a period that they like and stay there. You
can do that if you're looking at the full complex of things that a group
of humanists do, as Hans Baron did in Florence, and as others have, or as
Venetianists often do. But it seemed to me that to understand a technical form of scholarship it was important to see how further generations
responded to the arguments, in some detail. So I knew that Newton and
Giambattista Vico and Jacob Perizonius were in my future, as well as
Scaliger.

*Did your sense of the temporal and contextual breadth of
a tradition tie back to your earlier readings of Auerbach,
Curtius, and the Warburg scholars?*

I thought there ought to be a way of thinking of technical scholarship in
terms of tradition. Coming to the Warburg Institute in London, I found
that the history of scholarship was baked into the fabric of place, from
Aby Warburg himself—he connected Poliziano's scholarship to his poetry and both to Botticelli's paintings—onward. Even before, I began to
read my way into the work done at the Catholic University of the Sacred
Heart in Milan, where Giuseppe Billanovich and his pupils, like Mirella
Ferrari, had created a great journal, *Italia medioevale e umanistica*, and
were producing, mostly for early humanists, the kind of close readings
of commentaries and other technical works that I hoped to write.

But I had also made many individual discoveries in the vast open
stacks of Chicago's Regenstein Library. Carlo Dionisotti, a very, very demanding, acerbic historian and critic, was one of the most thrilling. The
single most exciting book I discovered was the Italian scholar Sebastiano
Timpanaro's *La genesi del metodo del Lachmann*. Timpanaro, unlike most
of the people I was reading, was knowledgeable about the history of science.[21] His father was a very distinguished Galileo scholar. He himself was
trained as a classicist and made his living as an editor, avoiding the universities, which he saw as terminally corrupt. His book followed scholars'
ways of trying to understand the relations between manuscripts, from

---

21. Sebastiano Timpanaro, *La genesi del metodo del Lachmann* (Florence, 1963); English trans.:
Timpanaro, *The Genesis of Lachmann's Method*, trans. G. W. Most (Chicago, 2005).

the Renaissance to the present. It was short, sharp, bitingly precise, and endlessly suggestive—as in an ironic passage where he refused to trace the connections between the genetic way of recreating a textual tradition and contemporary developments in linguistics. Timpanaro's book was always in my mind as one possible model.

I won the Fulbright, and my wife and I decided to go early; we arrived in London in the summer of 1973. I went and called on Arnaldo Momigliano before he went off to Italy, and he said he thought I should be reading the fifteenth-century Italian humanist Angelo Poliziano. I had no idea why he thought I should approach Scaliger by reading Poliziano—absolutely none! Also, I was very puzzled by Momigliano. As a little outsider from Chicago, I had a sense that many great European scholars were all in Bloomsbury now, where many of them had come as émigrés, and assumed they were all part of the same project. When I mentioned Roberto Weiss's book on Renaissance archaeology and antiquarianism, *The Renaissance Discovery of Classical Antiquity*, Momigliano described it as "An outsider's first look at an unknown thing."[22] Not like Timpanaro.

So I was not just out of my depth; I was miles, light-years out of my depth; dynasties were going to fall before I knew what I was doing. But I assumed that Momigliano knew more than I did, so I went back to the Warburg. In those days, the rare books were still on the shelves. They had the editions of Poliziano, and they had the complete secondary literature, offprint by offprint, bound and cataloged in the great Warburg way. I spent the whole summer reading Poliziano and reading about him. By the end of the summer I could see that there was one story about the history of textual criticism that started from the kind of work Poliziano did when he compared existing manuscripts in the new humanist libraries of Florence, Rome, and the Veneto and continued to the kind of work Scaliger did when he recreated lost manuscripts. In fact, Scaliger was talking about Poliziano, as Momigliano in some eerie way had intuited!

How did your relationship with Momigliano develop in that year?

Momigliano was amazing in many ways. I attended his seminar, which met at the Warburg rather than at University College. The seminar was

---

22. Roberto Weiss, *The Renaissance Discovery of Classical Antiquity* (Oxford, 1969).

an introduction to a capacious historical culture. Momigliano gave a talk on the Greek historian Polybius's reappearance in Western Europe, which was at once awe-inspiring and shaming—at least I could see that I would never know that much.[23] He would invite me to lunch every couple of weeks, which, by the standards of British PhD supervisors in 1973, was extremely generous. I was incredibly lucky.

In Chicago I had learned that Scaliger had discovered and published the list of the dynasties of Egypt compiled in Greek by an Egyptian priest of the third century BCE, Manetho of Sebennytos. So one of the things I did in the summer and fall, when I wasn't reading Poliziano, was to trace a kind of reception history of that discovery. I wrote that up very elaborately and gave it to Momigliano. He didn't think it was great, but he made some remarks that showed that he didn't think it was totally hopeless either. The way I knew this was that he invited me to speak in his seminar in the spring. About a week before the seminar met, he invited me to lunch with George Nadel, the founder of the journal *History and Theory*.[24] Nadel no longer taught but lived in some splendor in an English country house. Obviously this was an intelligence test, and the question was, Would Nadel think my work was interesting enough to be worth coming up to London again, to come to the seminar? He came to the seminar, and he invited me to publish the paper in *History and Theory*.[25]

I didn't just work with Momigliano, though. In the first place, he sent me not to Carlo Dionisotti but to Carlotta Dionisotti, one of Carlo's daughters. Carlotta—who is a legendary teacher at King's College London—saw me regularly. She was working in those days on French and Italian classical scholarship in the sixteenth century.[26] So she said, "OK, you've done Poliziano." I wrote something on that. She said, "Well, this is okay. Now you've got to work on Piero Vettori, and Pierio Valeriano and all these guys." So that's when I started dragging my weary length through sixteenth-century classical scholarship.

23. Arnaldo Momigliano, "Polybius' Reappearance in Western Europe," in Momigliano, *Essays in Ancient and Modern Historiography* (Oxford, 1977).

24. See, for instance, George Nadel, "Philosophy of History before Historicism," *History and Theory* 3, no. 3 (1964): 291–315.

25. Anthony Grafton, "Joseph Scaliger and Historical Chronology: The Rise and Fall of a Discipline," *History and Theory* 14, no. 2 (1975): 156–85.

26. Carlotta Dionisotti, "From Stephanus to Du Cange: Glossary Stories," *Revue d'histoire des textes* 14–15 (1984–85): 303–36.

It's striking that you worked with people who were classicists by training, but who were also active in the broader field that we now call the classical tradition, or classical reception. How did this shape your work?

It made sense to me, always, that the classical tradition would be something that you'd want to look at in many different ways, and from different points of view. I wouldn't confine myself to the history of technical scholarship. The Warburg Institute really encouraged broad reading, because you were always finding the good neighbor: the book you didn't know you needed, next to the book you were looking for. And the British Library encouraged endless reading of primary sources, so those were wonderful places to start out.

I was very interested in the classical tradition, and I wanted to work out ways of presenting some of that material to undergraduates and graduate students. At Cornell, where I began teaching the following year, all of my grad students were medievalists. We took a text by Erasmus on his theological method, read it very thoroughly in Latin, and then discussed it before the official seminar met. We sat and spent an hour and a half reading the Latin very closely. The combination of working through that text, seeing how Erasmus had developed his hermeneutics from the tools of classical rhetoric, while we also read primary and secondary sources in translation, made for a rich and novel way to encounter Erasmus and his generation.

Inspiration really struck one night when I was preparing a lecture. I kept thinking, I want to tell them about humanism. I want to tell them what humanists did. How in God's name do you tell people about how they edited texts? Well, they were like me: they taught. So why not talk about how they did that? At midnight I started working up a lecture on what it was like to be taught by a humanist. I pulled together a mosaic of sources from a wonderful old classic, Remigio Sabbadini's *Metodo degli umanisti*, and a few other books, especially Baxandall's *Giotto and the Orators*.[27] At the core I put a hunk of the Latin rhetorical treatise *Ad Herennium*, and then I translated a segment of the Italian humanist Guarino da Verona's commentary on the text. I came in the next day, drunk with fatigue, and said, "People always tell you that humanists taught about being independent moral beings. They may have done that, but

27. Remigio Sabbadini, *Il metodo degli umanisti* (Florence, 1922).

I'm going to show you what you actually did in a humanist classroom. I've been up all night. This may not make any sense, but let's give it a try." I got a standing ovation! So I was always hoping to find different approaches to my great secret.

When I got to Princeton, I ended up framing my course in terms of Joseph Levenson's *Confucian China and Its Modern Fate*.[28] He devised powerful images of ancient texts, starting their lives as the weapons in an armory—things that are practical, that do things, that could even be dangerous—and winding up as exhibits in a museum. That was the story that I tried to tell, a story that went from Petrarch to Montaigne. We wouldn't tell the same story that way now, but it was a way of making sense of intellectual history as a story of tradition transformed. It involved talking at some length about medieval ways of reading and looking at both humanist and Reformation kinds of reading. It made a good frame for Machiavelli, for example, but also for Machiavelli's contemporary, the Florentine historian Francesco Guicciardini. There's a piece, the first piece in my first collection of essays, *Defenders of the Text*, a very modest-looking piece now on different humanist ways of reading.[29] That came out of my early teaching. I used to emphasize the contrast between Machiavelli saying "Nothing we try in politics works, because we don't know how to read the classics" and Guicciardini saying "It's pointless to read the classics, because things are different now."

What was it like at Princeton to be surrounded not only by Thomas Kuhn and the revolution in the history of science, but also Robert Darnton, who was beginning work in the history of the book and the history of reading?

Completely terrifying. I went as an assistant professor, just twenty-five. Every name on an office door was that of somebody I'd read in paperback in college, like Theodore Rabb or Jerome Blum, or somebody like Darnton, who was even more brilliant but so young that I only had time to read him in hardcover in college. It was a very exciting place, charged with the sense that historiography was always moving and changing and that the best new books reshaped the field. Lawrence Stone would always talk about

---

28. Joseph E. Levenson, *Confucian China and Its Modern Fate*, 3 vols. (Berkeley, 1958–65).

29. Anthony Grafton, "Renaissance Readers and Ancient Texts: Comments on Some Commentaries," *Renaissance Quarterly* 38, no. 4 (1985): 615–49, reprinted in Grafton, *Defenders of the Text: The Traditions of Scholarship in an Age of Science, 1450–1800* (Cambridge, MA, 1991), 23–46.

Brucker's Florence or Goldthwaite's Florence or Lane's Venice as if writing such a book established title for you over the subject.[30]

One of the exciting new things was Geertzian symbolic analysis of culture. Clifford Geertz was working on *Negara*, the book about Balinese monarchy.[31] I remember him giving a seminar at Princeton's Davis Center in which he argued that royal processions kept England together. The symbolic capital Elizabeth had accrued by making formal visits to great houses and staying for their ritualized entertainments mattered more than armies. Lawrence commented by explaining how each great house that had a procession was made bankrupt for the next fifty years [*laughs*]. He also pointed out that Elizabeth never left the home counties. How much power did ritual have? Not long afterward Ed Muir's book about Venice came out. It is still one of the most impressive books in that mode.[32]

Historians were trying things out. Social history was booming but already showing signs of strain, partly because it seemed to be really hard to keep doing it. You could devote your thesis to social history, but then how could you ever get the time back in the country to keep doing the archival work for a second book? That was a clear problem. Some of the big syntheses, like Natalie Davis's Lyon, or Carl Schorske's Vienna, never actually came into being—at least as the totalizing histories those scholars had once hoped to write.[33] Something in the world of social history was amiss, but cultural history was clearly growing. Intellectual history suffered from malaise, as Robert Darnton wrote in his essay in *The Past before Us*. He argued that cultural history was going to take over from intellectual history.[34] There was a lot of intellectual history, but it was often pretty dry stuff. By contrast the books that Davis and Schorske did write were dazzling models of how to imagine past cultures and identify the forces that shaped them.

How did you find your own thinking about Scaliger evolving at this time?

A lot, because of the historians of science. Peter Dear, for example, arrived at Princeton quite soon after I did. He and other history of science

---

30. Gene A. Brucker, *Renaissance Florence* (New York, 1969); Richard A. Goldthwaite, *Florence: An Economic and Social History* (Baltimore, 1980); Frederic C. Lane, *Venice: A Maritime Republic* (Baltimore, 1973).

31. Clifford Geertz, *Negara: The Theatre State in Nineteenth-Century Bali* (Princeton, 1981).

32. Edward Muir, *Civic Ritual in Renaissance Venice* (Princeton, 1986).

33. Carl Schorske, *Fin-de-siècle Vienna: Politics and Culture* (New York, 1981).

34. Robert Darnton, "Intellectual and Cultural History," in *The Past before Us: Contemporary Historical Writing in the United States*, ed. Michael G. Kammen (Ithaca, 1980), 327–54.

students were very challenging.[35] They pushed me to think harder about what it meant to write an intellectual biography about what one would now, but didn't then, call practice. Practice wasn't really a term yet—like actors' categories and agency and all those other terms that are now indispensable.

But that was more and more what historians of science were doing. They were about to move into the world of *Leviathan and the Air-Pump*.[36] History of science was about to go local and emphasize practice, and my work was converging with that, unexpectedly. On my leave in '77 in England, I worked through Scaliger's edition of the Roman poet and astrologer Manilius and really got to understand just how deep and complicated and strange Manilius was.

I'd worked on Scaliger's edition of the Roman grammarian Festus in the summer of 1976, and that was a real learning experience. Festus's work was preserved only fragmentarily, and Scaliger reconstructed it, by collating every other work he could find by an ancient grammarian, by applying his deep knowledge of early Latin customs, laws and language, and by sheer divinatory brilliance. But Manilius was even more demanding. I spent seven months reading Scaliger's commentary against A. E. Housman's commentary and then trying to understand what Scaliger had been doing. As it turned out, he was using this Roman astrological poet to reconstruct the history of astronomy and astrology in the ancient world. That was an urgent question because the influential sixteenth-century reformer of logic and science, Petrus Ramus, had argued that Egyptian astronomy was far better than Greek. As Scaliger edited an elegant Latin poet, it seemed, he also took sides in a major intellectual controversy in his own time. No one—not even Housman, who was almost obsessed with Scaliger—had ever suggested that his work focused on these questions. So I was relieved when I found that both friendly readers in his time, such as Isaac Casaubon, and unfriendly ones had understood his work as I did.

I was toiling away when, in '77, I was faced with a tremendous decision. I was offered a job at the University of Amsterdam in the Neo-Latin Institute and, at the same time, Princeton hired Natalie Davis. I was going back to Princeton to face my renewal for a second three-year term with a largely finished manuscript in hand, but I also saw quite clearly

---

35. His dissertation was subsequently published as Peter Dear, *Mersenne and the Learning of the Schools* (Ithaca, 1988).

36. Steven Shapin and Simon Schaffer, *Leviathan and the Air-Pump: Hobbes, Boyle, and the Experimental Life* (Princeton, 1985).

that with Natalie in residence my department could very easily—and reasonably—decide to dispense with me. And I was happy with the prospect of going to Holland. So I came home, and I thought about what I was doing and why, and I wrote the introduction to the first volume of my book on *Scaliger*. This was my first real elevator speech. In that short introduction I actually tried to say not just that this was a book about practice but why it was sensible to write such a book about someone whose intellectual life was chiefly lived in practice.[37]

I wrote this piece—it wasn't very long, but it was quite hard to think through and get down on paper—just before school started. I handed it in and said to the chair, "Look, I have a great offer. If you're going to fire me in three years, fire me now. I'll go to Europe. We'll be happy to go live in Amsterdam on a better salary." It all seemed obvious. If a department had Natalie, whom I've admired—well, revered—ever since the first time I heard her speak, why would it need me? It seemed as if there wasn't any room. To my amazement, they called me in and said, "No, we actually think we're probably going to want to keep you, though we can't guarantee it. You certainly shouldn't leave because there's no room." So I decided to stick it out.

The introduction to the first volume of your Joseph Scaliger *very concisely argues for the study of practice.*

The main argument I made there still seems to me to have some merit, though I overstated my case. People who work as scholars spend the vast majority of their time doing scholarship rather than constructing elaborate intellectual syntheses, in much the same way that Newton spent much more of his time doing physics and astronomy than he did writing the "General Scholium" or thinking about whether space is the sensorium of God. And it seemed to me that part of intellectual history had to do justice to pursuits that could not be summarized by a sketch of a set of ideas or a system of politics.

I think the deeper point that I was working toward is this: the exciting mode of intellectual history at that moment was Skinnerian analysis, which took as its model the notion of a speaker's or writer's intention in utterance. The core notion here was that mastering the immediate context of a text gives you real explanatory leverage on it. I believe that a lot

---

37. Anthony Grafton, introduction to *Joseph Scaliger: A Study in the History of Classical Scholarship*, vol. 1, *Textual Criticism and Exegesis* (Oxford, 1983), 1–8.

of intellectual work is done on a scale of time and effort for which that's not the only useful category. How can you ask what the intention in utterance of Newton's *Principia* is, or Copernicus's *De revolutionibus*, which as Copernicus said, quoting Horace, took more than twenty-seven years to complete? As a model for political thought, it makes sense, because political thought is often an intervention in a distinctive political world. But not everything is political thought.

So that was really, I think, what was on my mind, how to make a case for a kind of intellectual history that really looked wildly different and in which the principal actors and the principal subject would be different. I had no idea at that point that doing this kind of work might make it possible to understand the nature and development of cultural contacts on a larger scale—as, for example, Thomas Burman's close study of Western versions of the Quran has done.[38] I hadn't thought about that at all.

This preface was published with the book in 1983. But in 1977 you had already voiced some of these programmatic ideas in a review in the Journal of Roman Studies.[39]

I could write reasonably well, and so I was offered reviewing assignments relatively early. Two of them have, I think, stuck in the memories of the recipients, as well as mine: my review of Ted Kenney's *The Classical Text*, published in the *Journal of Roman Studies*, and my review of Betty Eisenstein's *Printing Press as an Agent of Change*.[40] They're really pretty different, I think. Kenney was so clearly a wonderful classical scholar and a brilliant and generous man. He did the history of scholarship and found all sorts of interesting things but didn't attack it with the wholehearted power that animated his work on Lucretius.[41] Self-righteous as I was, I became annoyed at the fact that you would treat the field to which I was dedicating myself in that way.

In Eisenstein's case, the notion that printing really matters seemed to me to be obvious. Eugene Rice put printing in the first chapter of his textbook on early modern history, which came out in 1970.[42] I thought

---

38. Thomas E. Burman, *Reading the Qur'an in Latin Christendom, 1140–1560* (Philadelphia, 2007).

39. A. T. Grafton, "From Politian to Pasquali," *Journal of Roman Studies* 67 (1977): 171–76.

40. Anthony T. Grafton, "The Importance of Being Printed," *Journal of Interdisciplinary History* 11, no. 2 (1980): 265–86.

41. E. J. Kenney, *The Classical Text: Aspects of Editing in the Age of the Printed Book* (Berkeley, 1974).

42. Eugene F. Rice, *The Foundations of Early Modern Europe, 1460–1559* (New York, 1970).

we had agreed that printing mattered. But we haven't all agreed that it mattered as much as Betty thought it mattered, and her book promoted in all kinds of ways the flourishing of book history, printing history, and reading history.[43] It had a huge rhetorical or organizational or magnetic, or I don't know, galvanic effect, which other people appreciated much better than I did.

Princeton in the seventies and early eighties was a very polemical place. We argued ruthlessly with each other, no holds barred. That was really Lawrence Stone's version of Oxford method, and it became a local practice. The idea was you didn't take it personally, just be as sharp as you can. If something has a real fallacy in it, show the fallacy. If something is really hollow, argue that it's hollow. Over time, I've developed much more sympathy for the human fallibility that I richly share with the objects of such reviews, and I no longer write them. But I think, at the time, it probably did a certain amount of good, if only by suggesting that the issues mattered.

At the same time you were also pioneering a new set of practices in terms of research by working with annotated books, scholars' manuscripts, and similar sources.

Annotation, of course, was not a new interest: Italian scholars and their allies had always looked at annotations. There was already a wonderful body of work on Petrarch's annotations by Billanovich and others, going all the way back to Pierre de Nolhac's book on Petrarch and humanism, which first appeared in 1907.[44] On the whole, though, historians hadn't made much use of them. And for me, this interest grew up in constant dialogue with Robert Darnton and Lisa Jardine. Bob was working out what book history was and should be during years of great, great creativity, which went from *The Business of Enlightenment* and his *Literary Underground* essays, to *The Great Cat Massacre* and *The Forbidden Bestsellers*.[45] He was turning over and over the question of how you would study the history of books. The history of reading, he argued, was especially hard.

---

43. Elizabeth L. Eisenstein, *The Printing Press as an Agent of Change: Communications and Cultural Transformations in Early Modern Europe* (Cambridge, 1980).

44. Pierre de Nolhac, *Pétrarque et l'humanisme* (Paris, 1907).

45. Robert Darnton, *The Business of Enlightenment: A Publishing History of the "Encyclopédie," 1775–1800* (Cambridge, MA, 1979); Darnton, *The Literary Underground of the Old Regime* (Cambridge, MA, 1982); Darnton, *The Great Cat Massacre and Other Episodes in French Cultural History* (New York, 1984); Darnton, *The Forbidden Bestsellers of Pre-revolutionary France* (New York, 1995).

You could look for organized reactions, such as readers' letters to Rousseau, in which you could see a new mode of response to texts taking shape.[46]

But it was very hard to convince Bob that you could actually find physical traces from which you could reconstruct the experience of reading. Working through notes enables you to stand over the shoulder of a sixteenth-century person, watching him or her think about a text. You examine the original, you follow the hand as it writes its response, and you look for other sources to which the reader refers or on which he or she draws. Eventually you can recreate a partial but vivid version of his or her experience of a particular text.

From the seventies I had used annotated books as a tool for history of scholarship. In my Fulbright year a friend and colleague, Michael Hoeflich, who is now a law professor at the University of Kansas, was at Cambridge. He told me about the *Catalogue of Adversaria*, a catalog of annotated books in the Cambridge University Library done by a great bookman of the mid-nineteenth century, H. R. Luard, and available for forty-five pence from the University Library publications office.[47] From that I learned that Isaac Casaubon's copy of one of Scaliger's greatest books, his last immense chronology, the *Thesaurus temporum*, was in the Cambridge Library. I began to do something I've been doing ever since: to think about Casaubon as a reader and annotator and critic and to use him as a gauge of how plausible Scaliger's arguments were. This was the book in which Scaliger had published Manetho's list of Egyptian dynasties. Manetho's list was longer than what biblical world history would have allowed, but Scaliger argued that it still deserved study, as a genuine Egyptian relic. Was this argument plausible in period terms? I had thought so. But Momigliano disagreed. So, I discovered, did Casaubon, who dismissed the list as pagan fantasy. In this case, annotation helped me to read Scaliger without excessive sympathy—a trap into which biographers often fall.

A few years later, when Lisa Jardine and I were working on the history of education, we found all sorts of annotations interesting.[48] A wonderful bookseller whose shop was near Sing Sing prison, William Salloch, offered for sale a *Sammelband*, a collection of pamphlet editions of clas-

46. Robert Darnton, "Readers Respond to Rousseau: The Fabrication of Romantic Sensitivity," in Darnton, *The Great Cat Massacre*, 214–56.

47. H. R. Luard, *A Catalogue of Adversaria and Printed Books Containing Ms. Notes Preserved in the Library of the University of Cambridge* (Cambridge, 1864).

48. Anthony Grafton and Lisa Jardine, *From Humanism to the Humanities: Education and the Liberal Arts in Fifteenth- and Sixteenth-Century Europe* (Cambridge, MA, 1986).

sical texts from Paris from the 1550s to the 1570s with notes by a single student on a single identified teacher's lectures. I went to the rare book room and met Steve Ferguson, then Princeton's newly appointed curator of rare books, and asked him to buy it. He was willing to spend the large sum demanded—three thousand or so 1976 or '77 dollars. Fortunately, the books turned out to be worth the money. They were so richly annotated, and so neatly supported and complemented one another, that they could bring you into a classroom in one of the colleges of the University of Paris in 1572 and let you follow what teacher and students did from day to day. Lisa and I were constantly in dialogue about this and other documents for the history of education.

But the history of reading is a somewhat different story. I was slowly working on what turned into the second volume of *Joseph Scaliger*, which turned out to be a very long and protracted process and a long book.[49] In 1988 Lisa came to Princeton as a fellow of the Davis Center. She knew that the Princeton Library had on deposit a bunch of books that had belonged to a late sixteenth- and early seventeenth-century classical scholar, Cambridge Greek professor, and object of academic satire named Gabriel Harvey, a man about whom scholars have never been able to agree. It seems somehow historical justice that our image of him was partly formed by a woodcut in which he's taking down his codpiece to urinate, in terror of the news that Thomas Nash is writing another book against him. He was the kind of person to whom that kind of thing happens. Lisa had looked at these books in the early seventies. More recently, Virginia Stern had written a book about them, which listed them and included photographs of some of them.[50]

One of them, a copy of Livy's *History of Rome* in a Basel edition looked as if it might maybe tell us something we didn't know. I don't think I can say any more than that. It was drenched, saturated, soaked with annotation: a classic ruin overgrown by a thick mass of notes. Could secrets lie here? Lisa was working on Erasmus, and I was working on Scaliger, but in our copious spare time, the two of us spent a semester going in and out of the rare book room, pencil and paper in hand, making transcripts from the notes in this Livy. Very, very slowly, we began to understand that we could see in this Livy what we came to call a period style of reading. That had several meanings. It meant that Harvey read not in isolation, not in a study where he immured himself, but in public, and

---

49. Anthony Grafton, *Joseph Scaliger: A Study in the History of Classical Scholarship*, vol. 2, *Historical Chronology* (Oxford, 1993).

50. Virginia F. Stern, *Gabriel Harvey: His Life, Marginalia and Library* (Oxford, 1979).

he named the people with whom he read. It meant his reading was goal-oriented; he was reading with young men who were training for public careers and so his reading was designed to make the text usable for them in that context. It was not erudite reading—he wasn't concerned with the commentaries on Livy—but it was informed reading.

Harvey compared Livy with all sorts of texts, from axiomatic versions of Tacitean political thought to travel narratives. Slowly we began to get a sense of a style of reading and a style of person. We came to call him a facilitator, someone whose job was to be an intermediary between the world of learning, insofar as that was relevant to public life, and people who were going to lead a public life. We also began to realize there were other people like him. I don't think either of us would have claimed his was a remotely typical or dominant style of reading, even in its own day, but we did see it was *a* style of reading and one that had largely been forgotten. Admittedly, it was reading that had very few of the characteristics of reading a novel in the late twentieth century. Nonetheless, it seemed to be a kind of reading that could be reconstructed in some detail.

Lawrence Stone permitted us to present our work in a special Davis Center meeting, to which we arrived wearing identical neckties, and we got very curious reactions. It was one of the rare times in my life when I was ahead of the curve, and when you're in that position, nobody has any idea what you're talking about! But people were interested, and they saw that the evidence was very rich, and they didn't have any other way of interpreting it to propose. So we plunged on: we submitted our piece to *Past and Present* and received four mutually contradictory readers' reports. We did our best to respond—by cutting material but also by changing emphases—to the reports.[51] Writing that article with Lisa made me begin to think of myself as a historian of books and reading. I began to think about teaching courses in book history, which I've been doing more or less ever since.

The other thing that had happened imperceptibly to me—I really didn't expect it—was that graduate students started coming to Princeton to study with me, and they were working on reading, one way or another. For instance, Ann Blair came, hot off a year in Cambridge doing an MPhil in History and Philosophy of Science. She was tremendously skilled, and she worked with Natalie Davis and our historians of science, and she wanted to find a way to bring learning, humanism, and book history together. One day I suggested that she think about working on

---

51. Anthony Grafton and Lisa Jardine, "'Studied for Action': How Gabriel Harvey Read His Livy," *Past and Present* 129 (1990): 30–78.

Jean Bodin's natural philosophy. It indeed turned out to be a good topic for a tremendously original and brilliant first book.[52] Soon Carol Quillen was at work on a fine dissertation about Petrarch and Augustine and Kate Elliott on a very original study of Spanish humanism.[53] With time, the numbers grew, and the projects they devised became richer and more varied.

All of a sudden, I realized that I was doing something that actually could interest students: the history of scholarship and reading, seen as both intellectual and material practices, which left their traces, like inky tidemarks, in the margins of books. By the late eighties, it became clear that really talented students still wanted to do intellectual history. They enjoyed and were informed by cultural and social history but wanted to do something different.

It also became clear to me over time that other scholars were following related paths. In the 1980s James Hankins appeared, brilliantly using the evidence of books and annotations to transform the history of Renaissance philosophy—though he did a lot for philology at the same time.[54] Princeton was not the only place where people were welding intellectual history, the history of books, and the history of scholarship. Soon Paula Findlen offered another, equally original approach to these methods.[55] All of this makes much more sense in retrospect than it did at the time and has a logic to it that it certainly didn't at the time. But looking backward, it seems clear that several new ways of tracing and writing the history of traditions were blooming in what had seemed, until recently, the somewhat bare garden of intellectual history.

I suppose, if that came together anywhere besides my work with Lisa, it was actually working on volume two of *Scaliger*, in Oxford, where I spent a year in Duke Humfrey's Library, reading and comparing the books and notes of the erudite. Slowly I was coming to see that chronology also involved an art of reading and to realize that Scaliger and other chronologers read in just as goal-oriented a way as did Harvey and other political readers. For example, they read to process texts into evidence for dates, evidence about calendars, and evidence about the rituals that had given anniversaries and feast days meaning.

52. Ann M. Blair, *The Theater of Nature: Jean Bodin and Renaissance Science* (Princeton, 1997).

53. Carol E. Quillen, *Rereading the Renaissance: Petrarch, Augustine, and the Language of Humanism* (Ann Arbor, 1998); Katherine van Liere, "The Moorslayer and the Missionary: James the Apostle in Spanish Historiography from Isidore of Seville to Ambrosio de Morales," *Viator* 37 (2006): 519–43.

54. James Hankins, *Plato in the Italian Renaissance*, 2 vols. (Leiden, 1991).

55. Paula Findlen, *Possessing Nature: Museums, Collecting, and Scientific Culture in Early Modern Italy* (Berkeley, 1994).

*Historical chronology is an area that you were interested in
very early in your career. What did the study of chronology
reveal to you?*

Chronology revealed to me, more than anything else, what I see as a fundamental difference between the traditional humanities and other disciplines. The humanities bring you the methods that you use, as well as the texts to which you apply them. Many early modern scholars did acquire a sense of historical distance and difference, as Erwin Panofsky and Fritz Saxl argued, though none of them was a pure historicist. But much of that they learned from reading Virgil, for instance, who himself had a very rich and powerful sense of historical change. Technical and grammatical writers also taught lessons in method. Early moderns learned from reading the late antique scholars Macrobius and Servius to compare Virgil with other Greek and Latin poets and to see him as a learned writer whose erudition was a feature rather than a bug of his poetry.

Awareness of these points had been part of my work for a long time. But Scaliger made it explicit. He insisted, in his work on chronology, that he was not doing something new; he was reviving a Greek method. And I found myself thinking about that and moving back and forth again and again between him and his sources, trying to understand what he was doing with them.

Oxford in the early eighties brought together a tremendous concentration of people with fantastic technical skills in philology. During my year there, when I had a question in Latin, I could take it to Michael Reeve or Leighton Reynolds. If I had a question in Greek, I could take it to Nigel Wilson or Hugh Lloyd-Jones. If I had a question about a Near Eastern language, I could take it to Sebastian Brock or Joanna Weinberg. And that sense of collaboration gave me great joy as well as much enlightenment.

But the main thing I realized, which became one of the motifs of my book on Scaliger—albeit one that has attracted almost no comment!—was that he was very self-consciously doing something that contemporary students of nature regularly did. Andreas Vesalius saw himself not as devising a new medicine but as reviving true Galenic anatomy. Copernicus saw himself not as devising a new astronomy but as doing a better form of Ptolemaic astronomy. In the humanities, in philology itself, Scaliger and others also saw themselves as reviving the methods of ancient scholarship rather than inventing new methods. So chronology, esoteric as it may seem, looks like other millennial traditions that have been studied more richly. It has been a great pleasure to watch the younger scholars who are both continuing and correcting my work in this field—Nicholas Popper, Philipp Nothaft, Dmitri Levitin, Nicholas Hardy, and Kirsten Macfarlane—bear out this insight in multiple ways—often revising, and sometimes refuting, me.

One of the most enjoyable articles I've ever written is a piece that I wrote with Noel Swerdlow inspired by my work on Scaliger. It's on the chronology of the fall of Troy in the *Aeneid*. In Virgil's account, the Greeks sail back to Troy through the "friendly silence of the moon."[56] Later, with the help of the moon's light, they sack the city. What is the friendly silence of the moon, and why is it light later on? We found that a set of Greek scholars argued on the basis of fragmentary evidence from a lost poem that on the night that Troy was sacked the moon was at third quarter. That meant that it was dark early at night, and they could sail in—or get out of the horse—undetected, but it also meant that the moon would rise later and enable them to sack the city.

We reconstructed this whole little tradition of antiquarian scholarship as well as its bearing on Virgilian exegesis in one evening with the help of much ice cream. So I found myself for the first time—it's happened a couple of times since—writing about an ancient source, using the leverage that Scaliger and other premodern scholars gave me.

When I went to study with Momigliano, he insisted, as he always had, that one should study past scholarship in order to solve the problems of present scholarship. And I always said, as a fastidious historian of science, "No, you don't do the history of science in order to solve modern scientific problems. You do it as intellectual discipline." I've come in my old age to see that here, too, Momigliano was wiser than I realized.

A real hallmark of your work is showing how scholars read antiquity through the tools and methods of antiquity itself. What light does this shed on the differences between the humanities and the sciences?

One of the differences is that we don't really have progress in the humanities! The only reason I've always regretted my own flight from classics is that I actually think in the end that classical texts are the greatest things you can teach, and I regret that I only get to teach them in general education courses in English translation. I envy my friends who

---

56. A. T. Grafton and N. M. Swerdlow, "Greek Chronography in Roman Epic: The Calendrical Date of the Fall of Troy in the *Aeneid*," *Classical Quarterly* 36, no. 1 (May 1986): 212–18.

offer courses on them in the originals. That must be a wonderful thing to do every year.

In this regard, I have some worries. For example, Harvard has recently announced a series of new courses designed to attract students to the humanities. Some of these are very appealing and very innovative. But there's a sense that everything has to be innovative, that the world has changed, and the humanities have to be recast in a digital form or some other way. And that's where I feel some worries, because my own sense is that there are some kinds of humanistic learning that we can master only by joining a tradition; there just isn't another way in. Digital texts are wonderful. The website Perseus is wonderful. You can read a classical text while a little machine parses every word in it for you. That's huge; I wish I'd had that when I was learning to read Greek and Latin.

But I just don't think that we can replace the traditions of humanistic learning, of going to the text with the wisdom and the artisanal tools that the text has given you. Lots of people and lots of students know this. One of my Princeton undergraduates used to say, "Oh, I just want to read Latin and Greek. That's all I want to do, really." She ended up writing a wonderful senior thesis on the teaching of Horace in sixteenth-century France: a piece of work informed not only by her minute and insightful reading of commentaries but also by her own direct knowledge of what it takes to find meanings in Latin poetry. I can't really think of anything more wonderful than that! "Just reading," at least in my student's sense, seems like the best thing you could possibly spend your life doing. And I worry that the rhetoric of innovation makes that kind of person seem old-fashioned and their activities pointless.

The only analogy I've been able to make that I think does have some measure of validity is with food. I don't think anybody wants to destroy the old methods of making food. Some of them can be improved with scientific measurement. Baking is now a scientific pursuit. But I don't think anybody wants to eat cheese that's made by a twenty-first-century digital method. And I do think that a deep structure of the humanities is that it works by traditions, that you enter the tradition at a certain point, and you move in the tradition. And moving in the tradition is always different than moving outside.

Perhaps that is what Momigliano meant when he said, "Some of these people are just outsiders." They can't do something useful, because they don't know where their feet are in the stream. I agree. But I understand that it's very difficult to make that case now without sounding elitist, old-fashioned, and out of it. So I'm not sure what to say.

In some ways, it's easier to make the case for studying traditions now than it was when I was young. Classics departments now have people who study reception. They have members whose literary and religious and scientific interests sprawl outside the narrow bounds of the classical. And many of them devote considerable attention to what the classics meant—how they were read, understood, and performed—when they were the core of European civilization. When I was young, a classicist didn't need to know the tradition, because one assumed there was nothing of importance in any work before 1900. I think that idea is gone!

Jill Kraye

JILL KRAYE is professor emerita of the history of Renaissance philosophy at the Warburg Institute, University of London.

How did you start out? What were your early interests?

When I was an undergraduate at Berkeley, from 1965 to '69, one of the requirements for everyone was a course in either American or Californian history. There was a very popular American history class with around a thousand people in it, but I didn't want to do that. So, instead I took a tiny, very specialized class on seventeenth-century America. I was introduced there to the work of Perry Miller, which I found amazing. I had never read anything like *The New England Mind: The Seventeenth Century*; *The New England Mind: From Colony to Province*; or "Errand into the Wilderness."[1] It was these works that got me interested in seventeenth-century English history, and particularly theology. I had never realized its complexity and appeal—it was completely new territory to me, which, having been raised in a Jewish family, I approached almost as an anthropologist studying a remote tribal cult.

Later I took a course on historiography, which was eye-opening. The historian who most excited me was Marc

---

1. Perry Miller, *The New England Mind: The Seventeenth Century* (New York, 1939); Miller, *The New England Mind: From Colony to Province* (Cambridge, MA, 1953); Miller, "Errand into the Wilderness," *William and Mary Quarterly* 10, no. 1 (1953): 3–32, and reprinted in Miller, *Errand into the Wilderness* (Cambridge, MA, 1956), 1–15.

Bloch, again exploring a subject I had never thought about: French rural history.[2] Growing up in Chicago and Los Angeles, how could I possibly be interested in French rural history? But I found it absolutely fascinating, and likewise *The Historian's Craft*, where Bloch talked about what historians do and what they're concerned about: not facts and dates but how societies develop.[3] I never saw myself doing that kind of history: I certainly didn't think I would go out and investigate the fields of rural France or anyplace else, but I liked that you could approach history from this completely different angle.

For my senior thesis, I returned to Puritan theology, writing on John Jewel's *Apology for the Church of England*.[4] When I went to graduate school at Columbia, it was my intention to study English history, particularly seventeenth-century theology. But Eugene F. Rice, who ran Columbia's early modern seminar, convinced me that Italian humanism was an open area with texts that hadn't been studied and new things that needed to be done. Prompted by him, I started studying Italian. That's how I wound up doing Italian Renaissance history. Like most things that have ever happened to me, it was more or less by accident that I ended up at Columbia, working with Gene. I had thought I really wanted to study Puritan theology, but I was very easily moved away from it [*laughs*]. My commitment might not have been quite as strong as I thought.

Did any particular classes or seminars along the way prove pivotal?

Apart from the historiography course, the Berkeley course that made me realize I wanted to be an intellectual historian was Carl Schorske's European Intellectual History. Schorske, who went on to Princeton, was already famous at Berkeley as a great teacher. It was an illuminating experience: one week he would do Goethe's *Faust*, the next week Wagner, then Gustav Klimt, and the following one the rise of antisemitism. I think he was working at the time on the material that eventually became *Fin-de-siècle Vienna*.[5] I had had a narrower approach to intellectual history: I thought it was just about reading scholarly books and treatises. That it could include literature, music, and art was very exciting. The

---

2. Marc Bloch, *Feudal Society*, 2 vols. (Chicago, 1961); Bloch, *French Rural History: An Essay on Its Basic Characteristics* (London, 1966).

3. Marc Bloch, *The Historian's Craft* (New York, [1949] 1953).

4. John Jewel, *An apologie, or aunswer in defence of the Church of England* (London, 1562).

5. Carl E. Schorske, *Fin-de-siècle Vienna: Politics and Culture* (New York, 1981).

course had a few hundred people, and, though I never really got to talk to Schorske, my last paper came back with a scribbled note from him saying, "If you want to go to graduate school, I'm happy to write you a reference." It was a real shot in the arm to think that somebody like him, with whom I had never interacted in person, would bother to do that.

A course in graduate school that turned out to be important, although at the time I absolutely hated it, was historical bibliography. Gene Rice, when he was teaching us how to study humanism and intellectual history of the fifteenth and sixteenth centuries, decided that we needed to learn how to describe an incunable, a book printed before 1501. I didn't even know what an incunable was, but I learned, as we went through all the standard incunable bibliographies. Gene gave each of us an author and we had to prepare a detailed bibliography, learn all of the terminology and how you describe a book. This was my first year in graduate school, and I remember thinking, "If that's what intellectual history is, it's not for me. I want the big ideas. I want things to be exciting." I didn't want all of this trivial bibliography! Yet, of all of the courses I have taken, this one has stood me in the best stead. Once again, it opened up an area of history that I didn't know about. When I'm teaching students how to deal with early printed books, I say, "I know you think this seems trivial, but it will really be useful in the end." I had thought intellectual history was all about ideas, but I found out it's much more than that.

Finally, if I was going to work on humanism, I had to know Latin and Greek. The person from whom I learned both, Seth Schein, was very much a literary scholar, so when he taught Latin, he didn't just explain about declensions or how to translate, but also taught us how to pay attention to the language, and to the way things were said. When I originally decided to learn Latin, I thought, "I need to learn it in order to get access to the writings of humanists and know what they said." But what I learned from Seth, a lesson that has remained with me, was to think about not only what was being said but also about how it was said. I realized that I had to observe the literary devices even if I was reading philosophy or history, and that it was vital to do that in the original language, and to have a feel for style as well as content.

Did you read any seminal books in these years?

A book that inspired me as a graduate student was Francis Haskell's *Patrons and Painters*, his study of Baroque artists, especially Nicolas Poussin, and their intellectual context in seventeenth-century Rome.[6] I had learned from Carl Schorske that art history is a part of intellectual history. But Haskell shows you how to do it, how to interpret the antiquarian interests of artists and their relations with friends, colleagues, and patrons in the context of intellectual history. I don't in the least want to compare anything I've done to that classic book, but Haskell has often been a model to me. Even before I came into daily contact with art historians at the Warburg Institute, it gave me a way to bring this discipline into my own work, and not merely into intellectual history, but into the history of philosophy more specifically, because Poussin and his circle were interested in Stoicism, and Haskell says some very illuminating things about that. Looking at a total culture in a historical way and integrating its various elements has been my goal—it's not necessarily what I achieve, but it's what I'm aiming for.

How did you decide to pursue the history of philosophy?

As with most things, I didn't actually decide to pursue the history of philosophy. It just happened. I've only ever taken one philosophy course, at Berkeley, again because of a distribution requirement: I took a Descartes to Wittgenstein survey with John Searle. I was writing my senior thesis then, and realized, "If I'm working on history, I've got to go into the library and read a stack of dusty books. But if I'm writing an essay on philosophy I just have to sit on a grassy knoll and think." And I thought, "Wow, this could be a good thing!" [laughs]

In the end, however, I was more of a library and dusty book sort of person. I don't really remember how I drifted into philosophy; it might have been Gene Rice who suggested that I work on the Italian humanist Francesco Filelfo. I read Filelfo's work, especially his letters and treatises, many of which drew on Greek philosophy: Aristotelianism, Epicureanism, and other sects. Through him and through studying his sources, I became deeply interested in the history of philosophy and continued to pursue it.

When I came to England in 1974, I decided that perhaps an even more intriguing humanist was Lorenzo Valla. During my first few years in England, I worked on Valla, and that got me much more involved in the history of Epicureanism and the relationship between Epicureanism

6. Francis Haskell, *Patrons and Painters: A Study in the Relations between Italian Art and Society in the Age of the Baroque* (New Haven, 1962).

and Christianity, subjects which I'm still working on. But I never made a conscious decision that "I'm going to be a historian of philosophy." People started saying that's what I was [*laughs*], but if I thought of myself as anything it was as somebody who worked on humanism. Later it became humanism and philosophy and the connections between them. Then I started exploring philosophers who weren't humanists, because I wanted to see how humanism and philosophy fit together: I studied the late fifteenth- and sixteenth-century Italian philosopher Pietro Pomponazzi, by no means a humanist himself, so that I could see which humanists had been picked up by him and had influenced him and which translations by humanists he was reading.

I'm not a very typical historian of philosophy because of my historical background. Scholars who come to history of philosophy from philosophy approach it very differently from those who come from history. I've always been very firm that I'm a historian, not a philosopher—a historian who happens to work, at least part of the time, on philosophy.

What questions led you toward the Renaissance and the authors that you mentioned?

I'm not sure I had any specific questions. I simply wanted to know how people in the Renaissance thought, what they read, what issues were of concern to them, what it was to be a humanist. Why did they write treatises on certain issues? What kind of sources did they use? I didn't have a grand agenda; I just wanted—and this is the Marc Bloch influence, perhaps—to immerse myself in the fifteenth century and in the questions that interested people at the time. Why did Valla write a dialogue on pleasure? Why did Filelfo write a treatise on moral philosophy? Sometimes the answers were disappointingly straightforward: they wrote because they wanted to get a particular job, and that's what they had to do in order to get it. But sometimes the answers got right to the heart of what made Renaissance philosophy tick.

Gene Rice, my doctoral supervisor at Columbia, was probably a bit too laid back for my own good. Wherever my interests led me, he always had helpful suggestions and would never discourage me or tell me to stay focused. Now, at least in England, where you're under considerable pressure to get students through their dissertations in three years, you have to put your foot down. But Gene never did, and it was both a good and a bad thing. That's how I ended up meandering all over the place. Intellectually, it was good. Practically, it was a bit of a disaster [*laughs*].

Today one just doesn't have the luxury of taking that attitude, for better or worse.

How did you select a topic for your dissertation?

I did a rather odd dissertation. I was supposed to be writing on Filelfo, but, for personal reasons, I moved to England and got rather sidetracked. Gene Rice, who knew Charles Schmitt, had told me to look him up at the Warburg Institute, and that was one of the most pivotal events in my intellectual life. In the way that things happen, I ran out of money. So, I managed to get a job in the Warburg Institute Library. I worked there for sixteen years as the reading room librarian, which was a very instructive experience—I learned many things. Not good for writing your dissertation, though!

Largely encouraged by Charles Schmitt and by Tony Grafton, who by that time was a friend and was also very encouraging, I started writing: a couple of articles on Filelfo and one on an even more learned Italian humanist, Angelo Poliziano.[7] I thought that I was going to be one of those people who never finishes their PhD—which in England was not as uncommon as it was in America.

Then, in 1986, Charles Schmitt died suddenly, and I was asked to take over his teaching. A few months later his job was advertised, and I got it, which was a bittersweet moment, because he had been my friend and mentor. I had also been writing the article on moral philosophy for the *Cambridge History of Renaissance Philosophy*, of which he was the general editor.[8] On Charles's death, I was given the task of putting the volume together and bringing it to press.

At that point it dawned on me, "Maybe I am going to have an academic career after all." Up till then, I'd assumed that I was going to work in the Warburg Library forever! So, I decided I'd better get my PhD [*laughs*]. Gene organized what's called an *extra muros* dissertation, which you get by putting together a series of your published articles. My dissertation, in other words, was a grab bag of articles I had written up to that time. I started at Columbia in 1969 and got my PhD in 1991. I always

---

7. Jill Kraye, "Francesco Filelfo's Lost Letter *De ideis*," *Journal of the Warburg and Courtauld Institutes* 42 (1979): 236–49; Kraye, "Francesco Filelfo on Emotions, Virtues and Vices: A Re-examination of His Sources," *Bibliothèque d'humanisme et Renaissance* 43, no. 1 (1981): 129–40; Kraye, "Cicero, Stoicism and Textual Criticism: Poliziano on *katorthōma*," *Rinascimento* 23 (1983): 79–110.

8. Jill Kraye, "Moral Philosophy," in *The Cambridge History of Renaissance Philosophy*, gen. ed. C. B. Schmitt, ed. Q. Skinner and E. Kessler, assoc. ed. J. Kraye (Cambridge, 1988), 303–86.

used to tell my students, "Do not, under any circumstances, follow my example." [*laughs*]

So I never wrote a dissertation in the formal sense; I just produced a number of articles that I'd either been asked to write or had done off my own bat. That's been the pattern I've always followed. I would describe myself as an "article person"—it seems to be the genre I'm most comfortable in. If asked, "How did you develop a research program?," I'd have to admit, in all honesty, that I've probably never developed one. I've merely followed my nose and gone where it's led me.

Chance and accident have mattered a great deal. Moving to England also made a vast difference. As a librarian at the Warburg, I never felt that I was in competition with anybody; I just did my own thing. Colleagues were very nice to me: they helped and supported me. When an opportunity opened up, they encouraged me to seize it. I never really had a game plan and never really pursued a career path. Nowadays, both in England and America, you have to do that, but I'm not sure that if this had been the case in my day, I would've ended up where I am—wherever that is [*laughs*].

The historian of Renaissance philosophy Paul Oskar Kristeller was at Columbia during your time. What was your relationship to him?

When I first came to Columbia and became interested in humanism, somebody said to me, "I suppose you're working with Kristeller?" And I replied, "I've never heard of Professor Teller." [*laughs*] That's how benighted I was: I thought he was called Chris Teller. I soon found out, of course, who he was. At that time, Kristeller had already retired and moreover had been in the Philosophy Department, whereas I was in history, so there was no real possibility of working with him. He did teach some classes, which I attended. He was on my MA board, my orals board, and my viva, so he was always there, but, unlike my colleagues John Monfasani and James Hankins, who had a great rapport with him, I found him a rather intimidating, overbearing figure. All the things that Gene Rice was—friendly, open, encouraging—were the complete opposite of Kristeller.

To give you an example: at some point, Kristeller realized I was working on Filelfo. He said, "Well, you must edit the letters of Filelfo, because this is a great desideratum in the field." I said, "It is a great desideratum, and somebody should do it, but not me, because I'm not a philologist. You need a set of skills that I don't have, and it's not the kind of thing

I want to do. I'm much more interested in historical and interpretive work." But every time I would see him, which wasn't that often, he would ask me how my edition of the Filelfo letters was coming along, and I would say, politely, "Maybe you didn't realize I'm not actually doing that." I thought of it as a kind of running joke, but then I would get letters from people in Italy and Germany saying, "My friend Paul Oskar tells me that you're editing the letters of Filelfo," and asking me questions. And I'd have to write to them and say, "Terribly sorry. It's a misunderstanding." We never got it sorted out.[9]

An article I've recently published challenges Kristeller's interpretation of humanism or, rather, a very specific part of it where he describes the humanists' five disciplines of interest—grammar, rhetoric, poetry, history, and moral philosophy.[10] I call into question whether moral philosophy, rather than philosophy more broadly, was a pillar of the humanist program. This isn't really an anti-Kristeller argument but a counterblast against what people have done with his definition of humanism. Actually, in his own work, Kristeller took a very broad view of the relationship of humanists to philosophy. Yet his programmatic definition, which has been endlessly repeated, has made the relationship between humanism and philosophy seem much narrower, much more limited, than I think it was.

Many humanists were interested in moral philosophy, but many were also interested in other aspects of philosophy. Perhaps institutionally, in the fifteenth century, moral philosophy was favored to some extent, but, after that, humanists pursued anything to do with the ancient world—studying it, understanding it, reconstructing it. When it came to philosophy, they didn't say, "Our remit is moral philosophy," nor was that the view of historians who wrote about humanism and philosophy before the contemporary era.

To see humanists as scholars interested in just five disciplines rather than in the whole spectrum of ancient intellectual thought and culture is not really helpful, and it's particularly unhelpful for philosophy. Lorenzo Valla's major work on philosophy is about logic. Historians of science—Tony Grafton, of course, has been crucial for this—know that humanists engaged in all the different scientific fields. In philosophy, Kristeller's definition of humanism has instead become a mental barrier.

---

9. Filelfo's letters have now been edited: Francesco Filelfo, *Collected Letters: "Epistolarum libri XLVIII,"* ed. Jeroen De Keyser, 4 vols. (Alessandria, 2016).

10. Jill Kraye, "Beyond Moral Philosophy: Renaissance Humanism and the Philosophical Canon," *Rinascimento* 56 (2016): 3–22.

Kristeller was a very great man: his *Iter Italicum* transformed the study of Renaissance humanism, and his work on Ficino was one of the most serious works on a Renaissance philosopher up to that time.[11] But you don't have to accept his entire legacy; you can pick and choose.

Did your friend and mentor Charles Schmitt's view of Renaissance philosophy and Aristotelianism shape your own work or your own interest in philosophy?

Charles felt strongly that Renaissance philosophy was a chronological concept. Wherever you want to start Renaissance philosophy, say with Petrarch, and to end it, say with Montaigne or Francis Bacon, it covers everything that happened to philosophy in this time period. It was not one particular style of philosophy as opposed to another. Scholastics, as far as he was concerned, were as much a part of Renaissance philosophy as humanists such as Leonardo Bruni or political thinkers such as Machiavelli—and, for Charles, perhaps even more significant.

One of the first things I wrote for a general audience was a chapter on Italian Renaissance philosophy for *The Routledge History of Philosophy* that covered the fifteenth through seventeenth centuries.[12] The editor was a Leibniz scholar. When I handed my essay in, he said, "Very interesting, but you've included all of these medieval philosophers." He singled out Paul of Venice and Cesare Cremonini. I said, "Paul of Venice was the contemporary of Leon Battista Alberti, Cosimo de' Medici, and Leonardo Bruni. Cesare Cremonini was a colleague of Galileo. These are not medieval philosophers. They were walking around in the Renaissance and talking to Renaissance people. They belonged to the same world." He said, "Yes, but they're Scholastics." Eventually, though I think reluctantly, he agreed with me, and I got to keep them in.

I share Charles's view that Renaissance philosophy is what happened during the Renaissance. It's a very broad church that includes Scholastics like Pomponazzi and Cremonini and humanists like Filelfo and Valla. It becomes much more interesting to see the Renaissance not as having a unified ideological approach to philosophy but as encompass-

11. Paul Oskar Kristeller, *The Philosophy of Marsilio Ficino* (New York, 1943); Kristeller, *Iter Italicum: A Finding List of Uncatalogued or Incompletely Catalogued Humanistic Manuscripts of the Renaissance in Italian and Other Libraries*, 6 vols. (London, 1963–92), https://www.itergateway.org/resources/iter-italicum.

12. Jill Kraye, "The Philosophy of the Italian Renaissance," in *The Routledge History of Philosophy*, ed. G. H. R. Parkinson (London, 1993), 4:16–69.

ing a broad range of different approaches. Another thing I feel strongly as a historian: these figures knew each other. They taught in the same universities. Maybe they had disputes and didn't always agree on everything, but they belonged to the same historical context. To isolate one particular strand—to say that humanist Platonism was the new philosophy of the Renaissance and Scholastic Aristotelianism was the old philosophy of the Middle Ages—is artificial.

In this respect, intellectually Charles had a tremendous influence on me. But perhaps most importantly he believed in me—more than I believed in myself—and constantly encouraged me. He was always keen to support the work of young people. He used to tell me it was unfair that at conferences senior scholars like himself would often get an hour to speak, while junior ones would get only twenty minutes. He felt that it should be exactly the opposite, with more time allotted to younger scholars, who are new and fresh and working at the coal face of research.

Finally, I learned from him that there was a case for moving on to the next project rather than obsessively trying to get everything perfectly accurate and correct in the present one. At the time, I was working as a librarian, so I had learned to be very careful, methodical, and rigorous, to check, double-check, and even triple-check everything. I still believe that trying to get things right is fundamental for scholarship. But Charles used to say, "You can carry this checking too far, and isn't it better to get what you've written out there so that people can read it? Why not give the reviewers something to complain about and then go on to a new project?" I was rather scandalized by this. It was shocking to me that a scholar whom I looked up to took such a relaxed attitude to accuracy. But, of course, he was absolutely right! He himself opened up several fields, among them Renaissance skepticism, Aristotelianism, and the history of universities. He did so many things that have been so influential, which wouldn't have happened had he proofread everything as much as he probably should have!

What role has the library of the Warburg Institute played in your intellectual life?

Because I was the reading room librarian for sixteen years and then, after an interim, the librarian [an academic position] for another twelve, my relationship to the Warburg Library has been very close and intense. The library made me much more of a generalist than I had been. As a historian, you can focus on the periods and subjects that most interest you. But you can't do that as a librarian. The Warburg Library specializes in the history of the classical tradition; within that rubric, however, its coverage is extremely broad. I stopped thinking that I only needed to read within my own comfort zone. My field became the history of the classical tradition on the different floors of the library, following in the footsteps, as it were, of Aby Warburg. I would go to seminars and conferences on art history, literary history, philosophical history, history of science. And I began to see how I could bring all of these disciplines into my own work.

When I show people around the library, I tell them: you can go to the library, which is open stack and subject arranged, and spend all of your time in one area of one floor. But that's not the way to get the most out of the library. You should be going to all the different floors, moving from one to another. I think my research is at its best when I can bring together the various subject areas that I began to know about through the library.

I learned to embrace the idea of drawing on the entire library, telling myself, You're not just a second-floor person (this is where we have the material on humanism and literature); the second floor should be a springboard to other parts of the library. I gradually came to think that I could probably handle anything the library covered, at least as a starting point. So, if one of the thinkers I was studying worked on the history of the church fathers, I could also do that, because the library had a section on patristics, where I could read up about it and then pursue it further at the British Library. So, too, with bibliography, the history of printing, art history, the history of religion—whatever came my way.

The library's main organizing theme, the classical tradition, has always served as the interface between humanism and philosophy for me. I study philosophy as it relates to the classical tradition, and that approach has been shaped by the library. If there's an angle where the classical tradition can come into my research—whether it's art history or numismatics—that's the one I'll pursue.

To give you a practical example, I was hunting for a picture of Marcus Aurelius to illustrate something I was writing. In the Warburg Photographic Collection, I came across a wonderful painting by Rubens of a scholar dressed in characteristic seventeenth-century Flemish garb, sitting at a desk with a bust of Marcus Aurelius on it and writing, quill in hand, in a manuscript book. This being Rubens, there was a fascinating story: the scholar was a friend of his, Caspar Gevartius, who later asked the painter to help him by searching for manuscript readings of the *Meditations* when he went off to Spain on diplomatic and artistic business.

Gevartius advised Rubens on the design for a well-known triumphal entry and was in contact with some of the leading classical scholars of his day. I did almost all the research in the Warburg Library, just following the threads that made up this story. It's a very Warburgian article, because it's entirely guided by the topics one can pursue at the Warburg.[13]

There are many things you can't pursue at the Warburg. You can't do firsthand manuscript research, for example. Yet much that I've done elsewhere started from an experience I've had in the library, usually of running across a book on the shelves I didn't know about and then following it wherever it led, rather than thinking, "I'm a historian of humanism and philosophy. This is art history; it's not for me." Everything's fair game. Everything is for me. That's an attitude I first encountered with Schorske, but I developed it much further through working at the Warburg and particularly as a librarian, which taught me to think, "All of this can fit together just as it fits together in the library. One thing reinforces the other and enriches it."

How have the organizing categories of Aby Warburg held up? Do they still enable research?

When you tell people this is a classification system devised in the 1920s, they often say, "Obviously it can't work in the twenty-first century." But it works amazingly well both for librarians who have to buy books and decide the best spot to place them in the library and for readers who want to find the books they need, even—indeed, especially—if they don't know what these are.

If you come to the library and are asking the right questions, questions about the classical tradition and how different subjects were related to it, you'll find everything you need. If you come asking the wrong questions, you won't find anything. It's like the reaction British people have to Marmite, a brand of brewer's yeast: either you love it, or you hate it. But I've shown hundreds of people around the library, and the classification system holds up extremely well.

For example, there is a section on the second floor called Cultural Transfer. It's about the influence of one culture on another. You can use it to research the impact of Turkey on Hungary or of England on France,

---

13. Jill Kraye, "Marcus Aurelius and the Republic of Letters in Seventeenth-Century Antwerp," in *For the Sake of Learning: Essays in Honor of Anthony Grafton*, ed. Ann M. Blair and Anja-Silvia Goeing (Leiden, 2016), 2:744–60.

and vice versa. When I first came to the library, and obviously much more so in the 1920s, this was a very small topic, just one of the many things Aby Warburg was interested in. But, now, this topic has become very hot, and there's a steady stream of books about cultural transfer, particularly between East and West. A long-term reader said to me, "I used this library twenty years ago, and you had fifteen books in this section, and now you have several shelves."

Some areas have died out because the library is now part of a larger consortium, but most are alive, vibrant, and flourishing. For instance, we have a section on the afterlife of classical authors, something I've never come across in any other library. It covers the survival of classical genres, like the dialogue, poetry, et cetera, the classical tradition in various countries, and the later influence of individual Greek and Roman authors. Readers interested in reception studies, a very fashionable subject these days, will find shelves of books about the afterlife of Lucretius or of Virgil. These are topics that have come into their own, and the library is perfectly adapted to accommodate them.

If you want to learn about the history of psychology beyond the theory of humors and of genius along with other Renaissance notions, you'll find zilch. But, if want to know what people thought psychology was in the Renaissance, you'll find plenty of material, because this is an area where the library has always tried to keep up with current research. I can't really explain why the classification system continues to work, except that it was very well devised from the beginning. It's a kind of magic, but it does work.

I was giving someone a tour of the library not so long ago, and I said, "You're working on the right sort of topic for the Warburg. You'll find much more here than you anticipated, and this will mean that you won't get things done as quickly as you thought, but they'll be done in a much better way." And a reader who happened to overhear me turned and said, "Listen to her. This is what happened to me. I came to look for just one thing, and I've already been here a year." It works. It's magic.

How does your historical research relate to
contemporary philosophy?

From 2000 to 2003, I was involved in a project called The New Historiography of Seventeenth-Century Philosophy with two academics from other British universities. They both worked on the seventeenth century, but their background was in philosophy rather than history. They found my historical approach too unphilosophical, and I found their philosophical approach too unhistorical. Talking to one of them, a Descartes specialist as well as an analytical philosopher, I said, "You can't just look at Descartes on his own. You have to see who he was corresponding with, who his colleagues were, the constraints on him, the atmosphere in which he worked." And he replied, "All of that is completely irrelevant. All I want to know is, Is this a good philosophical argument or a bad philosophical argument?" Everything else, in his eyes, was pedantic obscurantism.

For me, however, the history of philosophy should be treated as part of intellectual history. As Schorske taught me, intellectual history includes music, art, and philosophy. It includes all the products of the human mind. Observing their interaction, you can begin to appreciate someone like Poliziano, who was a philologist but also taught philosophy and wrote poetry, or Henry More, who was both a poet and a philosopher. Philosophy had so much interchange with other areas that to isolate it from that wider history seems completely crazy. When you went to university in the Renaissance, you did a three- or four-year program of studying Aristotelian philosophy. It was the background of everybody who went to university, whether they became a doctor, a lawyer, or a theologian. Not taking that background into account when you study people who are doctors or lawyers or theologians means missing a very vital element of the story.

My approach differs even from that of more historically minded historians of philosophy. When I was asked to write the article on moral philosophy for the *Cambridge History of Seventeenth-Century Philosophy*, I decided to look beyond the big names and to read everything that could by any stretch of the imagination be considered moral philosophy in the period, from quasi-theological works to casuistry, from humanist commentaries and dialogues to Scholastic treatises.[14] I aimed to show that moral philosophy was an immensely broad field, written by a very wide range of authors. The reaction of Dan Garber, one of the volume editors, was, "This is bibliography not philosophy," which was very wounding. I tried to explain to him why, in a volume intended to give a historical overview of seventeenth-century philosophy, it was necessary to include thinkers even if nobody had read them since that time and their writings

---

14. Jill Kraye, "Conceptions of Moral Philosophy," in *The Cambridge History of Seventeenth-Century Philosophy*, ed. D. Garber and M. Ayers (Cambridge, 1998), 2:1279–316.

hadn't led anywhere. I'm not sure he was entirely convinced, but he pretty much let me do just that.

Many scholars believe that the history of philosophy is only about finding the path from what was thought in the past to what we think now. It's a teleological story, and they're convinced that any history of philosophy has to tell that story. Well, it's one story and one way of doing the history of philosophy. But dead ends—ideas that went no place and didn't have any influence—are also worth investigating. I'm interested in what Renaissance philosophy tells us about the Renaissance, about the fourteenth to the seventeenth century, and all the directions in which thought moved at the time are part of that investigation. Not all of these directions led to the twenty-first century. If that's all you want to know, then clearly many Renaissance ideas are irrelevant. But if you see philosophy as one element in the larger culture, then all philosophical thinkers and writers, even those who've since been forgotten, are as much a part of the story as those who went on to become influential. As an intellectual historian of philosophy, I study philosophy in whatever guise it appeared at a given time, regardless of whether it had any later impact. This may not shed light on what happened in the following century or on the present, but it seems to me a richer way to deal with the past. I also try to read very widely, not to interpret mainstream philosophers but instead to get to grips with the intellectual world in which they and other thinkers were operating—in other words, the historical milieu in which everyone was developing their ideas. All writers contributed to the general panorama of what was going on at the time.

To give you an example, the book in the Rubens painting I mentioned earlier is an edition of and commentary on Marcus Aurelius that was probably never written; if it was written, it's now lost. I'm not normally in the business of writing about nonexistent books, but I felt there was an interesting story there, one which could tell us why people in the seventeenth century were interested in Marcus Aurelius and what approaches they took to his thought. An unfinished and possibly unwritten book obviously had no influence. Yet the painting records a moment in Antwerp when a particular connection arose among art, antiquarianism, humanism, patristics, and Greek literature, all centered on Marcus Aurelius.

How do you develop a topic and decide its extent?

As I've said, it's basically a matter of following my nose. For example, when I first started working on Marcus Aurelius, it was one of those "the dog that didn't bark in the night" situations, because I realized that al-though he's now regarded as one of the most famous Stoic philosophers, he didn't seem to have played much of a role in the Renaissance. Why wasn't he there? Of course, he was there, but not in an obvious way. I started rooting around and realized that the rediscovery of Marcus Aure-lius was a seventeenth-century episode: this is when a number of editions, commentaries, and translations were made. I came across someone called Thomas Gataker, whom I had not known about, but who, in his spare time—his day job was as a Puritan minister—produced what is probably the most learned commentary ever written on Marcus Aurelius's *Medita-tions.* I became intrigued by Gataker and published some articles on him.[15]

You find someone like Gataker, and you ask, "What else did he write? What else did he do? Whom did he know? With whom was he cor-responding? What context produced such a figure?" And then, rather than taking a vertical approach, moving chronologically in time from point A to point B, you take a horizontal one, widening your perspective more and more. It's this wider picture, the way that you can use philoso-phy to go off in different directions, that appeals to me.

When I read Gataker's amazingly learned commentary, covering hun-dreds of double-column pages in tiny print, I found that there were more references to the Bible than to philosophical works. There's a story there. This was part of Gataker's culture. There's a reason why he was attracted to Mar-cus Aurelius. You might say, "He's distorting Marcus Aurelius, because you shouldn't be bringing in the Psalms or St. Paul in order to read a pagan Ro-man emperor." But, for me as an intellectual historian, I want to understand how people used philosophy to interpret their own world and their own con-cerns, and, for my money, that's not a distortion. That's a creative adaptation.

How do you think about the Christian adaptation of pagan thought in the Renaissance?

The humanist philosopher Justus Lipsius gets a lot of flak from histori-ans of ancient Stoicism, who say, "He Christianized Stoic philosophy. He brought in extraneous theological considerations, and he distorted the truth." It's not the truth of Stoicism that interests me. What's significant

---

15. Jill Kraye, "'Ethnicorum omnium sanctissimus': Marcus Aurelius and his *Meditations* from Xy-lander to Diderot," in *Humanism and Early Modern Philosophy,* ed. J. Kraye and M. W. F. Stone (London, 2000), 106–34; Kray, "Philology, Moral Philosophy and Religion in Thomas Gataker's Edition of Mar-cus Aurelius's *Meditations* (1652)," in *Ethik—Wissenschaft oder Lebenskunst? Modelle der Normenbegründ-ung von der Antike bis zur Frühen Neuzeit,* ed. S. Ebbersmeyer and E. Kessler (Münster, 2007), 293–307.

about Lipsius, for me, is what he did with Stoicism, how he adapted it, how he put it in conversation with the concerns of his own time, including religious ones. Distortion is not the right word. Philosophy was something that past thinkers used to understand their world. Recovering that is much more rewarding to me than the purist approach of understanding the ancient Stoics solely in terms of their own times. Lipsius wanted to make Stoicism relevant to his contemporaries. To do this, he didn't take it on its own terms but on terms that could be understood and applied in the sixteenth century. Personally, I don't think that's a betrayal of the humanist approach to the past. This can be a flashpoint for how you look at the history of philosophy. Do you see what Lipsius did as betrayal? Do you see it as distortion? Or, do you see it as adaptation aimed at making ancient thought relevant to his own day? If it's not relevant to a thinker's own times, it's antiquarianism in the narrowest and worst sense of the term.

Renaissance scholars felt that ancient philosophy had something to offer them and their contemporaries, but in order to do that it had to be malleable, adaptable. They didn't consider this a betrayal or a distortion of ancient traditions but rather a development that made them usable for their contemporaries, particularly in relation to religion. No philosophy could take off in the Renaissance or the early modern period until it worked out some kind of accommodation with Christianity, one way or another. As an intellectual historian, I study how people used past thought, and to use it they sometimes had to disregard its original context. I don't see this in a negative light. For me, it's one of the most positive things they did.

What are your working methods? How do you take notes,
and what technologies do you use when you read and write?

I read somewhere that when the impressionists got together, contrary to expectations, they didn't discuss theories about light, color, and nature, but instead talked about where you could get the best turpentine, the best brushes, and how to stretch canvases. "Yes," I thought, "this is the nitty gritty!"

When I'm in a library I tend to use pencil and paper, and I take notes on sheets of paper. Today most people type directly into a computer, but I don't do that; I find I make too many mistakes. For my research on Pseudo-Aristotle three decades ago, I took notes from heaps of different books. I had a large number of folders, one for each work that I was interested in. Every time I came across a reference to a particular work, I would scribble it on a bit of paper and throw it into the appropriate folder. Often the same passage would also contain references to other works, so I would photocopy those notes, and put copies into all the relevant folders. In the course of time, some of the folders got very large. When I realized that I had five fat folders on the pseudo-Aristotelian *De mundo* (On the Cosmos), I knew that it was going to be a big topic for me! What I did was work my way through the folders, trying to weave all the references together into a series of stories.

Nowadays, of course, it's a bit more complicated, because much of the material I have collected isn't on paper. It's on my computer as downloaded PDFs, and that has made a big change in the way I work. For subjects I'm currently researching, about half the material is on paper, and the other half is downloaded PDFs. So I have to move back and forth between my computer and my notebooks.

The ability to download books has been the key thing that's changed. I had an interesting experience not long ago when I decided to look at Renaissance editions of Seneca.[16] I thought, "I know what's in the British Library and what I've looked at elsewhere, but there are various editions that I haven't seen. I wonder if any of them are online." Some twelve Seneca commentaries were published in the sixteenth century, ten of which I found online and downloaded. By the time I came to write the paper, the other two were available online as well. As a result, I had digital copies of all the printed primary sources that I needed. That is really extraordinary, because in the past I would have gone and looked at as many of these as I could and would've taken notes but without yet knowing exactly what I was going to focus on when I finally got down to writing.

For the Seneca paper, I was examining the philological use of skepticism. I observed the way that various editors dealt with doubt when emending the text. But then I would find another editor doing something differently, so I'd have to go back to other editors to check what they had done. Once I had everything on my computer, I didn't have to rely on notes that I'd taken six months or a year before, when I hadn't known what I would now need. I could immediately consult my digitized copies of these editions. Before, if the book was in the British Library, only a ten-minute walk away, it was not a problem, but, if I had to go Paris to check it, that was a real drag.

Often I find when I take notes that I stop just at the most interesting point. When I come to write up the research, I realize, "Gosh, what did

---

16. Jill Kraye, "Coping with Philological Doubt: Sixteenth-Century Approaches to the Text of Seneca," in *The Marriage of Philology and Scepticism: Uncertainty and Conjecture in Early Modern Scholarship and Thought*, ed. G. M. Cao, J. Kraye, and A. Grafton, Warburg Institute Colloquia (London, forthcoming).

he say after that? What an idiot I am. I didn't bother to take it down." It's happened to me hundreds of times. Now, I can look at the original on my computer and say, "Yes, that was the most interesting point and I missed it." I still feel like an idiot, but it takes much less time to repair the damage. Digitized copies give you a new level of control over your material, as if all the books you need can simply be pulled off the shelf, like you can in the Warburg Library. For a paper I recently wrote on the pseudo-Aristotelian *De virtutibus et vitiis* (On the Virtues and Vices), I had a copy of every Renaissance and early modern translation on my computer.[17] So, when I asked myself, "I wonder how Veit Amerbach translated that Greek phrase?," all I had to do was go to my computer and check his version. In a few minutes I had the answer. It's made a huge difference—everything that I now do with electronic copies I could have done with physical books, but this is much quicker and more convenient. In the olden days, if you thought you had to go to Paris to sort something out, you might've decided to forget about it. But, now, there's no excuse!

In terms of putting an article together, as I write I figure out what it is that I want to say. When I get to the end of an article, it often says something rather different from when I started. I see writing as part of the research process. When I'm writing, I often discover what it is that I don't know, and then I have to go back and look for it. Instead of sifting through ring binders full of notes, as I used to do, I now scour the internet for digitized copies of the primary sources, so that I can reread them. It usually involves a lot more work, but the opportunities are amazing.

At the end of one of your essays, "Philosophers and Philologists," you write that the birth of modern philosophy was a revolution that also turned philology into an obsolete tool of philosophical inquiry.[18] Could you describe that process and also comment on the ways in which the enterprise of philology can still inform philosophy and vice versa?

The relationship between philosophy and philology, by which I mean classical philology as practiced by humanists—that is, the study of Greek and Roman language, history, culture, and thought—has been at the center of my studies. The issue continues to concern me, and I still more or less

17. Jill Kraye, "Translating Pseudo-Aristotelian Moral Philosophy: Giulio Ballino's Vernacular Version of *On the Virtues and Vices*," *Rivista di storia della filosofia* (forthcoming).
18. Jill Kraye, "Philologists and Philosophers," in *The Cambridge Companion to Renaissance Humanism*, ed. J. Kraye (Cambridge, 1996), 142–60.

agree with what I wrote then: during the Renaissance there was a close interaction between philosophy and philology. Philologists and humanists made a valuable contribution to the development of philosophy. Stoicism, Epicureanism, and skepticism could not have been put on the map of Renaissance philosophy without the labor of the philologists who pored over the Greek texts, edited, translated, and interpreted them, and gathered together collections of, for example, the surviving fragments of ancient Stoicism. This was essential for the practice of philosophy. And even for Aristotelianism, which had a long tradition since the Middle Ages, it made a difference that the original Greek texts were made available again in new humanist translations. In addition, it was mainly humanists who translated the ancient Greek commentators on Aristotle, enabling philosophers to gain access to them. So, in the sixteenth century, there was a very close relationship between philology and philosophy.

As Western philosophy in the seventeenth century started to detach itself from ancient philosophy—a process that took far longer than is generally assumed—the role of philology became increasingly marginalized. Humanist philology was less able to contribute to philosophy because influential thinkers like René Descartes and Thomas Hobbes self-consciously distanced themselves from the philosophy of antiquity. Hobbes did, of course, have humanist interests, but reviving ancient philosophy wasn't among them.

The early modern period is when the divide began to open. Ancient philosophy remained a subject of great interest but was more and more seen as part of the history of philosophy instead of belonging to the ongoing enterprise of philosophy. As such, it was left in the hands of historians of philosophy such as Thomas Stanley in the seventeenth century and Jacob Brucker in the eighteenth century. Since philology was so closely tied to ancient philosophy, it, too, became a tool more of the history than of the practice of philosophy.

As for the role of philology in the present day, again, it's pretty much limited to the history of philosophy. For those who study ancient philosophy, it's still a necessary tool. They have to know the ancient languages because many debates hinge on the meaning of terms, and they have to understand the relationship between one ancient philosophical tradition and another. Philology also has a role in the study of Renaissance and early modern philosophy in that new editions of texts from these periods, many of them written in Latin, continue to be produced. So, we're still doing textual criticism, and that requires paleographical, bibliographical, and philological skills.

In modern analytical philosophy, there's no place for classical philology. The famous quote "Just say no to the history of philosophy" also means "Just say no to philology": if you throw out the history of philosophy, you throw out philology along with it.[19] I hope, however, that philology will keep its function in the history of philosophy, that it won't disappear because the linguistic and critical skills on which it's based become obsolete. But there are no guarantees. Most of the medieval Latin translations of Aristotle were made by 1300. Throughout the fourteenth century no one bothered to translate Aristotle, as if it had somehow been decided: we've got Aristotle; we've got usable texts; now we can get on with doing philosophy. Philology more or less dropped out of the philosophical picture in the fourteenth century and didn't return until the fifteenth century, when humanists recognized the need for new, more philologically sound translations of Aristotle and other ancient philosophers. There is always the danger that philology could vanish again. Like the humanists, we have to fight for the role of philology.

What do you think you have unlearned as well as learned in the course of your career? Has what has seemed true or significant to you changed over time?

I'm not sure that I've unlearned anything. Instead, I've come to realize that many individual, discrete facts that I've learned, rather than needing to be abandoned—because, if you've done your job properly, they remain true—benefit from being placed in a broader context. When small, isolated facts and discoveries—little stories that I've pursued in one direction or another—are viewed from this wider perspective, they sometimes look rather different. Slowly, over time, I've learned to stand back and try to see this larger picture. When I first began researching and writing, I was very reluctant to put forward anything resembling a generalization or speculation. I didn't want to venture beyond narrow and strictly defined questions that I knew I could answer with a degree of certainty. That gave me a feeling of security.

Often when I was reviewing articles for journals or assessing grant applications, and someone would start speculating, I would think, "Aha, speculation. This is terrible." But now, though I'm still quite skeptical of grand theories and all-encompassing explanations, I'm much more comfortable with a midlevel framework than I was.

19. "The Eighties: A Snapshot," Department of Philosophy, Princeton University, accessed April 15, 2018, https://philosophy.princeton.edu/about/eighties-snapshot.

So, what strikes me as true has largely remained the same, but what strikes me as significant has changed. That was your distinction, wasn't it? I still think that verifiable facts are true, but on their own they now seem less significant than I thought in the past. I'm now prepared to admit that facts can gain considerable significance when seen against a wider background and used to answer larger questions, which I'm less reluctant to ask than I was.

This was brought home to me recently. In the late 1980s and early '90s, I wrote two articles on arguments over the authenticity of the pseudo-Aristotelian *De mundo*.[20] I then moved on to new topics; but around ten years ago I was asked to contribute a piece on the later reception of *De mundo*. So, I went back and looked at those folders I told you about, into which I'd continued to throw any mentions of pseudo-Aristotelian works I came across, and I found I had accumulated some thirty-five to forty additional references to *De mundo*. I thought, "OK, I'll say yes." When I wrote the article, however, I didn't merely supplement my previous work but attempted to construct a broader framework.[21] I traced how questions of authenticity had developed century by century. I now had a different perspective, which encouraged me to ask different questions from the ones I'd previously thought significant. I'd learned the value of asking bigger questions.

One such question that's occupied me in the last couple of years is whether the recovery of ancient philosophy from the late Middle Ages to the seventeenth century can be seen as a continuous story. That's a question that I wouldn't have touched with a barge pole in the past [*laughs*]. But attempting to chart the trajectory of ancient philosophical traditions over many centuries is something I'm now prepared to do, and it seems very significant to me. If you don't ever stand back and ask the bigger questions—maybe not too big but at least middle-range ones that can be answered with some level of credibility—then your work tends to raise the "So what?" response. So, I guess what I've learned is not to be overly frightened of speculation, of generalization—a bit frightened but not too much.

20. Jill Kraye, "Daniel Heinsius and the Author of *De mundo*," in *The Uses of Greek and Latin: Historical Essays*, ed. A. C. Dionisotti, J. Kraye, and A. Grafton (London, 1988), 171–97; Kraye, "Aristotle's God and the Authenticity of *De mundo*: An Early Modern Controversy," *Journal of the History of Philosophy* 28, no. 3 (1990): 339–58.
21. Jill Kraye, "Disputes over the Authorship of *De mundo* between Humanism and *Altertumswissenschaft*," in Pseudo-Aristoteles, *De mundo*, ed. J. Thom (Tübingen, 2014), 181–97.

What are your hopes for the history of philosophy?

My main hope is that the history of philosophy will survive as an academic discipline, because I think it's regarded as expendable, and that means it has to be fought for. If you work in a minority branch of a minority field, which the history of Renaissance philosophy certainly is, you're always aware that it's in danger of extinction. It's by no means a given that the history of Renaissance philosophy will continue to be taught at the Warburg Institute, let alone elsewhere. So, the history of philosophy, whether the whole genus or just certain species, could perish. I very much hope it has enough intellectual resilience to survive, but I'm by no means sure of that.

What insights can we gain by restoring the place
of the Renaissance in the history of philosophy?

It's been a bee in my bonnet for a long time that Renaissance philosophy is usually written off as a period when nothing of interest happened and that's only worth a couple of pages, if that, in histories of philosophy. Although this attitude is still around, thankfully it's starting to disappear. A hopeful sign is the podcast series called *History of Philosophy without Any Gaps*. The host, Peter Adamson, is working his way from the pre-Socratics to twenty-first-century analytical philosophy through a series of interviews. In one of these, John Marenbon, a historian of medieval philosophy, and I questioned the traditional boundaries between the Middle Ages, the Renaissance, and the early modern era.[22]

A way of understanding medieval philosophy is exploring its influence on later periods. I wrote an article examining which medieval philosophers were published in the first age of print—my hated graduate school training in incunable bibliography came in very handy for this.[23] What I found was that those philosophers who were considered worthy of being printed in the late fifteenth century were not necessarily the same ones who feature in modern histories of medieval philosophy: there were no editions of Peter Abelard or Roger Bacon, for example, while Giles of

22. "Jill Kraye and John Marenbon on Medieval Philosophy," *History of Philosophy without Any Gaps*, no. 200, posted November 30, 2014, https://historyofphilosophy.net/medieval-marenbon-kraye.

23. Jill Kraye, "The Role of Medieval Philosophy in Renaissance Thought: The Evidence of Early Printed Books," in *Bilan et perspectives des études médiévales (1993–1999): Actes du deuxième Congrès européen d'études médiévales, Barcelona (8–12 juin 1999)*, ed. J. Hamesse (Turnhout, 2004), 695–714.

Rome was a bestseller. Looking at the continuing impact of the Middle Ages in the Renaissance and beyond can be instructive.

As recent studies have shown, late Scholasticism continued to exert an influence on seventeenth-century philosophers, even those such as Hobbes and Descartes who repudiated it.[24] What hasn't been done enough, though some young scholars have made a promising start, is the same thing for late humanism.[25] In the period of transition from early modern to modern philosophy, ancient thought was still important for many philosophers, and this meant that humanists still had a valuable role to play. For example, Gataker's commentary on Marcus Aurelius is both a remarkable work of humanist scholarship and a serious study of late Stoic philosophy. Pierre Gassendi produced an outstanding humanist textual edition of Epicurus's extant writings, as well as a major philosophical treatise on Epicureanism. I'd like to see the approach that's transforming our view of the relationship of Scholasticism to seventeenth-century philosophy applied to humanism as well.

The history of philosophy never had any gaps. There weren't three centuries between the Middle Ages and the seventeenth century when nothing happened. It may seem like nothing happened if you don't know where to look. One of the reasons for the negative attitude toward Renaissance philosophy is that much of it took place in commentaries on ancient texts. To make any sense of Renaissance commentaries, not only do you have to know the languages, above all Latin, in which they were written but also the specialized terminology that they used. You can't just pick up a Renaissance commentary and start reading. You need to understand the philosophy and philology underneath the traditions and the questions that commentators asked. In a commentary, it's not so obvious what's new and what's traditional. That's much harder to dig out than when reading a straightforward treatise where authors tend to be much more explicit about their innovations. In an era like the Renaissance when much philosophical work went on in commentaries, the modern scholar often has to reconstruct what was new and interesting. This is what Charles Schmitt did so well, showing that Aristotelian commentaries in the Renaissance were vehicles for an eclectic range of ideas and approaches, from the old-fashioned to the newfangled.[26] But

24. Cees Leijenhorst, *The Mechanisation of Aristotelianism: The Late Aristotelian Setting of Thomas Hobbes' Natural Philosophy* (Leiden, 2002); Roger Ariew, *Descartes among the Scholastics* (Leiden, 2011).
25. See, e.g., Anthony Ossa-Richardson, *The Devil's Tabernacle: The Pagan Oracles in Early Modern Thought* (Princeton, 2013); Dmitri Levitin, *Ancient Wisdom in the Age of the New Science: Histories of Philosophy in England, c. 1640–1700* (Cambridge, 2015).
26. Charles Schmitt, *Aristotle and the Renaissance* (Cambridge, MA, 1983).

judging them superficially, from the outside, you might think, "They're all just writing commentaries on Aristotle, so what's new or interesting about that?"

The recognition that we need to look at the whole history of philosophy is helping. All of the different periods of philosophy, not just the Renaissance, gain when you see them as part of a continuous story.

Peter N. Miller

PETER N. MILLER is dean and professor at the Bard Graduate Center, New York City.

What were your early intellectual interests?

In my first semester in college, I took a course in Russian history at Harvard with Richard Pipes. On the reading list was Isaiah Berlin's *Russian Thinkers*.[1] I remember reading the essays in that book, in particular "The Hedgehog and the Fox." That was really my first glimmer of a certain kind of intellectualism: I admired Berlin's wide-ranging references and his ability to make sense of vast expanses of intellectual and cultural life. I subsequently read a lot of Berlin in college. Then, when I started my graduate studies in Cambridge, I read a lot of George Steiner, whom I later had the honor to meet and talk with on several occasions. I devoured *Language and Silence*, *The Death of Tragedy*, *Tolstoy or Dostoevksy*, *The Portage of A.H. to San Cristobal*, and *After Babel*.[2] Berlin and Steiner represented a certain ideal of learning that I admired. They could traverse, equally comfortably, seemingly limitless tracts of erudition, literature, art, and music. I found that immensely appealing. Was I aware

---

1. Isaiah Berlin, *Russian Thinkers* (London, 1978).

2. George Steiner, *Tolstoy or Dostoevsky: An Essay in the Old Criticism* (New York, 1959); Steiner, *The Death of Tragedy* (New Haven, 1961); Steiner, *Language and Silence* (New York, 1972); Steiner, *After Babel: Aspects of Language and Translation* (Oxford, 1975); Steiner, *The Portage of A.H. to San Cristobal* (London, 1981).

already that the man of learning was not necessarily identical with the professor? I don't know.

Berlin, in a way, got me to Cambridge by getting me interested in intellectual history. At the end of my first year at Harvard, I put together my own concentration in history and philosophy as a way of doing intellectual history. One of my teachers, Wallace T. MacCaffrey, a Tudor-Stuart historian, recommended that I read John Pocock's *Ancient Constitution and the Feudal Law*.[3] It so happened, because my mother was an English historian and had taught survey courses of early modern European history, that she had a copy of *Ancient Constitution* on our bookshelves. I read it over the summer and found it enthralling—and utterly persuasive. Mac-Caffrey was right, and that book turned me on to the history of political thought. I then read Quentin Skinner, first his methodological essays of the later 1960s, such as "Meaning and Understanding in the History of Ideas," and then *The Foundations of Modern Political Thought*.[4] After Skinner I read Richard Tuck's *Natural Rights Theories*.[5] I decided to apply to Cambridge to get my doctorate and work with Skinner and Tuck.

How did you find your dissertation topic?

Through failure. I had come to Cambridge to extend a research paper on the seventeenth-century English political theorist James Harrington's use of the notion of the "Hebrew Republic" in his *Commonwealth of Oceana*. I thought I would work on the late Renaissance literature of the "Respublica Hebraeorum." In the end, that project didn't work out, and neither did a subsequent one on the history of Jewish political thought as formulated by Jews in Italy in the fifteenth, sixteenth, and seventeenth centuries.[6]

By then it was March of my first year at Cambridge. In the back of my mind was a sense that the clock was ticking, that I had a three-year grant for my PhD, and already six months had gone by. The only way to figure something out in a hurry was to go back to a more familiar subject, English history. I hadn't read anything about the eighteenth century, so I decided that's what I would do—a crazy decision masquer-

---

3. J. G. A. Pocock, *The Ancient Constitution and the Feudal Law: A Study of English Historical Thought in the Seventeenth Century* (Cambridge, 1957).

4. Quentin Skinner, "Meaning and Understanding in the History of Ideas," *History and Theory* 8, no. 1 (1969): 3–53; Skinner, *The Foundations of Modern Political Thought*, 2 vols. (Cambridge, 1978).

5. Richard Tuck, *Natural Rights Theories: Their Origin and Development* (Cambridge, 1981).

6. On this topic see, for instance, Abraham Melamed, *Wisdom's Little Sister: Studies in Medieval and Renaissance Jewish Political Thought* (Brighton, 2011).

ading as a practical one. Skinner, who had very patiently followed me along through the two previous dissertation topics, had several concrete suggestions about the bibliography. It was a relatively easy dissertation to write—all printed materials. Cambridge was a very good place to do the reading, and what wasn't in Cambridge was in the British Library.[7]

But those failed topics and, maybe more, that ideal of cultivation, remained lodged in my mind. The following year, my second at Cambridge, I spent my spare time checking out musical recordings from the public library for my own education. Eventually, my weekend borrowings got me to Claudio Monteverdi's opera *L'incoronazione di Poppea* (1643). I signed it out on a Friday and spent the Saturday night sitting in the living room of my rickety apartment overlooking Midsummer Common listening to the opera while reading the libretto. I recognized many of the themes from early modern Venetian political writing. The same curiosity had also gotten me to audit a lecture course on Monteverdi that term. At a certain point, I put some ideas down on paper and wrote a letter to the professor who was giving the course, Iain Fenlon. This was the origin of a little collaborative book we wrote on Monteverdi and his local intellectual context. It was the road that brought my research back to the Continent, though I didn't then know it.[8]

Through the Monteverdi project I got interested in Stoicism, especially the early modern philologist and neo-Stoic Justus Lipsius. Through Lipsius I came to Peter Paul Rubens, because Rubens did the illustrations for Lipsius's works. A couple of years later I visited Antwerp and saw the Plantin-Moretus Museum and Rubens's House and became fascinated by Rubens the man. There I bought a paperback translation of Rubens's letters.[9] Among those letters were many written to one Nicolas Fabri de Peiresc. From the way Rubens wrote to him it was clear that his correspondent knew a huge amount about many different topics at a very serious level. I was curious about who this person was.

Peiresc was an unusual choice for someone who had written about eighteenth-century British political thought.

Yes. I often describe the Peiresc project as my *Habilitationsschrift*—a second work in an entirely different field. I was at a time in my life—the

---

7. Peter N. Miller, *Defining the Common Good: Empire, Religion and Philosophy in Eighteenth-Century Britain* (Cambridge, 1994).

8. Peter N. Miller and Iain Fenlon, *The Song of the Soul: Understanding 'Poppea'* (London, 1992).

9. Peter Paul Rubens, *The Letters of Peter Paul Rubens*, ed. and trans. Ruth Saunders Magurn (Cambridge, MA, 1955).

end of my six years in Cambridge—when I didn't have a lot of commitments. I was applying for jobs. My first book was out of my hands. In Paris in December of that year [1992], at Vrin's secondhand shop in the Place de la Sorbonne, I picked up both the *Life of Peiresc* by the seventeenth-century French philosopher Pierre Gassendi and Peiresc's letters to the Italian scholar Cassiano dal Pozzo.[10] After reading them, I turned to the riches of the Cambridge University Library. I wandered the stacks pulling books about Peiresc. It was entirely nonutilitarian; I had no idea that I would spend the next twenty-five years of my life doing this. I was curious: Who was this man? What was there to know about him?

In June 1993, I was in Venice for some research into what was intended to be a follow-up book on Monteverdi (it became an article instead). While in Venice, I read Peiresc's letters to the Italian humanists Lorenzo Pignoria and Paolo Gualdo. Going to the Biblioteca Nazionale Marciana every day, walking through Piazza San Marco, hearing the sounds of the lagoon through the open windows of the reading room during a month of glorious weather—it was dreamy. Peiresc's handwriting, which is clear enough that even without any training I was able to read it, took me back with him to Aix. It may sound a bit ridiculous, but we researchers are also humans, and human experiences can affect our research mind. I don't especially remember the content of those letters, but I certainly remember that the experience of reading them felt like the life I wanted to have.

The other life-changing experience that summer was a three-week seminar on early modern European intellectual history at the Folger Shakespeare Library in Washington, DC, organized by Donald R. Kelley and Constance Blackwell.[11] I worked there on Peiresc's studies in Egyptology, and did research both in the Folger and in the Library of Congress. The footnotes of a recent book on Peiresc and Egypt indicated the wealth of the surviving manuscript materials and how much there was yet to do.[12] My seminar presentation at the Folger was the first time I spoke about Peiresc in public.

---

10. Pierre Gassendi, *Vie de l'illustre Nicolas-Claude Fabri de Peiresc, conseiller au Parlement d'Aix*, trans. Roger Lassalle (Paris, 1992); Nicolas-Claude Fabri de Peiresc, *Lettres à Cassiano dal Pozzo (1626–1637)*, ed. Jean-François Lhote and Danielle Joyal (Clermont-Ferrand, 1989).

11. The seminar generated the volume *History and the Disciplines: The Reclassification of Knowledge in Early Modern Europe*, ed. Donald R. Kelley (Rochester, 1997).

12. Sydney H. Aufrère, *La momie et la tempête: Nicolas-Claude Fabri de Peiresc et la curiosité égyptienne en Provence au début du XVIIe siècle* (Avignon, 1989).

When did you start to see yourself as a historian of antiquarianism?

The Folger was a caravan stop between Cambridge and the University of Chicago, where I arrived in the fall of 1993 as a postdoctoral fellow. My thinking about antiquarianism emerged out of my work on Peiresc, but slowly. I spent my first year there reading about early modern European Oriental studies and preparing for a first research trip to Carpentras, where Peiresc's manuscripts reside in the municipal library. I made a list of the ones that seemed to contain the greatest concentration of materials documenting his interest in the East. Oriental studies, an expansion of my earlier interest in Egyptology, provided the guiding thread at the start, not antiquarianism.

At the core of what became, two decades later, my book *Peiresc's Mediterranean World*, are two volumes in Carpentras that I remember marking out for special examination on that research trip in June 1994.[13] I turned their pages but couldn't read a thing. Peiresc's handwriting was clear, but as I looked at those volumes with copies of his letters to the Levant I saw the hands of his secretaries—he had ten or twelve over the years—and thought to myself, "How am I ever going to do this?"

I was fascinated by the fact that in the dossiers of his outgoing correspondence, which were organized alphabetically by recipient, he sometimes filed the additional letters that accompanied those to the named recipient. The filing system marked out his lines of communication, tracing for us like some radioactive isotope the unknown people who marked the route of the letters to the Levant: in Marseille, the portuary fixers, ship owners, ships' captains, and then in Egypt, Syria, and Lebanon, the merchants, merchant-diplomats, and random itinerants. If the main letters tended to be addressed to the more intellectual types, such as aristocratic travelers or missionaries—the sort of people studied by my friend Joan-Pau Rubiés, from whose work I have learned so much—these others were aimed at those below the scholarly radar, at people whose names mean nothing to us now, people a bit like Robert Boyle's "invisible assistants."[14] I was interested in that plenitude of communication. But, again, what to do with it? I had no clue. This was not the kind of intellectual history that had interested me as an undergraduate, nor the kind I had myself written as a graduate student and assistant professor. I told

---

13. Peter N. Miller, *Peiresc's Mediterranean World* (Cambridge, MA, 2015).

14. See, for instance, the essays collected in Joan-Pau Rubiés, *Travellers and Cosmographers: Studies in the History of Early Modern Travel and Ethnology* (Aldershot, 2007).

myself I was bringing the kind of conceptual analysis used by the Cambridge school to the sort of history of scholarship practiced by Tony Grafton, and applying this combination to the study of nonscholars. But how?

I took away from that initial visit to the Peiresc archive both an enormous sense of possibility and of difficulty—there was no way I could make anything meaningful out of what I sensed was very rich material. I couldn't read the writing, and, even if I could have, I knew that I didn't yet know what questions would enable me to find interesting answers in those pages.

Instead, to buy myself time, I identified the more or less self-contained stories about how Peiresc studied Oriental languages and history. Imagining that archive as a giant marble slab, I planned to chisel off these self-contained blocks. They were materials in Peiresc's hand deriving from some of his discrete projects. I spent about a decade publishing these and they were eventually collected in *Peiresc's Orient*.[15]

While working on this I began, very much on the side, to collect later references to Peiresc. This was at first a passive endeavor. Later, I realized that the trail also marked out a rough history of antiquarianism. The narrow focus eventually became the appendix on Peiresc's reception in *Peiresc's Mediterranean*. The wider one turned into my recent book *History and Its Objects*.[16] It was only after finishing my first book on Peiresc, *Peiresc's Europe*, that I began to think about antiquarianism as the frame for understanding him.[17] Later, I probed the subject of antiquarianism with greater synchronic and diachronic range in two volumes I edited, *Antiquarianism and Intellectual Life in Europe and China* and *Momigliano and Antiquarianism*.[18]

What makes Peiresc so fruitful for thinking about early modern history?

For one thing, he left behind an archive. The fact that he was such a thorough self-compiler and that his materials remained unstudied for so

---

15. Peter N. Miller, *Peiresc's Orient: Antiquarianism as Cultural History in the Seventeenth Century* (Aldershot, 2012).

16. Peter N. Miller, *History and Its Objects: Antiquarianism and Material Culture since 1500* (Ithaca, 2017).

17. Peter N. Miller, *Peiresc's Europe: Learning and Virtue in the Seventeenth Century* (New Haven, 2000).

18. Peter N. Miller and François Louis, eds., *Antiquarianism and Intellectual Life in Europe and China, 1500–1800* (Ann Arbor, 2012); Peter N. Miller, ed., *Momigliano and Antiquarianism: Foundations of the Modern Cultural Sciences* (Toronto, 2007).

long—and thus preserved pretty much in the form he left them—made him a scholar's bonanza lying in wait. The material condition of possibility of Peiresc-as-observatory is that archive of over seventy thousand pieces of paper.

Then there is the way he refracts so many important themes. In the mid-1990s, just as I was discovering Peiresc's study of the Samaritans, and exploring the inclusion of Samaritan material in early modern polyglot Bibles, I was also trying to tie up a book about Stoicism in seventeenth-century culture. But then I realized that I could write a book on Stoicism in the seventeenth century that would at the same time serve as an introduction to Peiresc. His personal comportment, religion, social life, political activism, and, yes, his sense of the past seemed to exemplify what I had been reading in books about seventeenth-century England, Italy, Spain, and France. Moreover, I also realized that I couldn't really count on more than a handful of people to know who Peiresc was. If I was eventually to tackle all those manuscripts in Carpentras, with their stunning detail—and it was clear to me that it was in the detail that his interestingness, if not divinity, would be found—then I would first have to write a more general introduction to why he was worth knowing about. That was the conceptual origin of *Peiresc's Europe*.[19]

What has always excited me about early modern history is its ferment. New worlds, new continents, new genres, new learned disciplines, new technologies, new foods, new sources, new social classes, new political expectations—all these collisions, which made for much precariousness and suffering, also made for great intellectual creativity. Could we even say that Peiresc's kind of curiosity is an early modern thing? Or, maybe, an expression of what could happen to the right sort of mind living in a collision zone like the South of France at that time?

Finally, biography is an ideal means of capturing the encyclopedic ambitions of the Baroque period. We marvel at people like Peiresc, or the Jesuit scholar Athanasius Kircher, who seem to have ranged so broadly. The *Wunderkammer* is for us a puzzle because we think of its undertakings as separate and their pursuit by one person as extreme. It seemed clear to me that if one person were doing things that to us seem distinct from each other or that we categorize as different activities or disciplines it must mean those things were not so different for that person. The blunt fact of biographical reality provided me with a justification for assuming connections among studying nature, studying antiquities, and

19. Miller, *Peiresc's Europe*.

studying living peoples. If these three pursuits could coexist within one head, it seemed to me that there had to be some connection among them. This was biography as an answer, at least from a methodological point of view, to the narrow problem of writing about the idiosyncratic encyclopedism of the Baroque age and the wider one of the relations between disparate intellectual fields as then practiced. I hadn't read Dilthey on biography at the time I formulated this thought, but if I had I would have used his word, "nexus."[20]

The subtitle of Peiresc's Europe *is* Learning and Virtue in the Seventeenth Century. *How did the research for that book influence your understanding of the early modern Republic of Letters, and the moral dimensions of scholarly community?*

Learning and Virtue was my way of saying that an important element of the history of European scholarship had been ignored. Craig Clunas, a historian of Chinese art, said of Peiresc, "Ah! A Late Ming intellectual." He meant that the Chinese antiquarian tradition, both in itself and in how it has been studied, acknowledges the sentimental relationship that can exist between scholar and scholarship.[21] Not all European scholars may have felt this, or given expression to those feelings, but *modern* scholarship on European antiquarianism has almost entirely suppressed that side of the early modern venture.[22]

Learning is such a nonerudite term. By talking about it, I was suggesting, for those who had an ear for it, that this wasn't going to be just a history of erudition. In the world of classical Jewish learning people use the word to refer to a way of being. Not just "what are you learning?" but also "how's the learning going?" *Learning* does not refer just to content but also to practice and a whole set of experiential conditions. It could even approach devotion. By contrast, *erudition* seems thin and wan.

If *learning* referred to a whole way of life then it might actually have paired better with *Bildung*, a word that acquired its force in the German eighteenth century but that reeks too much of Goethe and Biedermeier

20. See Wilhelm Dilthey, *Selected Works*, vol. 3, *The Formation of the Historical World in the Human Sciences*, trans. Rudolf A. Makkreel and John Scanlon (Princeton, 2002).

21. See Craig Clunas, *Superfluous Things: Material Culture and Social Status in Early Modern China* (Urbana, 1991).

22. For an exception, see Charles Mitchell, "Archaeology and Romance in Renaissance Italy," in *Italian Renaissance Studies*, ed. E. F. Jacob (London, 1960), 455–83.

to use without qualification. And for those who did know what it connoted, it might have seemed too anachronistic to use it for the early seventeenth-century Franco-Italian world. So I chose *virtue*, which does much the same work, though without the specific social element and with a greater emphasis, in English anyway, on morality.

It never felt anachronistic to think about Peiresc in terms of this pairing of virtue and learning because it was how he lived his life, even if he did not self-consciously describe it that (or any other) way. This was clearly an advantage of a loosely biographical focus: it cut through the later categories we might want to impose on the past. Arnaldo Momigliano in his 1970 Harvard lectures on biography in ancient Greece made the point that the same word, *bios*, referred both to the world and to the life.[23] This dual meaning, he argued, provided the theoretical underpinning for the kind of reconstructive scholarship practiced by antiquarians and biographers. The antiquary and the biographer had only to place the facts on an existing scaffolding, not to assemble the scaffolding (the argument) and then mount the facts. Momigliano was probing this parallelism because he was interested in what the "parahistorical" genres—to use the term coined by the intellectual historian Mark Phillips—like biography and antiquarian writing could tell us about the more familiarly historical ones. I was interested in the relationship between professionalized learning and the person.

How did you find your way to your book Peiresc's Mediterranean World?

It goes back to trying, and failing, to read those two, big, bound registers of Peiresc's letters to merchants, ships' captains, and anonymous portuary folk which I looked at on my first trip to Carpentras in 1994. Not only could I not read them, I didn't know how to use them. They fell right into the category of source Francis Bacon described in *The Advancement of Learning* (1605) as "passages of books that concern not story."[24] Nothing I had done up to that point had prepared me for dealing with this material. I had to figure it out myself.

Eventually, of course, I did, mostly through the usual hitting-one's-head-against-the-wall-repeatedly approach. But then I realized that reading

---

23. Arnaldo Momigliano, *The Development of Greek Biography: Four Lectures* (Cambridge, MA, 1971).
24. Francis Bacon, *The Advancement of Learning* (New York, 2001), 77.

them wasn't actually the biggest problem. I could get the words, but the tiny little facts that studded the letters, like instructions about moving packages, or the shape of the quarantine regime in Marseille, or about grain prices, or the names of anonymous denizens of the quays—what to make of these?

I learned from archaeology, beginning with the medieval historian Michael McCormick's *Origins of the European Economy*. I admired how McCormick was able to squeeze information out of very few sources. My archaeological education then brought me to Ian Hodder and Michael Shanks and finally back to R. G. Collingwood.[25] Archaeologists are trained to extract information, to wring everything out of their sources, however few or many they have. I was thinking about this with Peiresc, who had a brilliant evidentiary imagination, which I would describe as the ability to imagine a particular thing as the answer to a number of different questions. I think that's something archaeologists are very good at doing. Historians, in particular we historians of more modern times, don't need to develop this particular muscle because we have so many sources to work with. The more sources there are, the less we need this ability to maximize the efficiency of extraction.

I took the archaeologist's approach to Peiresc's archive to see how I could squeeze as much as possible out of it. That got me thinking about Peiresc's connections with merchants and how to make sense of their presence in his archive. There were those two registers in Carpentras. I constantly asked myself the same series of questions. First, what did the presence of the merchants mean? But, then, how could I use it to illuminate Peiresc? How could I use Peiresc to illuminate his surroundings, whether the mass of those anonymous helpers or the physical setting in Marseille? How could I look at Peiresc against the public archive and the public archive against Peiresc? All those questions were just maneuvers to try and be like an archaeologist with my precious archive-tell and make sure that by the time I was finished I had done the best I could at squeezing data out of it.

Michael McCormick got me thinking about the Mediterranean in a serious way. However, I had written about Braudel's *Mediterranean* long before, in my graduate application to work with John Pocock.[26] The same sum-

---

25. Michael McCormick, *Origins of the European Economy: Communications and Commerce, A.D. 300–900* (Cambridge, 2001); Ian Hodder, *Entangled: An Archeology of the Relationships between Humans and Things* (Malden, 2012); Michael Shanks, *Experiencing the Past: On the Character of Archeology* (London, 1992).

26. Fernand Braudel, *The Mediterranean and the Mediterranean World in the Age of Philip the Second*, 2 vols., trans. Siân Reynolds (New York, 1972–73).

mer I read McCormick's book I also read Peregrine Horden and Nicholas Purcell's *The Corrupting Sea*.[27] Soon after, I taught a seminar on the Mediterranean that gave me a first chance to spend a lot of time with the six volumes of S. D. Goitein's *A Mediterranean Society*.[28] Discovering there the same pulsing, disorienting intensity of human detail I had encountered in Peiresc's archive, I began to read Goitein as a possible guide not only to medieval Cairo but also to early modern Marseille. His ability to find the stories in his fragments stayed with me as a model. Both McCormick's and Goitein's approaches resonated with me because they seemed also to be in harmony with how Peiresc himself had worked.

There's another thing about the archaeologists. What they do when they're turning an artifact around in different directions is ask questions. The artifact may give answers, but the answers are of much less weight, because they can be challenged from any number of directions. The questions can be much more fruitful. The work of R. G. Collingwood has been very important to me because he offers a hermeneutical theory based not only on question-asking but specifically on the question-asking of archaeologists. It helped that he was professor of both philosophy and archaeology at Oxford. I can't imagine there have been too many others who have held both of these chairs simultaneously! I had known about Collingwood for a long time. Quentin Skinner had told me the story about how walking past the Albert Memorial every day during World War I on his way to work had led Collingwood to formulate the notion that historical understanding had to be of "ideas in context." But it was only when I read Collingwood's *Autobiography* that I realized how his approach to the Albert Memorial—the "ideas in context" which gave its name to Skinner's book series in which my dissertation was published—derived from his practice as a field archaeologist.[29]

I started from the sources. But as the project on Peiresc unfolded over the course of many years, I followed a parallel process framed not around archaeology and method but place and method. A long conversation with the French historian Marc Fumaroli, who had been an inspiration when I was reading seventeenth-century French and Italian literature,

27. Peregrine Horden and Nicholas Purcell, *The Corrupting Sea: A Study of Mediterranean History* (Malden, 2000).

28. Shelomo Dov Goitein, *A Mediterranean Society: The Jewish Communities of the Arab World as Portrayed in the Documents of the Cairo Geniza*, vol. 1, *Economic Foundations* (Berkeley, 1967).

29. R. G. Collingwood, *An Autobiography* (Oxford, 1939), 30–31.

impressed upon me the stakes in recovering the story of the French Mediterranean.[30] I realized that this was Peiresc's story and that no one else would be in a position to rethink the early seventeenth century in terms of a French Mediterranean. Everyone interested in this subject was obsessed by the French conquest of Algeria and its aftermath—or by its prequel under Colbert and Louis XIV.[31] The conversation with Fumaroli led me to read Braudel again and Goitein for the first time.

Goitein's genizah-eyed view of the Mediterranean helped me realize that what I had been struggling with as the *how*—Bacon's "passages of books that concern not story"—actually constituted the *what* to a different set of questions. I was finishing my essays on Peiresc's Oriental studies and was faced with the choice of writing a book on the general subject of European Oriental studies or else pursuing Peiresc across the Mediterranean. Once the penny dropped, and I saw that a Mediterranean framing was a way of getting the Peiresc archive to tell a different kind of history, the decision was made for me.

We haven't yet talked about your intellectual interest in Arnaldo Momigliano. What did you learn from his scholarship?

Momigliano's point that modern cultural history had its origins in early modern antiquarianism was extremely important to me.[32] It's a throwaway line in his Sather Lectures (delivered at UC Berkeley in 1961–62 but left unfinished and published posthumously in 1990).[33] It got me thinking a lot about the much longer arc to that history. I was always looking at early modern scholarship, and Peiresc's scholarship specifically, with an interest in what we might call ethnography, customs, and rituals. These topics did not seem antiquarian in the strict sense, because the modern recuperation of antiquarian scholarship was driven by art historians interested in the classical tradition in art. However, Momi-

30. Marc Fumaroli, *L'Âge de l'éloquence: Rhétorique et "res literaria" de la Renaissance au seuil de l'époque classique* (Geneva, 1980); *Héros et orateurs: Rhétorique et dramaturgie cornéliennes* (Geneva, 1990); *L'École du silence: Le sentiment des images au XVIIe siècle* (Paris, 1994).

31. See *Levant: Guide du livre orientaliste: Eléments pour une bibliographie*, ed. C. and N. Hage Chahine (Paris, 2000).

32. Arnaldo Momigliano, "Ancient History and the Antiquarian," *Journal of the Warburg and Courtauld Institutes* 13, no. 3/4 (1950): 285–315.

33. Arnaldo Momigliano, *The Classical Foundations of Modern Historiography* (Berkeley, 1990).

gliano did think about antiquarianism broadly, most famously when he linked Peiresc to Galileo via their mutual commitments to empirical observation. By casting antiquarianism as the ancestor of cultural history, Momigliano provided an epistemic framework for thinking about how antiquarianism could have functioned in the seventeenth century.

You are recovering the role of antiquarianism in the genealogy of various modern scholarly disciplines. What is at stake in reclaiming the significance of the early modern antiquary in that genealogical sense?

There's no one red thread on which to pull and unravel the history of the disciplines. The antiquarians of the sixteenth and seventeenth centuries spent a lot of time working between traditions of learning, asking questions about past things and past institutions that no one had asked before, or at least not in a very long time. Their answers pulled data from different places, what we might consider different disciplines. But they were working *before* most of those disciplines existed. If, today, we imagine interdisciplinarity in an inevitably dialectical relationship with disciplinarity, then the antiquarians' predisciplinarity offers us an open field for thinking about how to find our questions.

And then there is the impact of antiquarianism on history itself. I'd argue that the modern discipline of history has in its DNA both antiquarian heritage and the rejection of that heritage. Above all, the main contribution of the antiquarian to the modern practice of history was a method of research. Before the antiquarians, as Momigliano pointed out, historians rewrote the work of their ancient predecessors. It was the antiquaries who made the discovery and harvesting of new sources the mark of success.

But just as exciting to me was what it might mean for antiquarianism to have been the seedbed of the modern cultural sciences—Momigliano's throwaway line in his Sather Lectures. To put it the other way around, it was exhilarating to think that the decay products of Renaissance antiquarianism were the modern disciplines of archaeology, art history, anthropology, and sociology. Knowing that genealogy seemed a way to unravel some otherwise hard-to-explain features of the modern disciplines. Moreover, the persistence of antiquarianism itself within the discipline of history—its survival in the practice of cultural history—was something to unriddle.

In a recent essay on Peiresc's medieval scholarship, you proposed
a theory of historiography in which nineteenth-century historical
scholarship, generally taken as canonical, emerges as an outlier,
whereas its twentieth-century counterpart shares many similarities
with early modern practices.[34] *Can we really see a deep continuity*
between modern historical scholarship and a historical practice
from hundreds of years ago?

My sense is that what we take to be the canonical form of history might actually have been an exception. The standard narrative has Edward Gibbon bringing the antiquary's toolkit to the writing of history and thus simultaneously creating modern historiography while relegating the antiquaries to the dustbin. We think of Gibbon, Ranke, Macaulay, and a few other nineteenth-century historians as the canon. Academic history-writing from Ranke onward, and then outward from Germany, ripples across the centuries all the way to us. At least that's the received view. But what about the antiquaries? They didn't stop doing work in 1776 when Gibbon published the first volumes of his *Decline and Fall of the Roman Empire*, and there's more than a little of the antiquarian still alive in the twentieth-century academic monograph.

When I described this perception to a neighbor, the literary scholar Morris Dickstein, in the elevator of my old apartment building, he told me that Robert Alter had written a book about the history of the novel whose argument had this same shape.[35] For both historical and novelistic writing there is a moment toward the end of the eighteenth century when the desire for a certain narrative illusionism takes over. The interest of the writer or the historian in talking about the sources in the Pompidou Center–like way of writing a book—think of *Tristram Shandy*, for instance, or even the kind of history that is *Joseph Andrews*—gives place to realism. Compare Fielding or Diderot, not to mention Cervantes and Rabelais, to Scott or Dickens or Trollope, and you have pretty much the same relationship of the antiquarians to Gibbon and Ranke. Alter argues that it's in the twentieth century, with Joyce and the Modernists, that the pendulum swings back to a reflexiveness about practice, voice, sources, and timing. And the academic monograph is also all about those things.

34. See Peter N. Miller, "Peiresc's *History of Provence*: Antiquarianism and the Discovery of a Medieval Mediterranean," *Transactions of the American Philosophical Society* 101, no. 3 (2011): esp. 88–91.
35. Robert Alter, *Partial Magic: The Novel as a Self-Conscious Genre* (Berkeley, 1978).

That's when I got to thinking that the canonical view of what historical scholarship is, just like the canonical view of what the novel is, might be upside down. Hayden White's *Metahistory*, for example, takes as representative of historical practice a group of nineteenth-century historians (Ranke, Macaulay, Guizot, Burckhardt).[36] My point is that, seen in the long view, this kind of historical writing is actually the exception. It was not true of the sixteenth and seventeenth centuries and much of the eighteenth, and it is equally untrue of the twentieth and the twenty-first, where the academic monograph has reigned supreme.

I made an additional point in *History and Its Objects*, a book I envisioned as the companion piece to *Peiresc's Mediterranean*. As I argued there, the nineteenth century is full of antiquarianism, full of object-based historical scholarship. The nineteenth century had far more than just academic history à la the German historical school. Its full spectrum included lots of other past-lovers: the local erudites, the historians working outside of the university, the curators, the connoisseurs, the reenactors, the novelists, the visual artists.[37]

The value of working with material culture is that standing in front of an artifact forces you to be much more aware that what you're really doing is writing about sources. It means acknowledging that you're writing about particular things from the past that have survived into the present and that you're fascinated by them. That's true of text as well; it can be a poem, it can be a manuscript. It doesn't have to be a rock or a piece of wood. But it's easy to be fooled and slip into the illusion that somehow a text or a book is only made of words and is therefore familiar, as opposed to artifacts, which are always threatening to escape from us. And more: with words we can easily slip into the habit of reading them with eyes trained in the intellectual traditions of the university. But the world is not carved up into disciplines. It comes at us as it is, and we have to figure it out on its own terms.

Historical objects almost always exceed our ability to explicate them fully. There's always more to them than we can recover. Object-focused accounts are therefore pitched from the start toward the imperfect part of the historical spectrum. Bacon identified the study of antiquities, the flotsam and jetsam of the past—"like the plank of a shipwreck" was his phrase—with just this type of "imperfect" history.[38] And so, finally, objects

---

36. Hayden V. White, *Metahistory: The Historical Imagination in Nineteenth-Century Europe* (Baltimore, 1973).

37. See Miller, *History and Its Objects*, 14–18.

38. See Bacon, *The Advancement of Learning*, 77.

can help us understand literary forms that reflect the inevitably fragmentary state of our knowledge of the past.

The attempt to tie things up with a bow is something else again. It's a different activity, motivated by different things. You can be fascinated by the past and be a splendid scholar at recovering it and yet have no interest in turning it into the kind of narrative that was so popular among historians and fiction writers from 1760 to 1860. We may actually have more of a tolerance for this kind of antiquarian-style "gappiness" than ever before. Walter Benjamin's desire to blow up historical narrative may itself have become "normalized" within the history of historical scholarship in just the way that the nonlinear, curatorial scholarship of the early modern antiquaries has been contextualized in a narrative of historical scholarship's own history—and then dismissed.

In your recent work, especially in Peiresc's Mediterranean, *you have been engaged in new, experimental forms of trying to tell history. How have you thought about new approaches to narrative and to presenting an archive?*

At a certain point, deep into finishing *Peiresc's Mediterranean*, I realized that there remained the problem that has always bedeviled those who have tried to write about antiquarianism: all of us are university-trained historians. How do we write about the kind of scholarship that academic history banished from academic training? This might not seem a huge problem; after all, anthropologists face it all the time. But, in fact, anthropologists write about their non-Western subjects using Western categories. Their empathy is about sustaining contact, not about the ways and means of interpretation and presentation. A historian writing about past beliefs, such as witchcraft, can try to think him- or herself back into the categories of those acting at the time. But the article or book that is then written is written as a scientist would write, not a shaman.

On the contrary, I wanted to write the history of the antiquarian as the antiquarian might have written it. Momigliano thought antiquarianism was over as a living thing and that we now study it the way we study all dead artifacts: contextually, scientifically. But if you didn't think the phenomenon dead, then autopsy, or the distanced prodding of an object with alien tools, might not be the best way of understanding how the thing moved and breathed. How does a thing work? The only way to answer the question might be to try and use it. Call it experimental archaeology for historians of scholarship. Somehow, modern historians have to shed their two centuries or so of accumulated ways of thinking. Then they can grasp the way of thinking that modern history so utterly replaced that no shred of it remains in the curriculum. The problem of a historian writing a history of antiquarianism is exactly the question that Derrida put to Foucault about writing the history of madness.[39] Can one write a history of a disposition or activity that seems the very opposite of historical writing?

Thinking about all of this, I wanted to find a way of writing *Peiresc's Mediterranean* so as to present the reader with as unfiltered an early modern experience as I could. I wanted to write the book as the actors themselves might have written it or at least in a way that accorded with how they thought and worked. As I thought about it more, it made more and more sense. Why, for instance, did every academic book have to look the same? Every chapter with ten thousand words, and every book with eight chapters? There's no good reason for this, though I can think of a few bad ones, including the general length of the journal articles that serve as the building blocks for many monographs.

There's a serious historical point in this too. Antiquaries were comfortable putting their research above the line, so to speak, presenting huge chunks of text or images without much comment. But by the eighteenth century, historians were not just exiling citations to the bottom of the page or back of the book; they were also silently stitching their narratives together so as to eliminate lacunae. If the research-forward approach of the antiquary represented to the reader the state of knowledge, gaps and all, the narrative approach had the effect of representing the state of knowledge as what the writer happened to know. I was interested in undoing this sleight of hand. Much better to make clear, as Laurence Sterne did in *Tristram Shandy*, with its blank lines, paragraphs, and pages, exactly what we know and what we don't.

This antiquarian, research-forward approach also gave me the chance to grapple with another of the historian's dilemmas: whether to go diachronic or synchronic. It might seem that some stories simply write themselves in one or the other of these modes. But the historian is usually making a choice, and it's a fateful one. Putting the sources above the line licensed me to treat them all differently, depending on what best brought them to life.

39. See Ann Wordsworth, "Derrida and Foucault: Writing the History of Historicity," in *Post-Structuralism and the Question of History*, ed. Derek Attridge, Geoffrey Bennington, and Robert Young (Cambridge, 1987), 117–18.

My asking, "Why does every book have to be written the same way?" also has something to do with my personal history. The eight years I spent trying and failing to get a job left me with an ambivalent relationship to the corporate side of academia. I questioned the need to fit a slot whose parameters, such as period and place, are vestigial but whose qualifications are determined by ever-shifting local contexts, such as professional and institutional factors. Leaving eighteenth-century British political thought for Peiresc meant leaving one very crowded and easily identifiable field and moving to a wide open but also barely tracked research space. I remember sitting in the living room with my parents and my mother saying, "You're going to abandon your book on the eighteenth century. Nobody's going to read it because you're not in the field to defend it"—which, of course, is how it works. "And," she continued, "you're going to go into an area where there is no field. Is that a wise decision?" It's true, there was risk involved! But you've got to take your chances. That's the point of being in a creative profession—the other side of academia, and the one I identify with more fervently, even now that I am a dean. I went off in my own direction, and I liked constituting my own intellectual community for myself, dispersed across different institutions and different continents.

It so happened that I wound up in a place that mirrors this, an institution in the form of a critique. The Bard Graduate Center (BGC) was founded as an answer to the limitations of art history as a discipline and as an attempt to embrace what was excluded from art history, such as study of the decorative arts. But, over time, both because art history as a discipline has changed and become more attentive to material and materials and because of our internal culture of conversation, Bard's institutional focus has changed. Now it's more focused on the different ways in which the human sciences help us understand the world through things. Another way to say this is that the BGC aims to reconstitute the antiquarian synthesis using the tools of its successor disciplines. Though I didn't know anything about the decorative arts when I arrived here in 2001, I was already dimly aware that the institution's telos could be found in the history of antiquarianism. Certainly the art historical study of objects had its modern origin with the antiquaries, but so did the history of studying objects as historical evidence. Over the course of the later eighteenth century and the first part of the nineteenth, the historical and aesthetic motivations for studying objects separated. The received account places this separation in the biography of the other great eighteenth-century historian of the ancient world, Johann Joachim

Winckelmann. He was an antiquarian, a historian, and an aesthete of great sensitivity. What he could hold together in a tension could not be sustained. So, too, the academic discourse that was launched by his contemporary and detractor Christian Gottlob Heyne. Winckelmann talked of "history of ancient art" (*Geschichte der Kunst des Alterthums*) and Heyne "archaeology of art" (*Archäologie der Kunst*). If Heyne's term kept much more explicit faith with the antiquarian heritage, the category he created eventually fell apart into historical and aestheticizing wings. This is, writ large, the tension at work today between history and art history and also between art historians who are more oriented to the objects as evidence and those for whom the primary connection is wonder at the thing itself. The legacy survives in the names of university departments: Art and Archaeology, Archaeology and Anthropology.

In a way, I have found in the history of my institution the history of a wider field. Being in this observatory has led me to pay a lot more attention to institutional questions but also freed me to experiment a lot more with my thinking about antiquarianism, outside of the constraints of those disciplinary frontier guards Aby Warburg spoke of in Ferrara in 1912.[40]

What about antiquarianism today? Is there any? Does it still exist?

Momigliano ended his famous essay by saying that antiquarianism was dead but that if it were to revive, this would happen in France.[41] I'm fascinated by what I take to be its contemporary forms among poets, artists, and writers who might know nothing of early modern scholars and yet produce work driven by the same passions. As I mentioned in passing, it's also true that the contemporary academic monograph is an ironically antiquarian piece of scholarship. It offers a thematic, structural, synchronic way of mastering sources and illustrating them. It's ironic, of course, because the monograph was part of the effort to overcome antiquarianism, once and for all. Even the persistent complaints about the narrowness of academic scholarship and writing echo those made two or more centuries ago about antiquarians. Replace *academic*

40. Aby Warburg, "Italian Art and International Astrology in the Palazzo Schifanoia, Ferrara," in *The Renewal of Pagan Antiquity* (Los Angeles, 1999), 563–91.

41. "France remained traditionally the best home for the antiquaries until not so many years ago." Momigliano, "Ancient History and the Antiquarian," 312.

in today's dismissiveness with the *antiquarian* of yesterday's, and there's a real continuity.

But, in fact, the antiquarian heritage actually allows for much more play in both writing and thinking, and it's closer to the reality of the past as it survives into the present. Part of being a historian is interposing a crafted narrative between those traces of the past and the reading public. But we don't have the answers, however much we historians have gotten used to representing ourselves as having them. At best, we can try to ask more interesting questions. In *Truth and Method*, Hans-Georg Gadamer identifies the historicist project of understanding the past in its own terms with the hermeneutics espoused by Friedrich Schleiermacher in the early nineteenth century.[42] He contrasts this approach with that of Hegel, who argued that the past as experienced, felt, and thought was to us a closed book. There simply was no way back. From this perspective, historicism is fundamentally *ahistorical* because it proposes a mythical encounter between past and present. But objects are different. They come from the past, but survive into *our* present. In them, Hegel's caesura is bridged. There is through them a connection between present and past. Not only, then, do objects offer a possible source for history, but I think the argument could be made that they are essential to doing history.

The antiquarian, source-based approach also has the effect of bringing the pursuers of the past into a much closer conversation with artists. David Macaulay's architectural illustrations, Erik Desmazières's prints of ancient and modern *Kunst- und Wunderkammern*, Mark Dion's reconstructions of early modern research spaces, and Grisha Bruskin's polemical archaeological installations all reflect serious thinking about the early modern study of historical objects. Michael Shanks, with whom I first connected over the way he studied the imaginative Scottish Borders antiquaries of the early nineteenth century, like Sir Walter Scott, is someone whose thinking about things spans the historical and the performative. With Mike Pearson he has been performing *Theatre/Archaeology* for over twenty years and using it to explore the way in which past things live on into our present and shape our futures.[43] All of this is a kind of living antiquarianism that Momigliano did not think about.

---

42. Hans-Georg Gadamer, *Truth and Method*, trans. Josel Weinsheimer and Donald G. Marshall (London, 2004).

43. Michael Shanks and Mike Pearson, *Theatre/Archaeology* (London, 1993). A second edition is forthcoming.

Looking ahead, what are the questions that you are interested in, and what questions are others asking that are interesting to you?

There's an inbuilt tendency to underestimate the impact of others on the formulation of our own questions, and I'm aware of that. After the war, whenever he was asked about a really thoughtful book, Fernand Braudel always asked whether it was written in prison. The point is that to be really original is always in tension with communication, with sociability, with community. I may have trained as a historian, but I've been in a history department for only two of the twenty-eight years since I received my PhD.

This means that there are some kinds of conversations that I have had fewer of and others that I have had more of. Over time this gives you a very different view of things. The conversation that began at the Folger in 1993, for instance, has taken me into many discussions about the Republic of Letters, history of philosophy, history of scholarship, and some history of science as well. At the BGC, because of the interests of my colleagues and the people they bring in, I've been immersed in the questions of art historians and anthropologists.

So, back to your question. I mentioned earlier that I came to think that research forwardness characterized the way antiquaries presented themselves to their readers. The contrast with historians' construction of narratives is one application to which I've put this thinking. Another is the question of research itself. I first paid attention to how Peiresc used the word to describe what he was doing and the ways research got parsed by him. But what is research, actually? Why do we do it? These are enormous questions. They point toward deep themes in the human psyche and in our collective life—and they span thousands of years.

If you were to give some advice, either to your former self or to someone starting out now and still trying to articulate an intellectual project, what would you say?

In 1869, at the age of twenty-four, Nietzsche was appointed to a chair in classical philology in Basel. He quit in 1879 and was on his winding way to Sils Maria. Over the course of that decade he gave his lectures—the introductory survey on classical philology, Greek sacred ritual, Homer— and wrote a few revolutionary books, *The Birth of Tragedy, Human, All*

Too Human, and the five *Untimely Meditations*. I have been reading the second *Meditation*, on history, now and again for the last thirty years. But only a couple of years ago did I read the fifth one, which he never finished, titled "We Philologists."[44] I was amazed at how valid his criticisms still are. When he says we train philology not the philologist, what he's really saying is, "We're making professional scholars but not intellectuals." We could read him as protesting the passing of the age of "learning and virtue" and calling out its consequences.

Nietzsche's exact contemporary was Wilhelm Dilthey—they just missed each other at Basel, the latter leaving as the former arrived. Very little has been written about their parallel projects. Dilthey's idea of hermeneutics, which identified the limits of understanding with the limits of self-understanding, could have been a possible answer to Nietzsche's challenge in "Wir Philologen." Dilthey argued that the more self-aware, the more developed, a scholar is as a person, the greater the opportunities for the scholarship that she will produce.[45] I think this is a powerful point. It's also one that isn't a part of professional training in the humanities.[46] So, my advice for those trying to find their question: in addition to "learn this language," or "learn this technique," or "master this data set," I would say, "pay attention to yourself. Be more self-conscious about your questions and your categories, and you will better be able to understand the human beings you study."

What do we lose by thinking of the past only in a historicist, contextual mode? Are there other forms of interpretation that might be dismissed as premodern or outdated, but that might offer resources for a closer, more affective relationship with the past?

We need to play more. My ears always perked up when I heard Peiresc ask a correspondent to indulge his "conjectures." That's when I knew I would catch him thinking out loud. Let's take the example of his conjecture of a connection between eruptions of volcanoes in Ethiopia and Sicily in 1631. He posited that there might be underground tubes that

44. Friedrich Nietzsche, *Unmodern Observations*, ed. William Arrowsmith (London, 1990).
45. See Wilhelm Dilthey, *Selected Works*, vol. 4, *Hermeneutics and the Study of History*, ed. Rudolf A. Makkreel and Frithjof Rodi (Princeton, 1996).
46. For an exception, see Paul Veyne, *Writing History: Essay on Epistemology*, trans. Mina Moore-Rinvolucri (1971; Middletown, 1984), 177–78.

connect the fire from one to the other. Of course, we know about plate tectonics. He didn't. But he was willing to speculate. No one then had the tools to explore this conjecture even had they taken it seriously. But, as we know, play is an essential part of discovery. We could learn worse things from the past.

It's somewhat ironic that humanists—but let's speak more narrowly of historians, who are no longer likely to believe in Truth with a capital *T*—have much more of a scholarly monoculture when it comes to format than the natural scientists, who are still committed to proving things about the world. Part of this may come down to writing and to the relationship between history and the novel. The nineteenth-century union between long-form fiction and long-form historical writing produced a one-size-fits-all approach. The diverse tribe of antiquarians wrote in many different formats, and fiction was written in different ways as well, both before Gibbon and after Burckhardt—but university-based history hasn't wanted to change.

When I was writing *Peiresc's Mediterranean World*, I thought a great deal about writing "as a cognitive tool," as Carlo Ginzburg once described it to me. Choosing a style, mood, or voice opens up scholarly possibilities. Think of what Arlette Farge was able to do in her history of the Parisian street in the eighteenth century, or Reyner Banham with his history of Los Angeles's highways in the twentieth.[47] Keeping to one style, mood, or voice the whole time actually limits one's thinking. Historians can learn a lot from writers. I'm not making a plea that historians turn from being analysts to raconteurs for a general public à la Macaulay. I'm saying that we can be better analysts when writing for other professionals if we are aware that writing is our particular technology and not some transparent container. The best writing isn't the clearest; it's the writing that best makes whatever argument we're trying to make.

There's a real opportunity here, and it's related to what we were just talking about: play. We need to incorporate much more play into our training of historians. Forget about big data as the solution to everything. It's imagination that we need to do interesting work, regardless of our sources and our tools. Without it we're the same sitting ducks Nietzsche took for target practice in 1874–75.

---

47. Arlette Farge, *Vivre dans la rue à Paris au XVIIIe siècle* (Paris, 1979); Reyner Banham, *Los Angeles: The Architecture of Four Ecologies* (1971; Berkeley, 2009).

A final question. You began by talking about the impact of reading Berlin's Russian Thinkers. Given the range of subjects, places, and periods you've written about, and with a nod to the most famous essay in that collection, would you describe yourself as a hedgehog or a fox?

I have always thought of myself as a fox. But I recently came across something I had written in 1986—it was actually my first published, learned article in a student journal—which has made me rethink that a little. It was a piece on the way Claude Lanzmann's 1985 documentary *Shoah* functioned as historical narrative. The central texts I worked through were Nietzsche's *On the Advantages and Disadvantages of History for Life* and Paul Veyne's *Writing History*. As I said before, I have returned to Nietzsche's second meditation many times since.

Veyne I did not read again until this past year. And yet there, in a text I read carefully three decades ago, is a discussion of antiquarianism (he calls it erudition and never mentions Momigliano) as the overlooked partner of history and even, perhaps, the core historical practice. He speculates about what a book written as erudition and not narrative might look like, insists on what historians can learn from novelists and playwrights, and even suggests that from this perspective the great age of history was not the nineteenth century, dominated by the narrativists, but the eighteenth, which was led by the erudites. In other words, the experiment I undertook in *Peiresc's Mediterranean World* was proposed here, in a work I had read thirty years earlier but whose existence, or at least content, I had completely forgotten![48]

Am I, then, a hedgehog in spite of myself? The historian of reading might note that these passages were not underlined or otherwise marked in 1986, so perhaps I had not taken in their meaning. Of course, maybe I could not have taken in their meaning without having read what I read and lived what I lived in the meantime. But still it is a stun-

---

48. Veyne, *Writing History*, 231–34: "The scholar does not tell stories or comment on the past, he shows it; in fact, he chooses and organizes it, and his work has the false impersonality of a documentary photomontage. Erudition is a variety of historiography to which we give too little thought; two centuries of historicist speculation have excessively associated 'history' with 'science' or 'philosophy,' whereas the natural place of history, the documentary knowledge of the concrete, is situated at the opposite pole, that of erudition. . . . One dreams then of a metahistory in which the account would be replaced by an assembling of documents chosen with as much flair as Shakespeare had for putting the right words in the mouths of heroes of historical plays. If the enterprise could be pushed to its limit, history would be a reconstitution and would cease to be discursive. . . . Is the great century of history the Romantic nineteenth century or the erudite eighteenth century?"

ning return, even if not to the same place. It's also a reminder of the magic in our encounter with books: you never know how what you read will affect you, will shape your future, will lodge in your memory. That's why giving books as gifts is such a wonderful thing. There are books that I received as gifts when a child that I read only as an adult—as gifts for a child they were spectacularly ill-chosen—with great profit. For the decades in between they just sat there on the shelf, biding their time, waiting for their moment.

Jean-Louis Quantin

JEAN-LOUIS QUANTIN is directeur d'études at the École Pratique des Hautes Études in Paris.

What were your early intellectual interests? When did you decide to pursue history, and intellectual history and the history of the Catholic Church in particular?

In France, the correct thing to say is that your intellectual biography started with an inspirational primary school teacher, but, in fact, I began entirely on my own. Although I had some very good teachers in French and Greek, I never had an interesting history teacher throughout primary and secondary school. But at eight I discovered the *History of the Dukes of Burgundy*, by the early nineteenth-century historian Prosper de Barante, which was famous in its day as a masterwork of Romantic history, a historiographical counterpart to Sir Walter Scott.[1] I remember finding that book in our country house and spending long Sundays reading its twelve volumes. Nothing at all to do with what I was taught at school! So I was always interested in history, but as a personal hobby. In France history is taught together with geography, and I had no interest in geography. In addition, we were chiefly taught modern history, which didn't attract me very much.

---

1. Prosper de Barante, *Histoire des ducs de Bourgogne de la maison de Valois, 1364–1477*, 12 vols. (Paris, 1824–26).

The first time I discovered the teaching of history was at seventeen, in the first of two years of classes that prepare students for the entrance exam to the so-called Grandes Écoles, in my case the École normale supérieure (ENS). In the second year, I specialized in modern literature and spent a lot of time reading what in the States you call French theory: Roland Barthes, and so on. I enjoyed myself immensely—it was quite fun—but all the same to a large extent I was trained as a charlatan. In Philip Roth's novel *The Human Stain* the French academic character, Delphine Roux, is portrayed rather cruelly as a complete fraud—the only thing that she masters is the idiom of literary criticism. It is a caricature, of course, but there is something to it. Especially when it came to English literature, I didn't know the language that well at the time, and yet I remember several classes in which we were made to imitate, if not to parody, Roman Jakobson's commentary on William Blake's "Infant Sorrow" without knowing very much either about Jakobson or about Blake![2] But, on the other hand, that training was not entirely a waste of time. It made me more alert than many historians, French ones at least, to how a text actually works. French social historians are often extremely naïve when it comes to using literary texts, and Dominick LaCapra has a point when he criticizes them for employing nineteenth-century novels as straightforward historical sources.[3] When I was seventeen, I was extremely impressed with Pierre Bourdieu's *Ce que parler veut dire*, which alerted me to the existence of layers of meaning.[4] For instance, when I later worked on the controversy of the Jansenists, the seventeenth-century Catholic reformers, against the Protestants, my literary training made it easier for me to realize that the Jansenists were not only writing against the Protestants but also testifying to their own orthodoxy, legitimizing themselves in the eyes of their Catholic peers. Their writings were also aimed at a hidden audience within the Roman Catholic Church.[5]

So those were my wild years! When I entered the ENS, serious things began; I decided to get over my dislike of geography and started studying history. Then, in my second year, I had to specialize in a period. I had studied quite a lot of ancient history in my first year: I had followed a course in Greek epigraphy, and I loved Greek. So I was strongly tempted to pursue a career as a Greek historian. But I also had a personal

---

2. Roman Jakobson, "On the Verbal Art of William Blake and Other Poet-Painters," *Linguistic Inquiry* 1, no. 1 (1970): 3–23, reproduced in Jakobson, *Language in Literature* (Cambridge, MA, 1987), ch. 29.

3. Dominick LaCapra, *History and Criticism* (Ithaca, 1985).

4. Pierre Bourdieu, *Ce que parler veut dire: L'économie des échanges linguistiques* (Paris, 1982). English version in Bourdieu, *Language and Symbolic Power* (Cambridge, 1991).

5. Jean-Louis Quantin, "De la Contre-Réforme comme monopole: Les anti-jansénistes et la *Perpétuité de la foi*," *Chroniques de Port-Royal* 47 (1998): 115–48.

interest in early modern history, largely on account of French literature. I had never been taught it as a subject, but, because of the status of seventeenth- and eighteenth-century literature in French traditional culture, I had read quite a lot of it. As a child, I used to read the seventeenth-century poet Nicolas Boileau (the French Alexander Pope) and knew his *Satires* by heart.

I tried to have it both ways: my idea was to work on the history of scholarship and on the way ancient history was studied in the seventeenth and eighteenth centuries. For what was called the *maîtrise* (which has disappeared now; it was a master's degree, and you wrote a minidissertation on a topic of your choosing), I worked on the myth of Sparta in the eighteenth century and, specifically, on the way Sparta was known through research at the Académie Royale des Inscriptions et Belles-Lettres, the French academy for philological and antiquarian studies. When it came time to decide on my doctoral dissertation, my initial idea was to continue studying the reception and study of classical antiquity, especially Greek. Just at that point, I met Chantal Grell, who was about to complete her large dissertation about ancient Greece and Rome in eighteenth-century France.[6] She pointed out that my work would likely overlap with hers and be redundant. She said, "Why don't you study Christian antiquity—there are comparatively few studies on it." So that is how I ended up studying the reception of the church fathers! I cannot pretend it was a deep intellectual calling; it was simply because initially I couldn't choose between early modern and ancient history and then because, comparatively, the field appeared less crowded than the study of classical antiquity. And I thought that by studying the reception of the fathers, I would be able to keep up my Greek, which has proved, I'm afraid, a delusion, because divines in the seventeenth century chiefly read the Latin fathers (and, when they did read the Greek fathers, they tended to use Latin translations).

When you became interested in the reception of Christian antiquity, to what books and scholars did you turn for orientation?

During my *maîtrise* on Sparta I realized that, if you wished to understand what early modern scholars had actually been doing, you needed

---

6. Chantal Grell, *Le dix-huitième siècle et l'antiquité en France, 1680–1789*, 2 vols. (Oxford, 1995).

to have some idea of what the sources and the challenges were. Having some tincture of Greek epigraphy proved very useful in order to understand, for instance, how Michel Fourmont, who was a member of the Académie des Inscriptions, fabricated a series of false Spartan inscriptions around 1730.[7]

In my fourth year at the ENS, I had the fortune of attending the seminar of Pierre Petitmengin, who was the librarian there and became an important influence. He had done some pioneering work on the history of philology and the study of the church fathers in sixteenth-century Rome, and he ran a small seminar group on Latin paleography.[8] This offered an initiation into Latin philology with a strong concentration, because of his own interests, on patristic texts. I was a member of this seminar for a year and, I must say, everything I know about Latin manuscripts and philology I owe to Pierre Petitmengin. He steered our small group in a piece of collective research on the reception of Irenaeus at the beginning of the sixteenth century, in the period immediately prior to the appearance of Erasmus's *editio princeps*, and this was a formative experience for me.[9]

As for early modern history, I relied for guidance on Bruno Neveu, my predecessor here at the École Pratique des Hautes Études (EPHE), which, like the ENS, is one of the bizarre institutions meant to supplement the universities. It was created under the Second Empire to do what French universities didn't do at all at the time, which now they are doing to some extent, namely primary research. Neveu couldn't serve as my official supervisor for institutional reasons but, through his own work on early modern French erudition, he was a major inspiration for trying to articulate the history of scholarship and the history of theology.[10]

---

7. Jean-Louis Quantin, "Connaître Sparte au XVIIIe siècle en France: Recherches sur les fondements historiques d'une représentation mythique" (maîtrise thesis, Université de Paris Sorbonne, 1988).

8. Pierre Petitmengin, "Deux 'Bibliothèques' de la Contre-Réforme: La Panoplie du Père Torres et la *Bibliotheca sanctorum patrum*," in *The Uses of Greek and Latin: Historical essays*, ed. A. C. Dionisotti, Anthony Grafton, and Jill Kraye (London, 1988), 127–53; Petitmengin, "*De adulteratis patrum editionibus*: La critique des textes au service de l'orthodoxie," in *Les Pères de l'Église au XVIIe siècle*, ed. Emmanuel Bury and Bernard Meunier (Paris, 1993), 17–31; Petitmengin, "Les éditions patristiques de la Contre-Réforme romaine," in *I Padri sotto il torchio: Le edizioni dell'antichità cristiana nei secoli XV–XVI*, ed. Mariarosa Cortesi (Florence, 2002), 3–31.

9. Jean-Louis Quantin (with Agnès Molinier, Pierre Petitmengin, Olivier Szerwiniack), "Irénée de Lyon entre humanisme et Réforme: Les citations de l'*Adversus haereses* dans les controverses religieuses de Johann Fabri à Martin Luther (1522–1527)," *Recherches augustiniennes* 27 (1994): 131–85.

10. Bruno Neveu, *L'erreur et son juge: Remarques sur les censures doctrinales à l'époque moderne* (Naples, 1993); Neveu, *Érudition et religion aux XVIIe et XVIIIe siècles* (Paris, 1994).

Neveu had worked at the EPHE with Jean Orcibal, whom I never met myself. But Bruno imagined a sort of apostolic succession from Orcibal to Neveu to me: there was a continuity of interest. In Orcibal's time, French religious history was dominated by quantitative history, by the idea that you should study so-called popular religion and primarily investigate what could be quantified: mass attendance, Easter communion, clauses in testaments, illegitimate children, you name it. It was a rather crude attempt to introduce the French methodology of the second generation of the Annales school into religious history, to produce what an Italian historian quite rightly described as an anti-institutional version of cultural history: don't look at theology because it was a discourse of the elite that had no interaction with what the peasants actually practiced, but measure those practices instead.[11] Orcibal was pretty much the only one in France at the time who thoroughly applied a philological method to religious history. He initially worked on Jansenism and wrote books on Cornelius Jansen, the founder of the movement, and Jansen's disciple and patron, the Abbé de Saint-Cyran. Later he wrote on the French archbishop François de Fénelon and mysticism.[12]

Bruno Neveu's original contribution was to introduce the huge corpus of early modern scholarship into religious history. He worked on the French scholar Louis-Sébastien Le Nain de Tillemont (1637–98), who was trained at Port-Royal, and who at the end of the seventeenth century produced a massive work, in twenty-two quarto volumes, on the history of Christian antiquity. Edward Gibbon relied on Tillemont's work greatly, and it remained influential until late in the twentieth century.[13] Neveu was able to show how the history of early modern scholarship could illuminate major topics such as religious feelings, attitudes to time, and conceptions of the church. Early modern scholarship constructed a model of the primitive church, the golden age of the church as they called it, which was very different from the present institutional papal church. Neveu was able to demonstrate that the Jansenist crisis— the movement of Jansenism within the French church and its critique of contemporary religious practice—should be understood to a large extent

11. Luigi Donvito, "Ricerche e discussioni recenti in Francia su un tema di storia della mentalità: Gli atteggiamenti collettivi di fronte alla morte," *Rivista di storia e letteratura religiosa* 13, no. 2 (1977): 376–89.

12. Jean Orcibal, *Jean Duvergier de Hauranne abbé de Saint-Cyran et son temps (1581–1638)* (Louvain-Paris, 1947–48); Orcibal, *Jansénius d'Ypres* (Paris, 1989); Orcibal, *Études d'histoire et de littérature religieuses: XVIe–XVIIIe siècles*, ed. J. Le Brun and J. Lesaulnier (Paris, 1997); *Correspondance de Fénelon*, ed. Jean Orcibal, 18 vols. (Paris-Geneva, 1972–2007).

13. Bruno Neveu, *Un historien à l'école de Port-Royal: Sébastien Le Nain de Tillemont 1637–1698* (The Hague, 1966).

as the opposition between an antiquarian, Augustinian, philological approach and what was later called the "living church" or the "living authority" of the church. From that point of view, I am greatly indebted to his work.

How did you go from working on French history to English religious history?

My dissertation studied the use of the church fathers in seventeenth-century France, chiefly during the last third of the seventeenth century.[14] It is largely an interpretation of Jansenism: I attempted to show how the return to primitive sources, to the church fathers, inspired a whole range of trends in French Catholicism; it influenced everything from spirituality and literature to liturgical reforms and pastoral choices. The result was to build a self-awareness of French Catholicism, a representation of the Gallican Church as especially pure and learned, albeit within the pale of Catholicism. This primitivist movement appeared to triumph at the end of the seventeenth century but it prepared the way for the crisis of the eighteenth-century French Church. It delegitimized many practices and institutions of post-Tridentine Catholicism, which were revealed to lack a proper foundation in antiquity. In effect, what happened in the church was the process that people were well aware of in the case of the state. In his *Pensées*, Blaise Pascal had explained that the surest way to overthrow a state was to claim to go back to its original constitution, because everything would be found faulty.[15] Moreover, religious primitivism inspired very harsh, "rigorist" pastoral practices (denial or delay of absolution, attempts to reintroduce forms of public penance, a crackdown on pastimes like dancing), as well as campaigns against some widespread forms of popular piety, of Marian devotion, et cetera, which created much resentment at the parochial level, and proved deeply divisive within the church.[16]

---

14. Jean-Louis Quantin, *Le catholicisme classique et les Pères de l'Église: Un retour aux sources (1669–1713)* (Paris, 1999).

15. "The art of criticizing and overthrowing States lies in unsettling established customs by delving to their core in order to demonstrate their lack of authority and justice. They say they have to go back to the fundamental and original laws of the State, which unjust custom has abolished. That is a sure way of losing everything; nothing will be just on those scales." Fragment Sellier 94, in Blaise Pascal, *Pensées and Other Writings*, trans. Honor Levi (Oxford, 1995), 24–25.

16. Jean-Louis Quantin, *Le rigorisme chrétien* (Paris, 2001).

After the ENS, unfortunately, I had to go into the vast world outside! I was a junior assistant at one of the universities of Lyon (Lumière–Lyon II) and not terribly happy there. Thanks to my Sorbonne supervisor, Jean-Pierre Poussou, the opportunity arose to go to Oxford on a fellowship from the French Ministry of Foreign Affairs for two years, from 1993 to 1995. I enjoyed total freedom. I completed my French dissertation there, since the Bodleian Library at the time was an extraordinary place for research even on French or Italian history. And then I started working on the Church of England. That was the origin of my second project, which turned me into a historian of England.

What was it like to study English history as someone coming from the outside?

In Oxford I always had the feeling that this was not my culture but something different. Yet it was close enough for me to have at least the illusion that I understood it—I don't think I would have been able to understand something completely different fully. I am not the sort of scholar who is able to go into a completely different culture! For instance, I enjoyed going to choral evensong in the chapels of the Oxford colleges. I remember being struck by the English of the Prayer Book, a vernacular language but not quite, with its subtle differences from the English I had learned, occasionally puzzling when you heard it for the first time ("our Father which art in heaven"), both familiar and strange. This was entirely new to me. But there were aspects of it—the restrained dignity, the seriousness, the dim religious light—that evoked seventeenth-century French religious culture. The Englishness of all that, the sense of a universal religion being enfleshed, as it were, in a national culture and a national history, I could relate to what I knew of Gallicanism. Even at a linguistic level, there was some analogy. You have to remember that, until it became Italianized in the 1920s, church Latin in France was pronounced in the Gallican manner: it was not French, of course, but it sounded like an archaic version of French, and people argued at the time that the French pronunciation kept Latin alive. Bruno Neveu, who attended Anglican worship regularly during his Oxford years, used to say half-jokingly, "It is the ancien régime church." This is not literally true, of course; the theological doctrines are not the same, but the religious styles are somehow akin.

Things have changed to a great extent in the last decades, but for a very long time English history and especially the history of the Church of England were written from a very insular perspective—from a point of view of English exceptionalism, of the unique English way. Coming at it from the Continent, with a background in Continental, especially French, history, gave me a different view. The notion, for instance, that interest in the church fathers was peculiar to the English Reformation was untenable. I knew that everybody at the time appealed to the fathers, albeit with different confessional agendas.

Were your English interlocutors receptive to your point of view?

I can say honestly that everybody I met in England was very generous. I never encountered the kind of confessional hostility that I experienced in the French Catholic context. In the aftermath of the Second Vatican Council, the idea of going back to the fathers became very trendy again in some sectors of the Catholic Church. In patristic studies in France, even in officially secular universities, there is still a massive presence of scholars with a crypto-Catholic agenda. My work on the seventeenth century suggested that patristic scholarship at that time had been very brilliant but had some unwanted and, from the point of view of its own practitioners and promoters, nefarious effects. Some people were outraged because they felt that I was somehow undermining the present position of their church and their interest in the fathers. And, since those people cannot even conceive that one might work on such topics without being driven by confessional motivations, one Catholic reviewer accused me of being nostalgic for nineteenth-century ultramontanism and its newfangled devotions!

In Britain, although these subjects were long studied in a very confessional way, people at present seem far less confessionally touchy. It may also be that people everywhere are more generous to a foreigner, a person who comes from outside and from whom you expect a different perspective anyway. Interestingly, when my book on the Church of England came out, the only review that assessed it in purely confessional terms appeared in a German journal: the reviewer concluded that I favored the American Reformed Episcopal Church, which, to my shame, I hadn't even heard of before—I know too little about the religious landscape in America![17] Some Anglican theologians, notably Paul Avis, who is a canon and was chaplain to the Queen, and therefore writes very much from within the institution, have expressed disagreement with my interpretation but in a very courteous and balanced manner.[18]

---

17. Review by Hanns Engelhardt, *Theologische Literaturzeitung* 136, no. 9 (September 2011): col. 924–26.
18. Paul Avis, *In Search of Authority: Anglican Theological Method from the Reformation to the Enlightenment* (London, 2014), 165–68 ("Critique of a Critique").

Could you tell us more about your encounter with the English scholar and theologian Henry Dodwell (1641–1711) and how you came to work on him?[19]

I don't quite remember how I encountered Henry Dodwell for the first time; it was during my time in Oxford, and it may have been through reading in a desultory way in the Bodleian Library. At the time, in the early 1990s, the Bodleian, and specifically Duke Humfrey's Library, the oldest reading room there, was a scholar's paradise. You could ask for as many books as you wanted, and you received everything; there was no limitation. Unfortunately, some unscrupulous people took advantage of it, which has obliged the library to be more restrictive.

I'm afraid it was not premeditated [*laughs*]: I didn't decide to work on Henry Dodwell. What I found fascinating is that his intellectual career was the perfect confutation of the standard whiggish narrative, according to which political and religious radicals were always at the same time intellectual radicals and vice versa. Dodwell undermined the idea that progress is somehow univocal, because here was someone who was extremely conservative in his political and religious positions—he was a church-and-state Tory during the Stuart Restoration and after 1689 one of the so-called Nonjurors (those who refused to accept the settlement that recognized William and Mary after the Glorious Revolution)—and at the same time entertained some extraordinarily daring views on theology and church history. He maintained that the canon of the New Testament had been defined very late and that there had been no clear-cut distinction between canonical and apocryphal books until the beginning of the second century. He held that there had been very few Christian martyrs during the Roman persecutions (whereas orthodox apologetics claimed that there had been a huge number and that their readiness to die for their faith demonstrated the truth of Christianity). He argued that the soul was naturally mortal and so on. What is more, he had radical scholarly views not in spite of his religious and political conservatism but *because* of it, because he felt that it was no longer possible to defend the established church and the divine right of episcopacy using traditional arguments. In fact, whereas English episcopalian writers had been at pains to prove the

19. Jean-Louis Quantin, "Anglican Scholarship Gone Mad? Henry Dodwell (1641–1711) and Christian Antiquity," in *History of Scholarship: A Selection of Papers from the Seminar on the History of Scholarship Held Annually at the Warburg Institute*, ed. Christopher Ligota and Jean-Louis Quantin (Oxford, 2006), 305–56.

divine right of episcopacy from Scripture, he accepted the presbyterian claim that you couldn't; no present model of ecclesiastical government (neither episcopacy nor presbyterianism) could be found in Scripture, which described an extraordinary, provisional structure. His entire, life-long endeavor—by means of a convoluted scholarly montage, which he kept revising throughout his life—was to demonstrate that episcopacy was still a divine institution, even though it could not be found in Scripture.

Dodwell believed that after the last writings of the New Testament, authority in the church had been permanently devolved to the new institution of diocesan, monarchical bishops on the basis of universal consent, and that this step was a providential disposition. He argued that you had no better proof for the canon of the New Testament than for the divine right of episcopacy. If you rejected the divine right of episcopacy, then the canon of the New Testament crumbled, since both were founded on the testimony of the second-century fathers. In other words, he tried to buttress a sort of radical orthodoxy with a remarkably learned and at the same time extremely precarious construction!

You mentioned the misconception that intellectual daring and political or theological heterodoxy come as a package. This, of course, is still a widespread notion. How have you come to think about that relationship?

Seventeenth-century England seems to me to be a very strong case against that equation. It's perhaps not as clear-cut in the Roman Catholic context, although people like Jacques Sirmond and Denis Petau—the French Jesuits of the first part of the seventeenth century—also went to great lengths to defend a vision of Catholicism that could be described as conservative, that is, very papalist, authoritarian, and anti-Jansenist, using a great deal of very up-to-date scholarship and coming to a more historical understanding of the process of doctrinal formulation.

But this combination is certainly not confined to the early modern period. In the late nineteenth century, people joked that Monseigneur d'Hulst, the first rector of the Institut Catholique in Paris, was always wrong! About 1890, Pope Leo XIII called upon French Catholics to reconcile with Republican institutions. Shortly afterward, he published an encyclical in which he insisted on a very strict, literalist understanding of biblical inspiration. D'Hulst, who came from an old royalist family, was a reactionary in politics, so he was out of step with papal politics. But he was a liberal in biblical exegesis and was willing to make concessions to modern science. Foiled again! In that field, according to the pope, you had to be a strict reactionary![20] That sort of paradox, that sort of difficulty interests me—obviously people who are in that position are criticized on both sides. Dodwell ultimately displeased everybody. Even when he became a Nonjuror, he didn't satisfy the heads of his little communion, who wanted their case to be made using much more commonplace arguments.

How does studying the early modern reception of Christian antiquity differ from studying the reception of classical antiquity?

At a certain point in the sixteenth century, scholarship became confessionalized. It's very clear that in Rome around 1550, classical antiquity ceased to be the dominant subject.[21] The study of the classical past did not disappear, of course. But, still, the subject favored and promoted by the papacy was now Christian antiquity. At that point, we can speak of a confessionalization or even instrumentalization of scholarship; scholarship was supposed to become a tool of religious orthodoxy. For instance, around 1570 a German Jesuit named Johann Rethius—an interesting figure, on whom there is no modern study—became obsessed with potential falsifications in Protestant translations of the Greek fathers into Latin. He wrote to just about every Greek scholar in Catholic Europe, pestering them to undertake new translations. In 1573 he traveled to Italy, where he hammered the same message home.[22] On his way to Rome he stopped in Bologna and met a local humanist who was working on Polybius: his immediate reaction was to persuade him to work on John Chrysostom instead. You might say that Rethius was a fanatic and an extreme case, but he was part of a major trend. If you look at the huge correspondence of Cardinal Guglielmo Sirleto, the prefect of the Vatican library, who was a sort of scholar-in-chief of the Roman Catholic Church until his death in 1585, you see an international network concentrating

20. Francesco Beretta, *Monseigneur d'Hulst et la science chrétienne: Portrait d'un intellectuel* (Paris, 1996).

21. Pierre Petitmengin, "À propos des éditions patristiques de la Contre-Réforme: Le 'Saint Augustin' de la Typographie Vaticane," *Recherches augustiniennes* 4 (1966): 199–251.

22. Bernhard Duhr, *Geschichte der Jesuiten in den Ländern Deutscher Zunge* (Freiburg im Breisgau, 1907), 1:755–79; Paul Holt, "Aus dem Tagebuch des Johann Rethius, 1571–1574: Ein Beitrag zur Geistesgeschichte und zur stadtkölnischen Politik," *Jahrbuch des Kölnischen Geschichtsvereins* 20 (1938): 77–138.

on biblical studies, patristics, and church history, in a vigorously, even aggressively Counter-Reformation spirit.

It seems to me therefore that there is a specificity to patristic scholarship as opposed to classical scholarship. At the same time, unavoidably, you should be aware that there is a degree of anachronism in isolating patristic scholarship, as if it were a specialty in the modern academic sense, a point well made by Nicholas Hardy in his Oxford DPhil.[23] Even to call seventeenth-century figures patristic scholars is problematic, as nobody at the time used that designation; the scholars in question described themselves as theologians or critics. On the other hand, for practical purposes you are obliged at some point to choose an object of study and to concentrate on it! So, keeping in mind the degree of artificiality and anachronism, it's not completely illegitimate, I trust, because specific theological points and specific interests were at stake. The idea that the church fathers enjoyed a special status is not a figment of historiographical construction!

Your book The Church of England and Christian Antiquity *also argues that appealing to the church fathers was not merely, or not primarily, a doctrine: "it was an* art *of manipulating authorities as part of what might be termed a technology of truth" (emphasis added). How were you able to recover this dimension of your work?*

The phrase "technology of truth" comes from Michel Foucault; it's a throwback to my youthful years in French theory.[24] A major part of a theologian's expertise was the ability to hold one's ground in a controversy, and especially in a public, ritualized, even theatrical, oral disputation. This was a craft that included a number of tools. To a large extent, these tools were inherited from Christian antiquity itself, from the way the church fathers had tried to solve the apparent contradictions or difficulties of Scripture. There was a transfer, I think, of biblical hermeneutics to early modern confessional controversy: you had to manipulate authorities and explain away the texts that your opponents produced as proofs of their own views and as objections against yours. Such a craft was transmitted partly in

23. N. J. S. Hardy, "The *Ars critica* in Early Modern England" (DPhil thesis, Oxford University, 2012), 14–15, 87–88, 165–66, now published as Nicholas Hardy, *Criticism and Confession: The Bible in the Seventeenth-Century Republic of Letters* (Oxford, 2017).

24. Michel Foucault, *Psychiatric Power: Lectures at the Collège de France, 1973–74* (Basingstoke, 2006), 235–47.

an oral way in schools, which makes it harder for us to reconstruct. I am thinking of a controversy in France at the end of the seventeenth century, when Paul Godet des Marais, the bishop of Chartres—an important figure, as he was the spiritual director of Madame de Maintenon, Louis XIV's wife—was criticized by the Jansenists, who challenged him with some texts from the fathers and church councils. He protested indignantly, as if his professional qualification as a doctor in divinity from the Sorbonne had been questioned: "These are very common texts, which every bachelor on the benches of the Sorbonne knows how to answer in disputations!" The art of answering problematic patristic texts was an essential part of the shared theological culture in which clerics were trained. In addition to the actual practice of disputations, a number of handbooks were devoted to providing clues to students: you might reply that the speech was figurative, that the author spoke only in passing, in the heat of disputation, and so on.

Irena Backus warned some years ago that the reception of the church fathers during the Reformation era should not be reduced to religious controversy.[25] This is perfectly true in the sense that one didn't merely read the fathers to find proof-texts to quote in controversy; their influence went much deeper. But I would object to the binary and rather schematic opposition that she draws between confessional uses of the fathers and what she calls a genuine interest in the past. Does that mean that, if a reading was confessional, it was ipso facto not genuine? That is the anachronistic view of a twenty-first-century specialist. People were trained to read the fathers within a confessional, adversarial culture.

Much history of scholarship has been written as intellectual biography, focusing on a particular individual. One remarkable aspect of The Church of England and Christian Antiquity *is its enormous scale. How did you decide to cover so many different individual scholars over such a long period of time? And what did that entail in terms of research and exposition?*

I started with only vague ideas of what the chronological boundaries would be, both for my French dissertation and for *The Church of England and Christian Antiquity*, which was originally the first part of a French *Habilitationsschrift*. In the case of my dissertation, my initial intention

---

25. Irena Backus, *Historical Method and Confessional Identity in the Era of the Reformation (1378–1615)* (Leiden, 2003).

was to cover a very large chronological ground, including a large part of the eighteenth century as well. This proved too enormous to be practical. So I ended up working on a more limited span of time: 1669 to 1713, quite precise dates that refer to episodes in the Jansenist crisis. The year 1669 marked the so-called Peace of the Church, when a temporary, ambiguous, reconciliation was achieved between the pope and the French Jansenists, and 1713 saw the promulgation of the bull *Unigenitus* that finally condemned Jansenism (or rather a redefined version of it). It appeared to me that, because of my focus on Jansenism, such precise dates made sense. And I tried to cover as many strands as I could, considering not only theological controversies and works of scholarship, but also sermons, popular works of devotion, and liturgical books.

In the case of England, without having really premeditated it, it turned out that I could try something different, focusing on debates over the authority of the church fathers and covering an ample chronology. What struck me, for I hadn't noticed that phenomenon to the same extent in France—there was probably some English originality—was the extent to which people in the Church of England were obsessed with the history of their own church. Theological debates were to a large extent debates about the nature of the Church of England and its evolution over time. Critics of the so-called advanced conformists at the beginning of the seventeenth century and then of the Laudians in the 1630s and of the High Church divines during the Restoration, kept saying, "You have deviated from the original, Elizabethan, orthodoxy of your Church"—a point that I think many present-day scholars would accept. So the debate was intensely self-referential; texts from the 1560s and '70s were constantly quoted in the 1680s. Although I do not consider myself a sixteenth-century scholar except on very particular subjects, I felt I had to go back to the sixteenth century because otherwise those debates and those references would have been unintelligible. The subject required a long time span, with the consequence that I was obliged to ignore many aspects, for instance, the use of the fathers in sermons and popular works. Even if I manage to revise and put out the second part of my *habilitation*, on English patristic editions, it will remain a top-down study, a study of elite discourse—and that's an obvious limitation. Because my work on France was chronologically narrower than my work on England, I was able to suggest how very learned, seemingly esoteric debates influenced the way sacraments were administered and the way the parish clergy actually engaged with so-called popular religion. I had to neglect this dimension completely in the case of England. But I suppose I also did not wish to follow quite the same pattern for my dissertation and my *habilitation*.

What are your working methods?

I started in the predigital age, so I gathered the materials for my dissertation entirely on index cards alphabetically arranged. I continued in the same way for some years afterward: most of my notes on Dodwell, for instance, are still on index cards. I found it a convenient way to access information! The problem was that, when I moved from France to Britain for the summer, carrying my files became increasingly difficult. I was a visiting fellow at All Souls College, Oxford, in 2002, and I carried all my English files in boxes in a very heavy rucksack. At the time, security on the Eurostar train was comparatively lax, so I managed to cross the border with my rather suspicious boxes. I was very anxious that security officers might search them and cast all my cards into disarray! Physically, though, it proved impossible to continue in that way, so I started taking notes on a computer, albeit without enthusiasm.

Another precipitating event took place in Rome while I was working in the Archive of the Congregation for the Doctrine of the Faith, the former Inquisition. One morning, as I was walking from my room at the French School, on Piazza Navona, to the Palazzo del Sant'Uffizio, there was a sudden frightful storm. I was drenched to the bone, and all the index cards I was carrying with me to check my transcriptions were sodden. Afterward I had to dry out two hundred index cards that this Roman storm had threatened to destroy. So I do see the practical advantages of taking notes electronically!

Even so, I much prefer, when I can, to look at a physical book. When I use Google Books because, say, the Bibliothèque Nationale refuses to make available the original, I am very grateful to have some access to the text, but it's always second best.

You wrote a major book in a foreign language. What went into that decision, and what was the experience of writing in English like?

Once again, major decisions in my scholarly life have all been suggestions from outside. In this case the suggestion came from Scott Mandelbrote, an old friend from my Oxford years, who pointed out that a book on English history would have no audience in France—nobody is interested in the Church of England in France!—whereas writing in English would really make sense. The problem was that, technically, the book was to be the main part of my French *habilitation*, which is a national degree, and it was not clear whether you were allowed to submit a work in a foreign language. It turned out that it was admissible—Jean-Pierre Poussou, who acted again as my supervisor, was very helpful with administrative questions. If, however, I had wanted to apply on the basis of this *habilitation* to a university professorship, the national committee of universities—we still have a centralized national system—could have ordered me to deliver a complete translation in French, and that at very short notice. Fortunately, I had already been appointed to my present position at the EPHE the year before and had no desire to move anywhere else, so I could afford not to bother.

Writing the book in French and then translating it into English would have been a maddening task. It was much easier for me to write in English from the beginning, even with a number of mistakes. I submitted an uncorrected version to the Sorbonne for the *habilitation*—only one of the examiners had English as a native language, and he was kind enough not to dwell on my linguistic mistakes—and then rewrote it. Scott very generously reread and corrected the entire manuscript. But it's very specifically an English book on English history. I don't know whether this is schizophrenia, but it comes quite naturally to me to write in English on England and in French on France. On a number of occasions when I have been asked to write about French history in English, somehow that didn't feel right! I find that, when I have to write in English on subjects on which I think in French, the result looks contrived or artificial. This is not entirely a bad thing—it imposes a distance, shatters the illusion of naturalness—but I don't like it.

I don't know what the future has in store for countries like France. In Denmark, for example, judging by my experience, they have moved to a fully English-speaking academic system; they write dissertations in English. In France we are still very reluctant about the idea of writing our own national history, in our own country, in a foreign language. We would feel this as a dispossession. There is clearly a cultural issue here.

Has studying early modern scholarship given you some perspective on your own scholarly practice? Do you see continuities between the two or do you rather view them as distinct activities?

This is a fundamental question. My first response would be to stress emphatically that early modern scholars—to paraphrase an oft-quoted point by a specialist in ancient history about Thucydides—are not our colleagues and should not be treated as if they were.[26] Many people dabble in the history of scholarship with a literary training in classics or in patristic studies. They are completely unaware of the historical context, and they tend to pass naïve judgments on seventeenth-century scholars, either to celebrate them as great forerunners or to denigrate them on account of their "mistakes." Some years ago, there was a conference on the Benedictine scholar Bernard de Montfaucon, and a distinguished specialist in ancient archaeology gave a caricatural paper on Montfaucon's *L'Antiquité expliquée* (1719–24), his great collection of archaeological *realia*, complaining that it was impossible to use the work as a textbook for present students since it included so many "errors"!

On the other side, there is a naïve teleology, which is still very strong in the French context, often with positivist overtones: for instance, saying that the Benedictines of Saint-Maur—whose numbers included such erudite monks of the ancien régime as Montfaucon or Jean Mabillon—were the predecessors of the École des Chartes, our specialized *grande école* for archivists. In the old lecture hall of the École des Chartes there is a late nineteenth-century fresco depicting the abbey of Saint Germaindes-Prés in the seventeenth century: the dead Benedictines watching over the living archivists.

My first reaction, then, would be to stress differences, especially in order to push back against that sort of crude ahistoricism. On the other hand, I do think that what early modern scholars were doing is not entirely foreign to the work of today's historians, especially in the context, to use a catchy phrase, of postmodern discussions or of claims about a post-truth world. Scholars at the end of the seventeenth century tried to defend historical practice against so-called Pyrrhonism, a radical form of skepticism that argued that there was no difference between history and the novel. They evolved an epistemology of moral certainty. What I find consonant with my own work is their notion that history is fundamentally a craft. Someone like Mabillon put it very strongly that with practice you acquire "taste," a sort of habitus. If the skeptics asked, "How can you prove that a document is genuine, and not a well-crafted forgery?," he replied that the ability to do so required an acquired taste, based on experience.[27] Ultimately, the criterion for determining authenticity was the community of scholars in the field, what they called *les personnes habiles* in French, *periti* in Latin—the community of experts. There was

---

26. Nicole Loraux, "Thucydide n'est pas un collègue," *Quaderni di storia* 12 (July–December 1980): 55–81.

27. Jean Mabillon, *De re diplomatica* (Paris, 1681).

scholarly progress in the sense that certain critical questions were set-
tled. For example, Le Nain de Tillemont argued that there was now a
consensus among *les habiles* that the Pseudo-Dionysian corpus was not
genuine. You could not go on and on trying to defend its authenticity;
the discussion was now closed.[28]

Responding to skepticism in that way didn't amount to sheer empiricism, because scholars like Mabillon or Tillemont were well aware of
contemporary philosophical debates in the wake of Cartesianism and
had studied closely the so-called *Logique de Port-Royal* by the Jansenist
theologians Antoine Arnaud and Pierre Nicole. One should of course
always remain wary of anachronism. The analysis of moral certainty in
the *Logique de Port-Royal* was explicitly connected with contemporary
controversies against Protestants, especially about the Eucharist. Religious controversy remained central in Gallican intellectual culture in a
way that differs greatly from our present division of knowledge.

How would you compare the presentism of seventeenth-century scholars with our own?

All the past scholars whom I have studied were presentist in as much as
they didn't study the past for its own sake. They believed that the past
should be studied because it would bear witness to a permanent, unchanging body of religious truth. They already knew this body of truth
because it had been defined a priori by church authority. However, there
was a shift at the end of the seventeenth century. Le Nain de Tillemont,
for instance, was aware that there could be a provisional gap, as it were,
between the results of historical enquiry and doctrinal certainties. He
declined to examine the consequences that could be drawn from the
facts he had established. He explained that he was only searching for
"the truth of facts" and that he wasn't afraid it could be misused, "because truth cannot be contrary to truth." Some commentators have concluded that he was espousing a two-truths doctrine, that he discreetly
suggested there were two kinds of truth, the truth of history and the
truth of theology. It seems to me, on the contrary, that he was fully sin-
cere: he was convinced that there couldn't be any lasting, real contradiction between what he found in original sources and Catholic doctrine,

28. Jean-Louis Quantin, "Document, histoire, critique dans l'érudition ecclésiastique des temps
modernes," *Recherches de science religieuse* 92, no. 4 (2004): 597–635; Quantin, "Reason and Reason-
ableness in French Ecclesiastical Scholarship," *Huntington Library Quarterly* 74, no. 3 (2011): 401–36.

because, ultimately, truth was one—truth was God. But Tillemont did not attempt to work at conciliation himself: that was a task for theologians. His concern, as he put it, was "to present the simple truth of what happened during the first centuries." His research, that is, was not *immediately* apologetic or doctrinal; there was at least a functional division of labor between the theologian and the historian. Thus, scholars like Tillemont overcame presentism or, at any rate, eschewed the distorting effects of presentism on their research. This was a foundational step.

To what extent is my own work presentist? It is very difficult to say; I am perhaps not the best judge. I tend to denounce very strongly whiggish biases, in their secular as well as religious versions. On the other hand, it is impossible to study early modern scholarship without having in mind what followed. What partly draws me to the Gallican scholars of the late seventeenth century, or the English scholars of Restoration Oxford, is the fact that they lived at the last time in Western history when it was still possible to be very learned, scrupulously honest, and a bona fide orthodox: to see no contradiction between your work and Christian orthodoxy as defined authoritatively by your church. Even someone like Dodwell, who was already half over the fence, was not aware of the contradiction. So I look at these seventeenth-century scholars knowing with hindsight that they embody a coherence, a confidence, a unity that are definitely lost. After them, scholars who worked from within one of the main Christian churches could no longer ignore or even plausibly pretend to ignore that historical evidence contradicted a number of crucial claims of their church—of any church. They had to make a choice. They could practice confessional history in the modern, deservedly pejorative sense—deliberately distorting evidence. Or they could leave their church, as so many did in the nineteenth century. Or they had to subscribe, at least implicitly, to a two-truths doctrine, to accept that the truth of history was not the same as the truth of dogma. They had to accept to live with a divided self. There is a moving letter of Louis Duchesne, who was an eminent Catholic historian of ancient Christianity—a late nineteenth-century equivalent of Le Nain de Tillemont—directeur d'études at the EPHE and then director of the French School at Rome, in which he evoked to a friend, in 1888, the deep-rooted Catholicism of his native Brittany, where he had returned for the summer. As Duchesne concluded: "I will not give up this paradise for the satisfaction of being in full agreement with myself."[29]

---

29. Brigitte Waché, *Monseigneur Louis Duchesne (1843–1922), historien de l'Église, directeur de l'École française de Rome* (Rome, 1992).

The essential question is whether historical and philological scholarship is critical or not. If it is purely accumulative, there is no problem reconciling it with orthodoxy. It can even become an apologetic tool: displaying massive learning is an obvious way to obfuscate the issues. And as long as you use criticism in a one-sided way, it is perfectly compatible with religious (or for that matter political or social) orthodoxy. But when scholarship and erudition become genuinely critical, things change (and this again is a point that is consonant with our own time). There was a fateful moment in the seventeenth century—in the case of France you can date it quite precisely to the late 1660s—when scholars decided that they shouldn't use criticism only as an ad hoc tool against confessional adversaries but that they had a duty to be critical all the time, because source criticism was the only way of approaching truth.

In your book, you refer to antiquity as a Pandora's box. Could you talk about the unintended consequences of scholarship, and how people dealt with them?

In the sixteenth and seventeenth centuries, as I said, there was a close link between scholarship and confessional orthodoxy. But confessionalized scholarship rebounded against its sponsors. What I have undertaken is to study from the angle of the history of scholarship a phenomenon that has been observed by several others: that of the orthodox sources of disbelief, as Alan Kors termed it.[30] Neveu once compared unbelievers to cuckoos laying their eggs in the nest of the orthodox Benedictine scholars.[31] That is a fascinating way of reading the evolution of the eighteenth century! Dodwell again is almost too obvious a case because his works were quarried by freethinkers and deists. Voltaire explicitly appealed to him in his campaign *écrasez l'infâme*—his massive pamphlet war against Christianity—in the 1760s.[32]

What is more interesting and more difficult to see is how not just individual conclusions but the entire process of orthodox critical scholarship in the seventeenth century was self-destroying. I have in mind Nietzsche's famous aphorism in *Die fröhliche Wissenschaft* on the unintended consequences of the Lutheran Reformation: the holy books eventually came

30. Alan Charles Kors, *Atheism in France, 1650–1729*, vol. 1, *The Orthodox Sources of Disbelief* (Princeton, 1990).

31. Bruno Neveu, "Communication de synthèse," in *Dom Bernard de Montfaucon: Actes du colloque de Carcassonne, Octobre 1996*, ed. D.-O. Hurel and R. Rogé (Saint-Wandrille, 1998), 2:135.

32. Quantin, "Anglican Scholarship Gone Mad?," 308.

into the hands of the philologists—that is, "the destroyers of every faith that rests on books."[33] I am also thinking of his point that, when a religion is turned into historical knowledge, when Christianity is resolved into "pure knowledge about Christianity," it is fatally destroyed at the end of the process. According to Nietzsche, historicized theology unwittingly "placed itself in the service of the Voltairean *écrasez*": a remark that I find fascinating as it is verified literally in the case of Dodwell, whom Nietzsche certainly didn't know.[34] How did religion respond to that massive infusion of historical criticism into Christianity? To what extent did Christianity reinvent itself to survive? This process is very clear in the case of Roman Catholicism.

Once the cultural authority of historical erudition disappeared, when it could be dismissed as pedantic hairsplitting, it ceased to be a threat to religious orthodoxy. Nobody cared about it anymore. Look at what happened in the nineteenth century with the doctrine of papal infallibility, which was defined by the First Vatican Council in 1870. Scholars in the seventeenth century had leveled so many historical objections at the doctrine of papal infallibility that it appeared to be definitely confuted, or so they believed in Gallican France at the time. There were so many incontrovertible instances of popes who had issued false doctrinal statements, who had contradicted themselves, who had been condemned as heretics by universal councils and by their own successors.

That did not prevent the definition of papal infallibility, that is, in Cardinal Manning's famous phrase, "the triumph of dogma over history." Historical objections were simply swept away. The ground shifted. Infallibility was deduced from a political conception of sovereignty: to put it bluntly, a sovereign authority needed to be infallible because it needed to have the last word. Infallibility, Vatican I proclaimed, is "included" in papal primacy. As Manning explained in a defiant apostrophe to "scientific historians": "the Church defines its doctrines in spite of you, because it knows its history better than you. . . . The history of the Church is the Church itself."[35] Ultimately, the living pope was the entire history of the church. Pope Pius IX, who had infallibility defined by the First Vatican Council, exclaimed, "I am tradition!" Somewhat in the same way as Scripture in Calvinist orthodoxy was said to be *autopistos*, self-authenticating, the pope became self-authorizing. This explains why the council did not merely de-

33. Friedrich Nietzsche, *The Gay Science*, trans. Josefine Nauckhoff (Cambridge, 2001), § 358.

34. Friedrich Nietzsche, *On the Uses and Disadvantages of History for Life (Untimely Meditations II)*, trans. R. J. Hollingdale (Cambridge, 1997), § 7.

35. [Henry Edward Manning], *Religio Viatoris* (London, 1887), 76–79.

clare the pope infallible but claimed that popes had *always* held themselves to be infallible. From the point of view of Pius IX and Manning, the two statements were synonymous. Provided you are willing to commit yourself to this position and to accept its full implications, it is unassailable.

What do you consider peculiar about the early modern period?

In France, at least, the peculiarity of early modern history at this moment is somewhat threatened. It is squeezed between very expansionist medievalists who argue that there is a "long Middle Ages" lasting until the early nineteenth century and modern historians who would annex at least part of the eighteenth century. From the point of view of the history of scholarship and specifically of religious scholarship, I see the originality of the early modern period in the rise of criticism as a fundamental activity. Medievalists have a point when they say that theologians in the Middle Ages were not acritical, that they did not accept everything on trust. Already in the ninth century, Florus of Lyon used both external and internal arguments to reject a treatise falsely ascribed to Augustine. In the fifteenth century, in the course of a controversy between the canons and the hermits of Saint Augustine over the respective antiquity of their orders, a series of spurious sermons ascribed to Augustine (the so-called *Sermones ad fratres in eremo*) were submitted to a thorough critical examination.[36] But even in elaborate debates such as those, criticism was not the fundamental principle; it was used as an ad hoc tool in a particular discussion to get rid of an embarrassing text. There was not the idea, which appeared in the seventeenth century and was ultimately a moral idea, that you had a duty to truth and that criticism was the proper instrument of truth. You now had a moral obligation to use criticism, a moral obligation to adopt—as Mabillon put it, using the categories of contemporary moral theology— the historical account that was not merely probable but "more probable."

In a very crude way, I would identify three stages in this process: the rise of religious criticism in the sixteenth century; its extension in the seventeenth century, when it was turned into a fundamental tool to bring Christianity back to its alleged original purity; and its questioning in the eighteenth century, when this huge ambition broke down and people started to recognize the self-defeating effect of criticism. From

---

36. François Dolbeau, "Critique d'attribution, critique d'authenticité: Réflexions préliminaires," *Filologia mediolatina* 6–7 (1999–2000): 33–61. Reproduced in Dolbeau, *Sanctorum societas: Récits latins de sainteté (IIIe–XIIe siècles)* (Brussels, 2005), 1:3–32.

my point of view, a certain unity defined the sixteenth, seventeenth, and eighteenth centuries. The nineteenth century was a great age of scholarship. But nonetheless it seems to me that, in that period, the critical impetus was marginalized or rejected, perhaps within all the main churches, certainly within the Roman Catholic Church, and it was chiefly pursued from outside. The precarious balance that obtained in French religious culture at the end of the seventeenth century had come apart, and the nineteenth-century church didn't attempt to restore it. The nineteenth century's contribution to the study of Christian antiquity was limited. It would be different if you considered biblical or classical scholarship. But in the case of the fathers, basically all you have is Abbé Migne's *Patrology* (to be exact his two *Patrologies*, Greek and Latin), that *cloaca maxima*, as German scholars called it, in which he reprinted early modern editions with minimal changes. I did some work on the reception of Pascal's *Provincial Letters* in the nineteenth century.[37] In France, ecclesiastical culture at the time was very rhetorical, apologetical, strongly politicized, and theologically quite impoverished. In Rome, if you look at the personnel of the Index and the Holy Office—divines, mostly members of religious orders who were employed as "consultors" and for whom a prosopography is now available[38]—you find able people still immersed in the theological controversies of the seventeenth and eighteenth centuries who appear rather cut off from the intellectual trends of their own time and who hardly contributed anything new to the field. From a purely intellectual point of view, the great endeavor of early modern Christianity exhausted itself in the nineteenth century. The early modern period is not merely an arbitrary historiographic construction; there is some unity to it, from my point of view.

What have you unlearned, as well as learned, in the course of your career?

It's perhaps a bit early for me to say. When I first arrived in Oxford I succumbed to the last enchantment of the Middle Ages, as the phrase

37. Jean-Louis Quantin, "Pascal, la République et l'Église: Les *Provinciales* pour les classes et devant l'Index (1881–1886)," *Mélanges de l'École française de Rome—Italie et Méditerranée modernes et contemporaines* 126, no. 1 (2014): 161–88.

38. Philippe Boutry, "Gli uomini della censura: Dalla storia istituzionale alla storia intellettuale," in *Verbotene Bücher: Zur Geschichte des Index im 18. und 19. Jahrhundert*, ed. Hubert Wolf (Paderborn, 2008), 427–40; Boutry, "La congregazione dell'Inquisizione e dell'Indice dal 1814 al 1917," *Quellen und Forschungen aus italienischen Archiven und Bibliotheken* 88 (2008): 547–55.

goes, and I wrote a premature little piece, of which I am now rather ashamed.[39] When you are at evensong in an Oxford college the notion of the special nature of the Church of England appears plausible. With age you become increasingly skeptical about it. In the same way, like Bruno Neveu, who then strongly reacted against it, I had imbibed the cultural Gallicanism that is traditionally common among French academics, the literary myth of Port-Royal. I have become less and less ready to take Gallican claims at face value. Broadly speaking, I am now wary of self-proclaimed exceptionalisms and even of any notion of fixed, unchanging religious identities.

What current trends in historical scholarship seem most promising to you? What do you hope for the future of the field?

There was a very interesting conference on the reception of the church fathers at Trinity College, Cambridge, in October 2016, where the speakers included very bright and promising young scholars who were just finishing their dissertations.[40] In 2013, Trinity had already hosted a conference on the history of early modern religious scholarship, the proceedings of which are about to be published and will include an exceptionally well-informed historiographical survey by Dmitri Levitin on "confessionalization and erudition in early modern Europe."[41] The field is very active in the English-speaking world. Perhaps this is my own fault, but it is not as flourishing in France, at least in the sense that in France the history of scholarship still struggles to be recognized as a field in its own right. This has been my own experience as it was that of Bruno Neveu: historians of scholarship are very much scholars' scholars, in the sense in which one speaks of a writer's writer. The most historically aware of my colleagues in philology are very interested in what I am doing, for instance François Dolbeau, who is my colleague here at the EPHE in Latin philology. Among the younger generation of ancient historians or medievalists, some are quite alert to the way early modern controversies

39. Jean-Louis Quantin, "The Fathers in Seventeenth-Century Anglican Theology," in *The Reception of the Church Fathers in the West: From the Carolingians to the Maurists*, ed. Irena Backus (Leiden, 1997), 2:987–1008.

40. "The Reception of the Church Fathers and Early Church Historians, c. 1470–1650," organized by Andreas Ammann, Sam Kennerley, and Kirsten Macfarlane, Trinity College, Cambridge, September 23, 2016.

41. Nicholas Hardy and Dmitri Levitin, eds., *Faith and History: Confessionalisation and Erudition in Early Modern Europe*, Proceedings of the British Academy (Oxford, forthcoming).

imposed enduring interpretative categories, from which you can hardly free yourself if you don't understand in what context and to what purpose they were created. But the main home of these scholars is still ancient or medieval history. In France, very few people of the new generation really specialize in the history of scholarship, largely because of the job market. I am more optimistic when I am across the Channel than when I am here.

Quentin Skinner

QUENTIN SKINNER is the Barber Beaumont Professor of the Humanities at Queen Mary University of London.

What first drew you to intellectual history? And what in particular attracted you to the political thinkers of early modernity?

My interest was quickened at school through the influence of one remarkable mentor, John Eyre. His death was marked by a full-page obituary in the *Independent* newspaper, rightly headed "Life-Changing History Teacher."[1] Altogether I received an extremely good secondary education. I attended one of the English public schools, as they are still quaintly called—quaintly because they are of course private schools, and it cost my parents more money than they could probably afford to give my brother and me such a privileged start in life. We studied a wide range of subjects in the sciences as well as the humanities, but in the final three years the syllabus became highly specialized, and at that stage I concentrated wholly on Latin, English history, and English literature.

We studied English history in considerable depth but with some important constraints. One was that the narrative of high politics was assumed to be what chiefly mattered; another was that we concentrated exclusively on what were held to be the two formative periods, the Reformation and

1. Richard Lindley, "John Eyre: Life-Changing History Teacher," *Independent,* January 28, 2006.

the English Revolution. My studies were consequently confined to the years between 1500 and 1700. These centuries were in turn treated as a whiggish story about the emancipation of the English state first from the Catholic Church and later from the absolutism of the Stuart monarchy, with the narrative culminating in the so-called Glorious Revolution of 1688.

It was agreed, however, that there was something called "the intellectual background" to these events. When we learned about the Reformation we were asked to read some polemical writings of the time, including Thomas More's *Utopia*. When we studied the English Revolution we were similarly invited to see in Thomas Hobbes's *Leviathan* the leading apology for absolutism, and in John Locke's *Second Treatise of Government* the definitive justification for the Revolution of 1688. I bought all these texts at that time, and somewhere I still have the copies I acquired and annotated. You ask what first drew me specifically to intellectual history, and my answer is that I found myself instantly and indiscriminately fascinated by all these works. Since those far-off days I have published a lot about More, Hobbes, and Locke. I sometimes think that much of my academic career has consisted of little more than an attempt to give better answers to some of the questions I was originally asked to think about in my adolescence.

The effect of these early studies was that, when I arrived as an undergraduate at the University of Cambridge in 1959, I was already a devotee of intellectual history. But if you ask—as you have—what drew me more specifically to political theory and to early modernity, then I'm afraid the answer is not a very intellectually interesting one. It was simply that these were the subjects to which I was first introduced, and they have continued to hold my attention ever since.

What were those burning early questions that carried you through?

I was a very bookish boy, or rather I became one. There was a long gap in my early education when, at the age of eleven, I contracted tuberculosis and nearly died. I had to spend almost a year in bed, and all I could manage to do was read and listen to music. The effect was profound, and I returned to school transformed. After that I really wanted to make a success of my studies, and I eventually decided that I wanted to become a teacher—which is how I have always primarily thought of myself.

I must confess, however, that the academic questions that I originally found most fascinating were not wholly or even primarily political or philosophical in character. My great intellectual passion as an adolescent was for the history of architecture; one summer I even wrote and illustrated a little book on the history of neoclassical building in England. When I went to Cambridge, however, it was not possible to become a historian of architecture; the subject was barely taught there at that time. But, in any case, I was becoming at least as much interested in the social and political theories associated with the historical periods I had studied, and the questions I began to consider at that time have never ceased to haunt me: questions about the concept of the state, the idea of representation, the grounds and limits of political obligation, and the nature and extent of political liberty.

Who were some of your early mentors and teachers at Cambridge, and what did you learn from them?

My chief teacher of political theory—my "supervisor," in Cambridge parlance, to whom I had to present a piece of written work each week—was John Burrow, who later became professor of intellectual history at Oxford. But I also learned a great deal from attending lectures by Peter Laslett on Hobbes and Locke, by Duncan Forbes on the Enlightenment and Hegel, and most rivetingly by Walter Ullmann on medieval legal and political thought. Some of my most important mentors, however, were not my teachers but my contemporaries. Of these, the one who most influenced me was John Dunn, who later became professor of political theory at Cambridge. More quickly than I, John sensed that the strong emphasis placed by most of our lecturers on a small number of classic texts meant that we were not perhaps being taught the subject in the most illuminating way. It was John who, as early as 1969, produced one of the most important revisionist books in modern intellectual history, his study of Locke's politics, which remains a model of how these things should be done.[2]

What do you see as the relationship between intellectual history writ large and the history of political thought?

I think of intellectual history as the name of the historical study of all the products of the human mind. So for me intellectual history encompasses

---

2. John Dunn, *The Political Thought of John Locke: An Historical Account of the Argument of the "Two Treatises of Government"* (Cambridge, 1969).

the history of art, architecture, music, and literature, in addition to the history of philosophy, of which political philosophy would simply be a subgenre. So I think of the history of political philosophy as a subgenre of a subgenre.

I like, by the way, the term *intellectual history* rather than the one most widely used in my youth, the *history of ideas*. When I first began publishing, everyone still spoke about the history of ideas, and I cleaved to that terminology myself in some of the articles I wrote in the 1960s.[3] I did so with an element of irony, however, because I was trying to argue that strictly speaking there are no histories of ideas but only histories of the different ways in which ideas have been put to use. I think it's also important to stress that many intellectual historians don't study ideas. A history of painting would for me be a form of intellectual history, but I'm not sure that it would be a history of ideas, simply because many paintings are not about ideas. I like the inclusivity of *intellectual history*, and nowadays I always describe myself in those terms, although I can see that a faint and possibly self-congratulating ambiguity hovers over the usage.

What books and courses marked pivotal points in your early scholarly life?

I recur to my sense that some of these pivotal moments occurred at school rather than at university. Before I went to Cambridge there were two philosophers who already mattered to me very much. One was Bertrand Russell. For a time he was my great hero, and I especially admired his *History of Western Philosophy*.[4] Methodologically speaking, I would now have to admit, the book is somewhat primitive: it's just a sequence of intellectual biographies, and his choice of philosophers also feels a bit random, except that these were the people in whom Russell was most interested. But to me it opened up, for the first time, an entire world of speculation that I found entrancing. I remember beginning to read the book and then thinking that I really ought to take some notes and eventually finding that I had more or less copied out the whole work.

3. See, for example, Quentin Skinner, "Meaning and Understanding in the History of Ideas," *History and Theory* 8, no. 1 (1969): 3–53.
4. Bertrand Russell, *A History of Western Philosophy, and Its Connection with Political and Social Circumstances from the Earliest Times to the Present Day* (New York, 1945).

Something else that attracted me to Russell was the brilliance of his prose. He wrote with a glittering lucidity, and at the same time with a continual play of irony. I now see this as a traditionally English and perhaps a somewhat elitist way of writing, but to some extent it has remained a model for me, I must confess. I can't begin to emulate the style, of course, but I certainly retain the aspiration to write as clearly as I can manage. I like George Orwell's remark that expository prose should be like a pane of glass.

The other philosopher to whose work I was introduced at school, and who has remained very important to me, was R. G. Collingwood. I was told to read his *Idea of History*, a posthumous collection of essays on the philosophy of history.[5] That in turn led me to his *Autobiography*, a ruthlessly polemical work, in which I encountered his celebrated discussion of "The Logic of Question and Answer."[6] I took from Collingwood the idea that you shouldn't think of texts merely as bodies of propositions; you should think of them as answers to specific questions. Viewed in this way, philosophy no longer appeared as a subject in which we encounter different answers to a canonical set of questions. Rather it begins to look as if the questions as well as the answers continually change. Nor does the study of philosophy seem so obviously a matter of examining a canonical body of texts. If the aim is in part to recover the questions to which any given work of philosophy can be seen as an answer, this requires us to look beyond the texts to the circumstances in which they were formed. I am putting these points far more straightforwardly than I could have done when I first read Collingwood, but they have been with me in an inchoate way from an early stage.

At university, two specialist works particularly excited me. One was Peter Laslett's edition of John Locke's *Two Treatises of Government*, first published in 1960.[7] I started my university course in 1959, so I was studying Locke in the first year in which Laslett's work became available. Examining the circumstances in which Locke was writing, Laslett was able to show that, although Locke's *Treatises* were first published in 1689, they were drafted nearly ten years earlier. So the usual belief that they were written to celebrate the Revolution of 1688 simply collapsed, and it became necessary to ask anew why Locke composed the work. Laslett's answer was that, writing in an increasingly authoritarian climate at the end of Charles II's reign, Locke was seeking to vindicate the right of

5. R. G. Collingwood, *The Idea of History* (Oxford, 1946).
6. R. G. Collingwood, *An Autobiography* (Oxford, 1939).
7. John Locke, *Two Treatises of Government*, ed. Peter Laslett (Cambridge, 1960).

resistance to arbitrary and tyrannical rule. The reason why I found this analysis so arresting was that it managed to identify the specific questions to which Locke's *Treatises* were designed as an answer. Laslett's scholarship was, in short, thoroughly Collingwoodian in style.

Another scholarly work that excited me as an undergraduate was John Pocock's *Ancient Constitution and the Feudal Law*.[8] Pocock showed how a particular reading of English history—in which Parliament was taken to be an immemorial feature of the constitution—was deployed to challenge the drift toward absolutism in the decades preceding the English Revolution. As Pocock made clear, the evidence for this claim about Parliament was doubtful, but its ideological value to the parliamentarian cause eventually helped to guarantee its acceptance. I think this may have been what set me thinking about ideology in relation to political theory and about whether there is any clear distinction to be drawn between the two. This became the subject of one of my earliest articles,[9] and from that starting point I developed the suggestion that even the most abstract works of political philosophy can generally be shown to have a strong ideological component. We can safely assume, that is, that they will be aiming to legitimize or delegitimize some existing political arrangement or commitment. It was in an attempt to illustrate this suggestion that I turned to the philosophy of Hobbes, which had generally been considered to be above the battle. I tried to show that Hobbes was deeply implicated in the political debates of his time and that perhaps the history of political theory is basically a history of such battles.

As for my peer group at university, we were all reading Wittgenstein. Wittgenstein had been professor of philosophy at Cambridge between 1939 and 1946, and had died there in 1951. His *Philosophical Investigations*, posthumously published, was being hailed as the greatest work of philosophy of the century, which I still think may be true.[10] Anyone interested in philosophy in Cambridge when I was an undergraduate was reading the book. I think we mostly took it to be a work about the theory of meaning, although obviously it covers a huge range of themes. But certainly the parts that struck me most were those in which Wittgenstein exhorts us not to talk about meanings, but instead to ask about the use of words in language games and in constituting forms of life.

Of even greater importance to me was the publication of J. L. Austin's *How to Do Things with Words* in 1962, just at the moment when I was

8. J. G. A. Pocock, *The Ancient Constitution and the Feudal Law: A Study of English Historical Thought in the Seventeenth Century* (Cambridge, 1957).

9. Quentin Skinner, "History and Ideology in the English Revolution," *Historical Journal* 8, no. 2 (1965): 151–78.

10. Ludwig Wittgenstein, *Philosophical Investigations* (New York, 1953).

starting research. Wittgenstein had said, Don't ask about meanings, ask what words and concepts can be used to do. Austin went on to ask, What exactly is the range of things we can do with words?[11] I found his resulting typology exactly suited to my purposes. I took him to be telling us that there are two different dimensions to language and hence two different hermeneutic tasks. On the one hand there are words and their meanings, but on the other hand there is what Austin called the force of utterances. So one central interpretative task becomes, in the case of any utterance whatever, that of decoding what the speaker may have been doing in issuing it. Austin's underlying assumption here—that writing and speech need to be appraised as forms of social action—provided me with the basic hermeneutic principle I have tried to follow ever since.

It's very striking that the two key figures to whom you have devoted yourself are Machiavelli and Hobbes, because each represents a dramatic turning point in the history of political thought. Would you venture some thoughts about how you came to work so intensively on those figures? Lurking behind this is the question, How does one choose where to dig?

I follow extremely conventional protocols in relation to the question of where to dig. Sometimes this embarrasses me, although so far I haven't noticed that it unduly worries my audiences. But sometimes I find myself wondering, especially when I'm about to lecture in China or the United States, if it is still acceptable to talk about elite Western European culture. Because that's emphatically what I do. I have chiefly written about Thomas More, about Shakespeare, about Milton, about Locke, and especially, as you say, about Machiavelli and Hobbes. But if this worries me, why is this where I still choose to dig? My answer is not that I particularly admire Machiavelli or Hobbes. In fact I find some of what they say detestable. But one reason why I was originally drawn to them was that they both offered such perfect illustrations of some of the more general claims I wanted to make about intellectual history.

As I've already intimated, one of the claims I have most wanted to make is that even the most abstract works of political philosophy need to be apprehended as interventions in existing conversations or debates. To understand them, you need to identify the specific discussions to

---

11. J. L. Austin, *How to Do Things with Words* (Cambridge, MA, 1962).

which they were intended to contribute. If this is the approach you want to commend as well as practice, then Machiavelli offers a perfect means of illustrating its distinctive strengths. Machiavelli had inherited the humanist assumption that the goal of politics is greatness and glory and that the means to attain these ends is to possess *virtù* or *virtus generalis*, that is, the "cardinal" virtues of prudence, justice, courage, and temperance. Machiavelli agrees in *Il principe* that the ruler's goal should be greatness and glory and that this requires *virtù*. But he then declares that it is a ruinous mistake to suppose that the concept of *virtù* can be cashed out as a list of the virtues. Rather, he argues, what political leaders must recognize is that *virtù* is the name of whatever qualities succeed in bringing glory and greatness. Will the resulting actions always be instances of virtue? According to Machiavelli, no chance. So there, to put it crudely, you have the Machiavellian revolution. But to understand it is a matter of identifying the precise type of subversive intervention he was making in a generally accepted discourse about political morality.

Machiavelli goes on to say, in chapter 18 of *Il principe*, that the true *virtuoso* in politics is the leader who understands the value of imitating the lion and the fox; that's to say, who understands that force and fraud are indispensable to political success. To grasp the significance of this pivotal claim, you have to see that it is, among other things, a satire on Cicero. Cicero in his *De officiis* had declared force to be characteristic of the lion and fraud of the fox and had denounced both qualities as beastly, brutish, and hence as unworthy of men. Machiavelli is saying that these are the very qualities that men must cultivate if they are to be successful leaders. He is not only repudiating Cicero's humanism but also ridiculing his earnestness. To go back to the formula I take from J. L. Austin, this is what Machiavelli is *doing* in this celebrated passage. This is the kind of understanding, I want to say, that intellectual historians should seek: an appreciation of what is going on in the works they study, an understanding of what their authors are up to. One of my original reasons for concentrating on Machiavelli, in short, was methodological almost as much as historical: he illustrated so well some of the more general claims I wanted to make.

How did your time in America, particularly at the Institute for Advanced Study in Princeton, shape your work and interests?

I went to the Institute for Advanced Study in 1974 on a year of sabbatical leave from Cambridge. I was invited by Professor Sir John Elliott, the great historian of early modern Spain, and I spent the year in the Institute's School of Historical Studies. But while I was there I was invited to return for a five-year fellowship in the School of Social Science, which was then being built up by Albert Hirschman and Clifford Geertz, who had already recruited Thomas Kuhn and William Sewell. As things turned out, I only remained for a further three years, because my wife and I were both offered tempting positions back at Cambridge and decided to return home. But my four years in Princeton were of great importance to me, and I hugely enjoyed that period of my life.

You ask how my time at the Institute shaped my work and interests. I have to say, although this will sound pompous, that it didn't result in any major shifts in my outlook or style of work. I arrived as a fully paid-up Wittgensteinian, having by then published almost all my purely methodological and philosophical articles, about half-a-dozen of which appeared in the late 1960s and early '70s.[12] But Clifford Geertz was likewise deeply influenced by Wittgenstein, as he explicitly noted in the preface to his last book.[13] As a result, I found the atmosphere at the Institute congenial rather than challenging, and my time there mostly served to cement and deepen my existing intellectual commitments.

Nevertheless, being at the Institute was the most intense scholarly experience of my life. I found myself in an environment far more deeply committed to research than Cambridge was in those days—which unquestionably raised my own game—and I was granted a large expanse of time in which to get on with my work. I had been laboring for several years at Cambridge on what I hoped would be a large-scale work on the emergence of the modern state, but I could never manage to write it. But after three years at Princeton I succeeded in finishing the book, and it was published in 1978 as *The Foundations of Modern Political Thought*.[14]

Besides enabling me to do a lot more research, my time at Princeton introduced me to the most brilliant group of academics I have known, which greatly sharpened my philosophical as well as historical interests. One person who made a particularly deep impression on me was Geertz himself. He wasn't easy to get to know, because he could be shy as well

12. E.g., Quentin Skinner, "The Limits of Historical Explanations," *Philosophy* 41, no. 157 (1966): 199–215; Skinner, "Conventions and the Understanding of Speech Acts," *Philosophical Quarterly* 20, no. 79 (1970): 118–38; Skinner, "On Performing and Explaining Linguistic Actions," *Philosophical Quarterly* 21, no. 83 (1971): 1–21. See also the essays gathered in Skinner, *Visions of Politics*, vol. 1 (Cambridge, 2002).

13. Clifford Geertz, *Available Light: Anthropological Reflections on Philosophical Topics* (Princeton, 2000), xi–xiii.

14. Quentin Skinner, *The Foundations of Modern Political Thought*, 2 vols. (Cambridge, 1978).

as ferocious, but he became a highly valued mentor and friend. He was one of the most original and widely read scholars I have had the good fortune to know, equally at home in literature, philosophy, and a broad range of the human sciences. As an ethnographer he was always interested in how concepts hold together to make viable forms of life, even if the concepts may appear alien to us. This approach gave rise to one of his most powerful works, *Negara*, his study of what he called the "theatre state," which appeared in 1980.[15] I remember reviewing it for the *New York Review of Books* and being much impressed.[16] This was a book about the concept of the state but a book in which the state does not figure as the name of an apparatus of coercion at all. By challenging us to see that states can be about display as much as power and that display can be a form of power, Geertz was not only able to explicate a seemingly alien way of thinking but at the same time to challenge us to ask about the relations between power and display in our own societies. This seemed to me exactly the right kind of approach for intellectual historians as well as ethnographers to adopt, and it undoubtedly influenced my own later work on the theory of the state.

I also want to mention Thomas Kuhn, whose office at the Institute was next door to mine and who frequently burst in to talk about the work he was then beginning to do on meaning change. By the time I came to know him I had already been greatly influenced by his *Structure of Scientific Revolutions*, first published in 1962. I was especially taken by his core idea that what we call knowledge exists within a paradigm and that changes only occur when counterexamples to the paradigm build up until the paradigm itself begins to be doubted. Meanwhile the paradigm will be deployed to dismiss apparent anomalies—exactly the opposite of what Karl Popper had argued with his claim about the role of so-called crucial experiments. Like Geertz, Kuhn tended to argue that what it is rational to believe depends in part on what else you believe and not on anything that can uncontestably be called "the evidence."

I also spent a lot of time, very profitably to me, with two leading philosophers up the road at Princeton University, Richard Rorty and Raymond Geuss. Richard was then writing *Philosophy and the Mirror of Nature*, which he published in 1979. This, too, was a book I reviewed with great admiration in the *New York Review of Books*. I was particularly struck by the boldness with which Richard pushed his analysis of Witt-

---

15. Clifford Geertz, *Negara: The Theatre State in Nineteenth-Century Bali* (Princeton, 1980).
16. Quentin Skinner, "The World as a Stage," *New York Review of Books*, April 16, 1981.

genstein, W. V. Quine, and Kuhn in a relativist direction, and I had extensive discussions with him, in print as well as in conversation, about the extent to which intellectual historians are committed to some form of conceptual relativism.[17] I spent even more time with Raymond Geuss, who later became a colleague at Cambridge, and it was from him that I learned to think about genealogy as a tool for intellectual historians to use. Raymond was primarily interested in Nietzsche's suggestion that the act of tracing the origins of our beliefs can serve to discredit them. I eventually came to think of genealogy, perhaps in a more Wittgensteinian vein, simply as a useful means of tracing the disputes that frequently arise about how concepts ought to be individuated and defined. It was largely due to my discussions with Raymond that I was prompted to write the genealogical studies I later published on the concepts of liberty and the state.[18]

In your Foundations of Modern Political Thought *you complicate and challenge certain views that assigned novelty to the Renaissance— particularly by showing that ideas of classical republicanism and the like possess far deeper medieval origins. How do you understand the relationship between change and continuity in the history of ideas, especially in the early modern period?*

You are right to suggest that one of my aims was to challenge the traditional periodization of early modern history. It is true of course that one can't easily get away from the usual labels, and in book titles it is particularly difficult to avoid betraying oneself. The first volume of my book was subtitled *The Renaissance*, conventionally enough. But I was trying not merely to evoke but also to deconstruct the Burckhardtian image of a distinctive civilization that sprang into existence in fifteenth-century Florence. When I was writing, this way of thinking was still strongly prevalent, and it served to structure not merely Hans Baron's *Crisis of the Early Italian Renaissance* but even John Pocock's masterpiece of 1975, *The Machiavellian Moment*.[19] By contrast, I tried to trace the emergence of the theory

---

17. See especially Quentin Skinner, "Interpretation, Rationality and Truth," in *Visions of Politics*, vol. 1, *Regarding Method* (Cambridge, 2002), 27–56.

18. Quentin Skinner, *Liberty before Liberalism* (Cambridge, 1998); Skinner, "A Genealogy of the Modern State," *Proceedings of the British Academy* 162 (2009): 325–70.

19. J. G. A. Pocock, *The Machiavellian Moment: Florentine Political Thought and the Atlantic Republican Tradition* (Princeton, 1975).

and practice of republican self-government in the Italian city-states back to twelfth- and thirteenth-century debates about *suprema potestas* or "supreme power" in Roman legal as well as political thought.

The second volume of my book was called *The Age of Reformation.* Here I sought to question the thesis that, as Michael Walzer and Julian Franklin had influentially formulated it, the crystallizing of the modern vocabulary of constitutionalism was one of the distinctive legacies of the Protestant Reformation.[20] I tried to show that the relevant theories of authorization, limited government, and the right of political resistance had all been worked out in connection with longer-standing debates about the proper organization of the Catholic Church. Francis Oakley had already begun to argue in similar terms, but here I was chiefly indebted to the work of F. W. Maitland's great pupil, J. N. Figgis, who had demonstrated in *From Gerson to Grotius* the deep influence of debates about conciliarism on the formation of the modern secular state.[21]

You mentioned Hans Baron earlier. Did you also go back and reread his debate with Paul Oskar Kristeller?[22]

I was always on the side of Kristeller, and when I later coedited the *Cambridge History of Renaissance Philosophy* I was especially proud that I helped to persuade him to write the chapter on humanism. I was much influenced by what I take to have been Kristeller's basic contention, that *humanism* can best be understood as the name of a curriculum. He not only cleared away a lot of romantic nonsense about the alleged invention of humane values in the Renaissance, but also reoriented the historiography by showing that the *studia humanitatis* was largely derived from Roman rather than Greek sources. As he showed, the curriculum comprised five elements: grammar (the study of the Latin language), followed by logic and rhetoric, and then by the study of history and moral

20. Michael Walzer, *The Revolution of the Saints: A Study in the Origins of Radical Politics* (Cambridge, MA, 1965); Julian Franklin, *Constitutionalism and Resistance in the Sixteenth Century: Three Treatises* (New York, 1969).

21. John Neville Figgis, *Studies of Political Thought from Gerson to Grotius, 1414–1625* (Cambridge, 1907).

22. For Baron and Kristeller's positions, see Hans Baron, *The Crisis of the Early Italian Renaissance: Civic Humanism and Republican Liberty in an Age of Classicism and Tyranny* (Princeton, 1955); and Paul Oskar Kristeller, *Studies in Renaissance Thought and Letters* (Rome, 1956–96). See also the discussions in James Hankins, "'The Baron Thesis' after Forty Years and Some Recent Studies of Leonardo Bruni," *Journal of the History of Ideas* 56, no. 2 (1995): 309–38; and Patrick Baker, *Italian Renaissance Humanism in the Mirror* (Cambridge, 2015), esp. 6–8.

philosophy. Cicero emerged as a central figure, an expert on the theory and practice of rhetoric as well as an influential purveyor of moral and political advice. From as early as the thirteenth century, Kristeller showed, an essentially Ciceronian rhetorical culture developed in the *Regnum Italicum*, eventually giving rise in the sixteenth century to such histories and political advice books as those of Machiavelli and Guicciardini and in northern Europe those of Erasmus and Thomas More. Although Kristeller always presented his findings with caution and modesty, their effect was to suggest a new way of approaching Renaissance political theory, one that partially bypassed the alleged influence of Scholasticism and united the whole period between the thirteenth and early sixteenth centuries.

You have had a long-standing interest in the legacy of the ars rhetorica *and the history of rhetoric, culminating in your recent* Forensic Shakespeare.[23] *What first sparked your interest in the legacies of the ancient rhetorical tradition, and how has it shaped your approach to intellectual history and the history of political thought?*

My interest in rhetoric was first sparked by reading Kristeller but also by Jerrold Seigel's pioneering work of 1968, *Rhetoric and Philosophy in Renaissance Humanism*.[24] These works drove me back to reading Cicero, some of whose speeches I had already studied at school. I now turned to his theoretical writings on oratory and especially *De oratore*. There I encountered his crucial distinction between two types of argument, one characteristic of the sciences and the other characteristic of what he already labeled the human sciences. A science such as grammar or mathematics, Cicero suggests, can hope to furnish proofs that depend exclusively on *ratio* for their force. But in the human sciences we need to rely in addition on the force of persuasion and hence on the power of *oratio* or speech if we are to succeed in making our case. To put the point another way—as Cicero did—the human sciences are distinguished by the fact that there will always be two sides to the question, so that we can always hope to mount a persuasive argument *in utramque partem*, on either side of the case.

23. Quentin Skinner, *Forensic Shakespeare* (Oxford, 2014).

24. Jerrold E. Seigel, *Rhetoric and Philosophy in Renaissance Humanism: The Union of Eloquence and Wisdom, Petrarch to Valla* (Princeton, 1968).

For Cicero, accordingly, the principles of argument in the human sciences—including law and politics—need to be supplied by the theory of rhetorical *inventio*, that is, by the kind of theory that Cicero outlines in his *De inventione*. A mastery of *inventio* enables us to find out (*invenire*) what kinds of reasoning are likely to be most persuasive in different circumstances as well as showing us how to deploy our arguments in the best order and with the most potent combination of *oratio* and *ratio*. Nowadays, I think, we tend to equate rhetoric merely with verbal ornament, especially by means of figures of speech. But for Cicero and the Renaissance tradition of rhetorical education it was the name of a distinctive and indispensable art of argument.

You ask how the study of rhetoric, thus understood, has shaped my work as an intellectual historian. My answer is that it lies at the heart of two of my monographs. One is *Reason and Rhetoric in the Philosophy of Hobbes*, which I published in 1996. Hobbes states at the outset of his earliest work of political theory, *The Elements of Law*, that his aim is to articulate the principles of politics in such a way that there will be no place left for any argument on the other side of the case. I tried to explore the significance of the fact that this is at once a reference to and a repudiation of the Ciceronian view of explanation in the human sciences. I tried in particular to trace Hobbes's animus against the art of rhetoric as a means of accounting for the structure of *The Elements* as well as his *De cive* of 1642. I then contrasted this approach with Hobbes's later concession, in the conclusion of *Leviathan*, that the faculties of reason and eloquence must "stand together" if there is to be any prospect of constructing a science of politics. I tried to show how this rapprochement with the art of rhetoric affected Hobbes's mature presentation of his civil science, leading him to deploy a much wider range of arguments, and in particular to embrace rhetorical techniques of satire and ridicule in dealing with his adversaries.

My other book in which the theory of rhetorical invention provided me with my theme was *Forensic Shakespeare*, which appeared in 2014. I should explain that, as for many people of my generation in England, Shakespeare was a central figure in my education, and we studied a number of his plays in remarkable depth. While I was writing my book on Hobbes's shifting engagement with the art of rhetoric, I couldn't help noticing that much of the advice purveyed by the writers of rhetorical handbooks seemed to be echoed in the language and structure of several Shakespearean plays that I already knew well. I do not think, however, that I would ever have had the confidence to explore these intuitions if I had not been invited to give the Clarendon Lectures in Literature at

Oxford in 2011. I delivered the series under the title "Shakespeare and Rhetorical Invention." I attempted to show that, in a group of plays from Shakespeare's middle years, the most important of which are *Hamlet* and *Othello*, a number of pivotal speeches and scenes are organized around the use of classical rhetorical techniques to argue both sides of a case.

Would you tell us about your working methods? How do you begin a project and how do you write?

I once read a collection in which a number of scholars explained exactly what happens when they begin to study a specific topic and eventually sit down to write about it. I found these accounts fascinating, but I was also bemused by them, since I realized that I would have no such story to tell. I really have very little idea how I do it. I know that I take a lot of longhand notes, and then make more systematic notes out of those notes, trying to shape them into a draft as I go along. Then my habit used to be to type out my drafts, although since the early 1980s, like everyone else, I have used a computer. And, like everyone else, this means that nowadays I probably write more than I should.

I have come to recognize, however, that for a long time my note-taking has followed a structural principle. I see something in a text I am studying that reminds me of something in some other text, and I begin to juxtapose the two texts. This is how I worked, for example, in the case of the articles I wrote on Ambrogio Lorenzetti's fresco cycle known as the *Buon governo*.[25] I noticed that the program for the cycle was taken from a number of early humanist political treatises and specifically from Brunetto Latini's tract on city government. My resulting study begins by offering an exposition of this literature on tyranny and virtuous rule, after which I try to show that most of the details in Lorenzetti's master-piece can be explained by reference to this body of texts.

I followed the same principle when taking notes for my book on Shakespeare's forensic plays. I noticed, as I've said, that there is one group of plays in which Shakespeare makes extensive use of the rules of rhetorical invention in judicial causes. My book accordingly begins by offering a survey of Roman and Renaissance theories of judicial inven-tion, after which I try to illustrate the application (and sometimes the

25. Quentin Skinner, "Ambrogio Lorenzetti: The Artist as Political Philosopher," *Proceedings of the British Academy* 72 (1986): 1–56; Skinner, "Ambrogio Lorenzetti's Buon Governo Frescoes: Two Old Questions, Two New Answers," *Journal of the Warburg and Courtauld Institutes* 62 (1999): 1–28.

defiance) of these rules in each of the plays concerned. The merit of this essentially Collingwoodian approach is that the argument is easy to follow. But one weakness is that there is a danger of special pleading; another is that my books are so much designed to identify interventions and explain puzzles that they may seem rather mechanically organized. I continue to feel that the strengths of my approach outweigh the weaknesses, but some of my critics disagree.

While juxtaposition has always been my main scholarly technique—if you can describe it so grandly—I must also confess to a weakness for narrative closure. In my *Foundations of Modern Political Thought* my main aspiration was to trace the process by which the modern concept of the sovereign state arose out of a medieval background of multiple jurisdictions and authorities. I brought the book to a close at the moment when political writers began not merely to comment on this outcome but also to describe the overarching concept they had acquired as *lo stato, l'état,* or the state. I found this closure a satisfying one, although I was subsequently denounced—not unfairly, I fear—for having produced a grand narrative in place of the many conflicting stories that could have been told. I wrote in similar terms—while successfully avoiding the criticism, I believe—in my book *Hobbes and Republican Liberty,* published in 2008. I traced the evolution of a way of thinking about individual liberty in which the antonym of freedom was taken to be dependence on the arbitrary will of others. I sought to show how Hobbes contested this analysis and attempted—with epoch-making success—to replace it with the view that the presence of freedom is marked by nothing more than an absence of external constraints. I drew my narrative to a close at the moment when this new view of freedom successfully challenged the established one, treating the latter's resulting loss of hegemony as another form of closure.

Are research and writing private processes, or do you talk with other people while you're still working on a project?

For me the process is, preferably, a wholly private one. I have never liked talking about my research while I'm engaged in it. During my years at Princeton I found this difficult, because it seemed to me that most people wanted to discuss their academic projects all the time. There may have been a cultural difference here, because I was brought up to believe that it is bad manners to talk about oneself. But I think my diffidence is mainly rooted in a fear that, if I talk to experts on the topic I am trying to think about, I shall simply find myself blown off course or discouraged by comments and criticisms. I prefer to wait until I have finished, at which stage I become positively eager to send my work to experts with a view to being told what's wrong with it. Sometimes the responses can be depressing, but I have never failed to find that they lead to improvements, and in some instances I have been given an almost embarrassing amount of help.

You alluded earlier to still having some of your student copies of books with your notes in them. How do you interact with your personal library? Do you take notes in books?

Like all scholars of my generation, I imagine, I have a large personal library, and I have always treated my books simply as tools, scribbling in the margins and adding copious underlining to the text. But my scholarly life has been transformed by the availability of databases. Of course there have always been concordances for some of the writers I discuss—most obviously Cicero, Milton, and Shakespeare. But nowadays it is possible to download searchable versions of an immense range of texts, as a result of which the standard of scholarship in intellectual history has risen to previously unimaginable heights. When I was starting out, you would have had to be Keith Thomas to be able (thanks to having read everything) to say things like "there is no occurrence of the term X until time Y." But nowadays anyone can speak with the same amazing degree of precision after an hour or so of checking online.

In your Liberty before Liberalism *you explore some of the contemporary implications of your historical work.*[26] *What sorts of dialogues would you like to see between intellectual historians and political theorists? What can historians contribute to contemporary political debates and discourses?*

It is difficult, I think, for historians to have much in the way of a dialogue with philosophers at present. Philosophers who write in the prevailing analytical mode tend to assume that it is possible to offer definitions

---

26. Quentin Skinner, *Liberty before Liberalism* (Cambridge, 1998).

of concepts on which everyone might at least in principle agree. But historians of philosophy are more prone to emphasize that many of our central concepts have never ceased to be subjects of contestation and debate, so that any prospect of arriving at agreed definitions looks like a lost cause.

If you ask what historians can contribute to contemporary political debates, I'm inclined to suggest that perhaps I have just given you one element of the answer. It may be that intellectual historians can help us to see that some of the concepts we are prone to naturalize were in fact historically and contingently constructed. As I have already intimated, this is what I tried to argue in my book *Liberty before Liberalism*. There I noted that, in the *Digest* of Roman law and in endless commentaries on that text, the discussion always begins with a taxonomy of persons in which the basic distinction is between free persons and slaves. We are being told, in other words, that to understand the concept of liberty, what we need to grasp is what it means to live in servitude. The answer given in the *Digest* is that to be a slave is to live *in potestate*, in the power and hence in subjection to the arbitrary will of someone else. It follows that to be a *liber homo*, a free person, must be to live in a condition in which you are *sui iuris*, able to act independently of the will of anyone else.

As I hardly need to add, this is not how we currently tend to think about individual liberty. Rather it is a commonplace of contemporary political theory that liberty is simply a predicate of actions: to be free is to be unimpeded in the exercise of our powers. But is it possible, the historian will want to ask, that this prevailing understanding may amount to little more than an ideological construction that masks from us some of what we need to think about when we ask what it means to be a free agent? This is the question I tried to raise at the end of *Liberty before Liberalism*, where I proposed that the past may sometimes be a repository of buried treasure. Historians may be able not merely to help us stand back from our current assumptions and prejudices but also to show us alternative readings of some of our concepts that may be well worth picking up, dusting down, and reappropriating for our own purposes.

That lack of essence must be empowering.

Yes, that's the Foucauldian thought. The historian may be able to show that some of the definitions and descriptions we regard as most natural are nothing more than cultural constructs. I take it that this was the general contention underlying Foucault's later writings on the history of sexuality: sex may appear to be the most natural thing in the world, but it's largely a failure of imagination to believe so. There is also a Nietzschean epigram hovering hereabouts: that if a concept has a history then it cannot have a definition.[27] The task of apprehending the concept then becomes inherently historical. No concepts and definitions are above the battle, because the battle is all there is.

It's a very inspiring view of intellectual history. It prompts the question, What can historians do to be heard, to offer these possibilities that they recover to other thinkers or to broader publics?

It is not always easy to make this view heard, if only because of the divisions I have mentioned between analytical philosophy and the history of philosophy. If we want the view I have been sketching to reach a wide audience, we have to create the means to propagate it. The most obvious means is to persuade academic publishers to foreground it. I have been involved in several such projects myself, the most successful being the series that Richard Rorty, Jerry Schneewind, and I established with Cambridge University Press in the early 1980s under the title *Ideas in Context*. I eventually coedited the series with James Tully, and by the time we handed over the editorship about five years ago the Cambridge Press had published over a hundred monographs in what seemed to us, to put it crudely, to be the right style.

The scholars who have, I think, done most to propagate and encourage the study of intellectual history in recent times have been those who have founded new journals in the subject. When I was starting out, the *Journal of the History of Ideas*—still of course one of the leaders in the field—stood almost alone. Two notable additions were *History of European Ideas* and *History of Political Thought* in the 1980s. Since then we have seen the founding of the *Intellectual History Review* in the 1990s, *Modern Intellectual History* in 2004, and many similar initiatives, all of which are providing significant outlets for valuable research.

27. "Definirbar ist nur Das, was keine Geschichte hat." Friedrich Nietzsche, *Zur Genealogie der Moral*, ed. G. Colli and M. Montinari (Munich, 1980), 317.

What do you think that you have unlearned, as well as learned, in the course of your career? Has what seemed true or significant to you changed over time?

I really like the idea of unlearning. There's no doubt that, if you've lived through such extraordinary intellectual convulsions as we've witnessed over the past half century, it would be extraordinary if you hadn't unlearned quite a lot. I have certainly had to unlearn some of what I used to believe about historical method. When I published a collection of my articles in 2002, I was obliged to reread a number of essays I had written as early as the 1960s.[28] I was shocked to discover how unselfconsciously I had spoken about "the facts" that historians uncover and how many other ghosts of positivism haunted my texts.

I have also had to unlearn an excessively strong disposition to try to arrive at unambiguous interpretations of texts. For example, I was recently writing a piece about Hobbes's theory of political representation. I couldn't work out if Hobbes wanted to say that sovereigns represent individuals or if they represent the people as a whole. Sometimes he seemed to be saying one thing, sometimes the other. I spent a long time trying to decide which he really meant before I concluded that he must have meant both.[29] Why am I so inclined to think in terms of either/or? It's a weakness against which I continually need to be on my guard.

When I first started out as an intellectual historian, I also held a number of substantive beliefs that I have subsequently had to unlearn. I used to assume without thinking that the canon of leading political thinkers was male. I am ashamed when I now reflect on how many writers this led me to neglect and also how much I was led to sanitize, so to speak, the thinkers about whom I wrote. For example, Hobbes tells us that the political covenant agreed to in the state of nature involves everyone. But what subsequently happens to the women? It wasn't until Carole Pateman raised questions of this kind in her book *The Sexual Contract* that I began to wake up.[30]

I have also had to unlearn most of what I used to believe about the place of religion in public life. I have often been accused of ignoring theologico-political issues in my historical work, but this strikes me as

28. Quentin Skinner, *Visions of Politics*, 3 vols. (Cambridge, 2002).
29. See Quentin Skinner, "Hobbes on Political Representation," in *From·Humanism to Hobbes: Studies in Rhetoric and Politics* (Cambridge, 2018), 190–221.
30. Carole Pateman, *The Sexual Contract* (Stanford, 1988).

an ignorant criticism, if only because my book *The Age of Reformation* is largely concerned with religious warfare and its impact on the political realm. But it certainly seemed to me justifiable to refer at the end of that book to what I took to be a permanent and valuable cultural shift. As I showed, Jean Bodin and other writers on sovereignty began to argue that, in the name of public peace, states must give up trying to impose religious uniformity. They must treat religion as a private matter distinct from politics and consequently as not incompatible with public peace. I saw this as a real intellectual advance, and it shaped the narrative of my book. Few things have been more difficult for me to unlearn than the assumption that religious faith is somehow by definition separate from the public sphere.

Finally, and perhaps most importantly, I have had to unlearn the belief that I am probably fully aware of the beliefs that I would do well to unlearn.

What do you see as the future of intellectual history, and what would you like the future of intellectual history to be?

On the subject of how I should like the future of the subject to look I am liable to sound conservative. It seems to me that, during the past generation, many intellectual currents have converged in such a way as to provide us with a strong rationale for pursuing the subject in the kind of way I have been outlining in this interview. At the same time, as I have been stressing, a number of technological advances have enabled us to practice the subject at a new level of rigor and exactitude. There is much to be said, I think, for continuing our journey with our present maps, while refining them in such a way that we can hope, in Beckett's immortal words, to fail better.

Meanwhile the subject is of course continuing to evolve. One interesting development, promoted in particular by David Armitage and his associates, has been to move away from the pointillist approach that I and others have followed in our attempts to situate individual texts within the political and intellectual frameworks that help to explain them. David's most recent book is a history of the concept of civil war, in which he explores the different uses of the term and their changing significance over a period of two millennia.[31] A further striking innovation has been that, like so much historical scholarship, intellectual history

---

31. David Armitage, *Civil Wars: A History in Ideas* (New York, 2017).

has gone global of late. This seems to me all to the good, and I have even been trying to make a modest contribution to this development myself. Recently I agreed with the Cambridge University Press to revive the series that Raymond Geuss and I used to coedit, *Cambridge Texts in the History of Political Thought*. Aided by a distinguished editorial board, I am now in the process of commissioning a large number of additional texts, all of them from non-Western traditions of political thought, with the eventual aim of giving the series something like a global reach.

You also ask how I see the future of intellectual history. When I first started out, it would not have been much of an exaggeration to say that many leading historians shared two connected and governing beliefs. One was that social and economic history, pursued in a quantitative style, was what most mattered. The other was that, because social and political principles are largely ex post facto rationalizations of economic interests, they play no independent role in historical explanation and are consequently best ignored. No one thinks like that anymore. As a result, the study of intellectual history has been able to throw off its earlier marginality, and its future looks to me bright. It is true that, in some of my gloomier moments, I am not sure if the future looks bright for any of us. It will undoubtedly be much warmer but not necessarily brighter. When I reflect, however, on the current state of intellectual history, it seems to me healthier than at any previous stage in my professional career. There are many brilliant and original young scholars in the field, and they show every sign of continuing to surprise as well as educate us.

Acknowledgments

The authors would like to thank

All of our interviewees for participating in this project.

Ann M. Blair and Anthony Grafton for early encouragement; Lorraine Daston for wisdom at a crucial juncture.

Amelia Atlas, Dmitri Levitin, and Claudia Roth Pierpont for their advice and enthusiasm.

The Harvard Society of Fellows, especially Diana Morse and Kelly Katz.

Heidi Muir and her team at Mediascribe for transcribing seven of the interviews; Leitha Martin for transcribing the eighth; Felice Whittum for expert copyediting and creating the index.

Douglas Mitchell and the two anonymous readers for the University of Chicago Press for taking seriously the proposal of two graduate students, and Doug also for his unremitting enthusiasm.

Randolph Petilos, Kyle Wagner, Christine Schwab, and Carol McGillivray for their work on behalf of this project.

This book is dedicated to our many teachers and mentors, in gratitude for their generosity and inspiration.

Index

Aeschylus, 95
afterlives (of works and ideas), 6, 10, 25, 128
Alter, Robert, 154
amanuenses, 6, 35, 36
anachronism, 149, 177, 178, 183
ancient constitution. *See* Pocock, J. G. A.
Anglicanism, 53, 117, 172, 173, 177, 178–79, 185, 189
Annales school, 1, 24, 25, 170
annotation, 19–22, 24, 29, 95, 107–9, 111, 192
anthropology, 1, 11, 52, 58, 153, 156, 159, 161
antiquarianism: approach to church history, 171; diversity among, 163; French, 97, 168; history of, 4, 146; in history of ideas, 6, 119, 145–46; and learnedness, 148, 164; as a negative, 132; relation to modern field of history, 149, 152–57, 159–60, 161, 168; relation to other disciplines, 130, 153, 158–59, 163; Renaissance, 99; scholarship, 113
antiquity: Christian, 170, 177, 188; Christian vs. classical as field of study, 168, 176; dangers in studying, 185; early modern distancing from, 135; late, 7, 95; modern study of, 113; Renaissance revival of, 10, 12, 99. *See also* classics (Greek and Latin language and scholar-ship); Greek (language and authors); Latin (language and authors)
archaeology: contribution to historical method, 150–51, 156; negative relation to history, 182; relation to antiquarianism, 153, 160; relation to other disciplines, 159; in the Renaissance, 99
architecture, history of, 4, 63, 160, 193, 194
archives, 30, 57, 63, 180; Peiresc's, 146–47, 150–52, 156
Aristotle: anti-Aristotelianism, 16, 19, 20, 26; Aristotelianism, 19, 26, 50, 119, 135; editions of, 22, 23; humanists and, 135; and the Renaissance, 6, 7, 124–25, 129, 139–40; translations of, 136; vindication of, 62
Armitage, David, 211
Ars rhetorica. *See* rhetoric
art history, 20; and Bard Graduate Center, 158; origins of discipline, 158; relation to other disciplines, 119, 126, 152–53, 159, 161
artisans, 12, 56
Auerbach, Erich, 11, 92, 98
Augustine, Saint, 94, 111, 187
Austin, J. L., 196–97, 198
authenticity, 75, 77, 137, 182–83, 186

Backus, Irena, 178
Bacon, Francis, 26, 46, 50, 63, 124, 149, 152, 155